PROSPERITY
IN CRISIS

By the same author

THE FALLING RATE OF PROFIT

PROSPERITY IN CRISIS

Joseph M. Gillman

MARZANI & MUNSELL, Publishers

26169

To
Len and Bob

CONTENTS

LIST OF TABLES AND CHARTS

ACKNOWLEDGEMENTS

If there is clarity and coherence in the argument of this book it is due in large degree to the help given me by many friends who have great concern for the subject. Among these I mention but a few: Professor Ronald L. Meek of the University of Leicester, England; Professor John P. Henderson of Michigan State University, and Professor Martin Bronfenbrenner of the Carnegie Institute of Technology, who read the longish first draft and pointed out many shortcomings; Angus Cameron who as head of Cameron Associates guided me through early drafts; Professor H. D. Dickinson of Bristol University who made several suggestions for improving the argument and the text, although he disagreed with the central thesis of the book; James S. Allen, editor and publisher of International Publishers who showed me how to reduce a manuscript by 100 pages without doing injury to pride of authorship; Dr. Hyman Lumer who read the first shortened version; Professor Eugene D. Genovese of Rutgers University who pre-edited the manuscript and purged it of duplications. Etta Gillman, perpetual target of a writing husband, would not let me escape into technical jargon when a concept became too complex.

At an early stage I discussed the main theses of the book in person with Dr. Maurice H. Dobb of Cambridge University; with Professor Henri Denis of the University of Rennes; with Professor Ronald L. Meek, and with Professor Antonio Pesenti of the University of Pisa.

To all these and to all others who would listen to my "dissertations" on the subject I owe profound gratitude. In addition, I should like to thank The Louis H. Rabinowitz Foundation for a grant that enabled me to pursue my work.

Joseph M. Gillman
Hartsdale, N. Y.
May 1, 1965

PREFACE

This book deals with theoretical and practical problems of providing peacetime full employment in America on a continuing basis.

Since the end of the war, the United States has experienced four recessions, each tending to leave a larger pool of unemployment than the preceding one. The fear of a serious depression stalks the country. This fear arises from the gnawing awareness that much of the employment in the post-war years was born in war and has been largely nurtured by preparations for war. Genuine peace and massive disarmament, it is feared, would bring a major depression.

The problem of finding an answer to the question of full employment dates back to the depression of the 1930's. It had become clear then to all who would see that another depression of such magnitude would not be tolerated by the American workers. The very survival of the capitalist system appeared threatened by repeated breakdowns and mass unemployment. As some economists have since put it, provisions for the maintenance of full employment would be provisions for saving capitalism.

The theoretical basis for such provisions have been derived, in the main, from the economics enunciated by John Maynard Keynes in 1936 in *The General Theory of Employment, Interest and Money*. In accordance with Keynesian economics, the state is called upon to use its taxing, monetary, and spending powers to assure full employment when private investment and private consumption fail to do so.

The depression of the 1930's lasted nearly 10 years and was brought to an end mainly by the rising military expenditures incidental to the outbreak of the war in Europe. Early Keynesians saw in that experience a vindication of their theory of the role of government spending in the prevention and cure of depressions. Can that experience apply to a capitalist economy at peace?

We know that in the postwar years prosperity did not come in response to any undue increase in civilian expenditures by the government, or in response to an undue increase in the rate of private capital formation, except in housing for which there had been an accumulated shortage dating back to the Great Depression. After the wartime shortages had been made up, prosperity developed in the face of a declining trend in the rate of net private investment in plant and equipment. The big stimulus came from unprecedentedly large peacetime military expenditures by the government, supplemented by wasteful and unproductive sales promotion expense; by the mortgaging of future consumer income in the purchase of housing and of household durable equipment; by an inflation of capital values; by government stockpiling commodity surpluses, from grains to metals, at inflated prices, and a general price inflation. Civilian-type expenditures of government, as a per cent of the nation's total output, remained about the same throughout the postwar years and the rate of capital accumulation has been slow and even declining.

The question, therefore, is what would substitute for the military and other wasteful expenditures, for stockpiling and for inflation, that is compatible with the viability of the system and continued full employment?

Keynesians say, build the Welfare State: Expand the public expenditures for the public education, the public health, public housing and for the other social services to the full needs of the people. This is easier said than done. Capitalism is a system of the private accumulation of capital. The Welfare State, to be meaningful and not a shibboleth, would tend to negate this basic characteristic of capitalism. It is not only a matter of cost — of taxes or even of deficit spending. Equally if not more important is the fact that the Welfare State thus conceived would set up worker-capitalist relations which would challenge the domination of the capitalist class over the production and distribution of the national income.

These, then, are some of the questions that this book seeks to explore. Evidently, they are not easy questions. They involve widely debated theoretical and practical considerations of the nature of capitalism as a system of social production and of the possibility of disarmament and of peaceful coexistence with the socialist bloc of nations. They involve an appreciation of the growing dissolution of centuries-old colonial empires and its impact on continued capitalist viability. They involve the need for peace and disarmament as the precondition for any meaningful advance in social welfare. All this must be seen in the context of the rising political challenge of the socialist world.

PART I
PREVIEWS

1.
THE PROBLEMS WE FACE

Capitalism is an economic system with a tendency to fluctuate in cycles between periods of prosperity with reasonably full employment and periods of recession and depression with various degrees of mass unemployment. No one disputes this fact, which is a matter of every-day observation as well as of theoretical analysis and measurement. What has been and continues to be in dispute are the origins of these cycles and the reasons for the failure thus far to arrest their course.

It is true that much learning has been bestowed on these questions, especially since the disastrous 1930's. The "business cycle" has been the subject of innumerable books and essays, Government Reports and Congressional Hearings, and newspaper editorials. But each time a depression, or "recession" hits us, we seem to be starting all over again in search of an explanation, only to end up where we had started. Not long ago, in 1956, the National Bureau of Economic Research, the most prominent and scholarly *collegium* devoted to the study of the business cycle, held a symposium on *Policies to Combat Depressions*. In reviewing the contributions to this symposium,[1, *] Professor Lorie Tarshis of Stanford University wrote:

> In a way, the papers make depressing reading. For one thing they do not suggest that our understanding of the problems of depression has shown any real advance since the war. There is very little here which could not have been written before 1941 . . . what was obscure then . . . remains obscure.

In this book we make a fresh start. We develop the thesis that capitalist economies experience booms and depressions because they operate within a framework in which more profits, more social surplus we will say, is produced than can be absorbed in the expansion of their productive assets on a *continuing* basis, and that this condition has worsened under the impact of the new technologies and concentrated business organization. A qualitative change has taken place

*All numbered references will be placed by Chapter, in Notes at the end of the book. All starred (*) references will be footnotes in the text.

in the creation of investment funds and in the ways of absorbing them. Present-day industrial technology is, to an ever increasing degree, capital-saving as well as labor-saving.[2] Unit for unit, in constant dollars, productive capacity costs less to build now than in former years and its expansion requires relatively less investment capital. At the same time, under large-scale business organization and management, operating as monopolies and oligopolies, the productivity of labor is so heightened by the new technology that it tends to produce a volume of investment capital which exceeds existing private investment outlets.[3] It was the growing disparity between investible capital and potential real investments in the 1920's, we will argue, that was the basic condition underlying the crisis and depression of 1929-1939. And it is the potentially still greater disparity between the two which the latest technologies generate today that threatens the American economy with still sharper crises and with more severe depressions. What, in the main, has prevented this growing disparity from generating a major depression, we will see, has been the absorption of much of the uninvested capital in unproductive and wasteful expenditures: in the multi-billion dollar "business" of racketeering;[4] in the $15 billion advertising and sales promotion; in recent years in the $50 billion+ annual expenditures for the military.

In the late 1920's much of the excess social surplus was apparently "invested" in the stock market, but was, in fact, consumed in luxury expenditures of paper gains. It has been estimated[5] for 1962 that about 7,500,000 Americans, including military and government civilian personnel, were engaged in national defense occupations. That was over 10 per cent of the total labor force. The government now siphons off a large portion of the country's social surplus in taxes (and in loans), which if not otherwise invested would exert a downward pressure on the economy. By spending it, the government puts this portion of the social surplus back into the country's production stream where private investors might not find profitable outlets. That a recession may, nevertheless, develop despite such large government expenditures as it did, for example, in 1960-61 for the fourth time in a dozen years, simply testifies to the insidiousness of the capitalist tendency to depressions.

We are concerned in this book, however, not with the cyclical ups and downs but with the long-run trend of capitalist economies, in particular of advanced capitalist economies, in the direction of a growing disparity between their emerging social surplus and their *productive* investment potentials, and how this growing disparity

15

gives shape and magnitude to the business cycle of twentieth century capitalism. Capitalist production now increasingly depends on the unproductive use of the uninvestible capital of the system, and capitalist depressions are shallowed by the large employment of unproductive workers. Unproductive employment lifts the bottom of depressions by offsetting the effects of the tendencies to unemployment of productive workers. In these respects, modern capitalist prosperity is often but the manifestation of a continually existing unemployment crisis. Always now, it would seem, the system can prosper and unemployment can be mitigated only by the expansion of investment outlets of an unproductive nature. Else there would be a chronic depression.

In the next chapter I shall explain in some detail what I mean by uninvestible social surplus and unproductive expenditures. Here we must call attention to the emergence, from the current dependence of employment on military expenditures, of a new fact of life which holds grave dangers to the American people. That is a growing delusion that the militarization of the economy may be offering a permanent solution to the problem of full employment. So much has this delusion penetrated the consciousness of many of us that when a depression threatens, leaders in Congress and leaders of labor seem unable to think of any way out other than by still more military spending, while States vie with one another for an increased share of "defense contracts." When in December 1962 it became known that the Defense Department was planning to close 35 military bases with 75,000 jobs, Congressmen from the affected States joined in a strong protest to the Pentagon.[6] Additional defense contracts in the amount of $8½ billion to be let during the second quarter of 1961 were held out as a promising stimulus to recovery from a nagging recession. The subsequent rise of defense expenditures from $45.7 billion in 1960 to the $55.2 billion in 1963 in no small way explains the lift in the economy these years. Twenty years of full employment or near full employment supported in great part by military expenditures, has created an illusion among American workers that they have a vested interest in war and preparations for war. The military as a factor in the maintenance of full employment has become structured into the American economy.

For the capitalists, the militarization of the economy fits in with their institutional and private interests. It holds many economic and political advantages for them. For munition manufacturers there are the economic advantages of high profits. For the exporting manufacturers and American investors, expenditures for the military safeguard and expand profitable foreign markets. With all of them, perhaps, the political advantages weigh most tellingly. Expenditures for the military create the war loyalties which help tie most people and millions of workers to "our way of life." They help tie people to the defense and preservation of the capitalist system, when the alternative system of socialism is developing attractions. The militarization of the American economy causes the "enemy," the socialist states, to extend themselves in their war expenditures, to the detriment of the standard of living of their people.[7] The American capitalists can then tell their own workers how much better off they are than the workers who are "compelled" to live under socialism, and they can tell Congress that the war expenditures of the socialist countries compel us to increase ours. These new war expenditures absorb still more of the otherwise uninvestible social surplus and give more workers jobs. Hence the general apathy in America to peaceful coexistence with the socialist nations, and even fear of it.

For the workers, individually and as a class, this illusion, even though fostered and abetted by its present leadership, leads to a weakening of their economic and political class-power potentials. They tend to become economically and politically subservient to the interests of the capitalist class and to a war economy, which serves as a serious barrier to the development of worker class power.

Continued dependence on ever-larger military expenditures for the maintenance of capitalist viability cannot be a permanent solution to the problem of full employment. First, the preparations for war may actually lead to war — a war which, waged with thermonuclear weapons and chemical poisons, would cause the slaughter of half the human race and the mutilation of the other half. That indeed would end the problem of unemployment.

But assuming away a Third World War, the militarization of the economy cannot offer a permanent solution to the problem of full employment for still other immediately pressing reasons. Continued large expenditures for the military give rise to social, moral and political tendencies incompatible with the well-being of a free people. The war spirit, which the military expenditures generate, and on which they are projected, brutalizes the national conscience, leads to the deterioration of the public morals, the constriction of the social services, and to stultification of the intellect. In an atmosphere in which violence is extolled, crime and juvenile delinquency multiply and a President is assassinated. At the same time, the drain on the public purse for military expenditures spells a denial of adequate provisions for the education, public health and medical care, decent housing, recreational and cultural facilties in which the "beat generation" might find wholesome outlets for its restiveness — might find William James' "moral equivalent of war."

In the great city of New York, public libraries are open fewer and fewer hours. "Whole floors of museums are darkened much of the time and educational activities at these institutions have had to be restricted sharply," Robert Alden reported in the New York *Times*, July 20, 1959. The Metropolitan Museum of Art, after having been open seven days a week for nearly 70 years, is now closed on Mondays, for lack of $35,000. The Brooklyn Museum, which in November 1960 "had the highest attendance for any November in its sixty-three years," announced that beginning with the new year (1961) it will close two days of the week for lack of some $50,000 a year for necessary guards. (N.Y.T., 12/22/60). Throughout the country, in one school dictrict after another, "tax-payers' associations" defeat proposed bond issues to finance essential school needs.

Suppose, then, that the armed truce of the cold war is ended and real peace comes, as sooner or later it must if the world is not to end in a war of self-destruction. The allies may find the continued military burden intolerable. Sooner or later the United States will have to give up its forlorn hope that threat of a military build-up will bring on the collapse of the Soviet Union, the initial motivation of the cold war, and begin to roll back its military expenditures. In that case, what will take the place of these expenditures to serve as the principal means for the maintenance of full employment? For the workers, the question is: How can we have peace *and* jobs? It is as simple as that.

As a rule, before the 1930's, capitalist economists largely ignored the question of full employment. The "business cycle" until then, remained generally an exercise of academic discipline. The effects of depressions were something that happened "out there." The depression of the 1930's was something else again. It brought the world capitalist structure near to political ruin. It was then that Keynes saw fit to write (in the *Yale Review*, Summer 1933):

> The decadent international but individualistic capitalism . . . is not a success. It is not intelligent, it is not beautiful, it is not just, it is not virtuous — and it does not deliver the goods. In short, we dislike it and are beginning to despise it. But when we wonder what to put in its place, we are extremely perplexed.

A generation, two wars and four recessions later, America was still without a solution to the full employment problem.

2.
WORKING CONCEPTS

From what has already been said it should be clear that we will be discussing in this book subjects of a highly controversial nature. There are almost as many theories about business depressions as there are economists that write about them. And there are almost as many prescriptions for curing them.

One reason for the diversity of opinion on the cause and cure of the business cycle is that most economists and politicians come to these discussions with ready-made points of view which shape their conclusions—points of view of practical political and economic policy. For all economic theory, in various thicknesses of disguise, aims at the propagation of practical objectives. In this sense, economic theory is a form of propaganda. In the words of that brilliant economist, Joan Robinson:

> Economic doctrines always come to us as propaganda. This is bound up with the very nature of the subject and to pretend that it is not so in the name of "pure science" is a very unscientific refusal to accept the facts.[1]

Often, the propaganda of an economic "theory" is quite transparent. Such, for example, was the "full dinner pail" theory of the protectionists at the turn of the century. In most academic economic theory the propaganda angle is disguised under the halo of the cap and gown as "objective economic analysis."

This, of course, does not in any way disqualify men of different points of view from participating in the debate, if only they declared the points of view from which they start. If they had no points of view they would not even debate the issues. People do not think in a vacuum. They think because certain objective conditions in their lives, which impinge upon their consciousness and interests, make them "think." Thus individual as well as group points of view and policy objectives are formed.

The present writer is no exception to these general rules. To be fair with his readers, therefore, he feels incumbent at the very outset to make his point of view known to them. It pertains, in this context, to his concept of the nature of capitalist economies — to his definition of "capitalism." The "propaganda" part is the book.

It may come as a surprise to most readers that "capitalism" requires defining at all. Does not everybody know what capitalism is? Maybe so, but capitalist economists have never yet agreed on a definition of that historical phenomenon. "Despite the fact." wrote Werner Sombart in his article "Capitalism" in *The Encyclopedia of the Social Sciences*, "that capitalism tends to become the sole subject matter of economics, neither the term nor the concept has as yet been universally recognized by representatives of academic economics."[2] This is one reason, one might say, why capitalist economists have to date failed to construct an adequate theory of capitalist economic crises. Imagine physicians disputing on the nature and cure of smallpox or pneumonia, without the prior agreement on the physiology of the human body!

For the present purpose it is not necessary to consider the various concepts of capitalism which capitalist economists have used over the years. What is necessary is a clear definition of the concept which will be used in this book. It forms the frame of reference for our treatment of the questions of prosperity and depression; of economic crises and economic growth.

1. *Capitalism, Profit, Surplus-Value and Social Surplus.* — We define *capitalism* as a social-economic system in which the means of production — plant, equipment and materials, and labor-power — are all commodities, things produced to be sold in a market. So also is land a marketable property, although only its improvements are a product of human hands. In this system one class, a small minority of the people, the class that owns most of the means of production and called capitalists, live by buying labor-power, transforming labor and materials into commodities and services, selling them at a profit and cumulating most of the profit in the form of additional means of production. The other class, the workers, who constitute the majority of the people, own only themselves and live by selling their labor-power of brain and brawn, for wages and salaries. Profit-making and the conversion of profit into capital are the prime movers of capitalist production.

True, this class division of a capitalist society is not as rigidly monolithic as the above definitions might seem to imply. *Within* the capitalist class, sub-groups exist whose interests may be antagonistic to one another. Such antagonisms may exist, for example, between producers of raw materials and producers of finished products; between farmers and manufacturers; between exporting and importing industries; between Big Business and small business; between money capitalists and entrepreneurs. In the era of the cold war, antogonisms exist between the cluster of high-profit munition makers and the majority of business men who get no direct benefits from cold war expenditures, but who pay cold war taxes. However, all capitalists have one interest in common as *one class*: the accumulation of capital through the controlling ownership of the means of production and the appropriation of the surplus-value produced by labor, defined below.

Similarly, *within* the working class, sub-groups may be identified which bear different attitudes toward their place in society and toward the capitalist class. A large and increasing proportion of the working class, white-collar employees, or the "salariat," tends to identify itself with the capitalist class rather than with wage earners or blue-collar workers. In the United States, antagonisms have tended to emerge between workers of different national origin, color, race, and creed. In the era of the cold war the concentration of government spending in the employment of munition workers in a few favored geographical areas points up the concurrent creation of stagnant pools of unemployment elsewhere and the inadequacy of expenditures for the social services everywhere in the United States. But all workers, of all national origins, color, race or creed, have this in common: they can live only by selling their labor-power, brain or brawn, to a capitalist.

In this aspect of cold war expenditures, potentially, the interests of large segments of the working population and of the majority of businessmen coalesce in favor of peace, a reduction of armament expenditures, reduced taxes, and a shift to the production of civilian-type goods and services, especially of a socially productive nature.

The "profit" we just talked about is a broader category than is the conventional term. It is used here as the equivalent to Marx's "surplus-value" — the difference between the value of the commodity workers produce and their wages and salaries plus the value of the material capital consumed in that production. Thus, surplus-value comprises, besides the conventional profit, also rent, interest, royalties and all other payments to property ownership. As we will see later, it is also the source of all payments to government, taxes, and to the unproductive workers of the system, shortly to be defined.

Surplus-value as here defined may also be called the gross social surplus of a community. When from this gross amount we deduct the portion used by capitalists for their own personal consumption, we get what I shall call the net social surplus. Wherever in this book we treat of the "social surplus" it is to this net concept that we will refer. We call it social surplus because it is generated in a system of social production. People now mostly work for each other and with each other, not by themselves or for themselves as they did in precapitalist days. The concept of the social surplus as here defined is crucial to the argument of this book, for, we will argue, it is the failure of all of the potential social surplus of the economy to find outlets in its further productive expansion and in social consumption that emerges as the chief characteristic of business depressions and, in recent years, of its tendency to a secular decline. The portion of the social surplus which cannot find its way back into the further productive expansion of the economy (and that happens now, even in periods of business booms) we shall call "excess" social surplus. In the text in this connection we will speak interchangeably of "excess surplus-value," of "excess social surplus" and of "uninvestible social surplus" as expressing the same idea in its several aspects.

2. *Distinction Between Productive and Unproductive Labor.*

a. *First criterion: Production of Surplus-Value.* As originally conceived by the classical economists and by Marx, workers who produce surplus-value are called the *productive* workers of the system; they perform "productive" labor. Workers who do not produce surplus-value are "unproductive" workers; these perform "unproductive" labor. This is one criterion for the distinction between productive and unproductive labor — that to be deemed productive a worker must produce surplus-value for a capitalist. For this reason, self-employed artisans and farmers are deemed unproductive. Also, under this criterion the usefulness of the product is not the test, nor is its social desirability. Neither the police nor the public school teacher nor the fire warden who protects our forests nor the admirals and generals who defend and extend "our way of life," nor college professors, useful as their services may be deemed to be, are "productive" workers under this criterion. They do not produce material commodities and services which enter into the production of material values, which are sold at a profit for an employer.

b. *Second criterion: Production of Commodities and Productive Services.* On the other hand, workers may be deemed "productive" who combine their labor-power with material means of production to produce material products and such services as transportation, the public utilities, teaching and research which facilitate production.[3] Thus, workers who engage in selling or who perform any other promotional and non-factory adminstrative duties are not deemed

22

productive workers. They do not transform material means of production into material products or into productive services. As unproductive workers, therefore, they do not produce surplus-value. On the contrary, their wages and salaries are paid directly or indirectly from the surplus-value produced by the productive workers. But this does not mean that only workers in overalls are productive. The engineer who designs the factory or the product is also productive in this sense as is the physicist whose research leads to the production of new products or to the improvement in the quality of existing products. So also are the managers who organize the work and the foremen who supervise it. They all participate in the transformation of labor-power and material means of production into commodities and productive services for sale at a profit for the capitalist.

   c. *Third criterion*: *Production of Capital*. Finally, workers are unproductive whose labor does not eventuate in an asset or service that can be used in further production. Thus, workers who are engaged in the production of armaments are unproductive in this sense, even though their labor produces products and surplus-value.[4] In other words, only such labor is productive whose product is capable of re-entering the cycle of production, either as a means of production, as producer goods and services or as a means of consumption, as consumer goods and services. A steel beam and a blueprint can be used in the construction of a bridge, and a can of soup and a steam bath in the reproduction of the labor-power of a laborer. A cannon or a missile cannot be thus used in a new cycle of production, except perhaps as scrap. These are a sheer economic waste. To be sure, some of the munitions plant and equipment may be convertible to civilian production and to that extent represent productive investment. But this is a one-time investment and in the continuing military output and the cost of the military establishment is relatively a negligible amount.

   To be productive, then, a worker must (a) produce surplus-value in the course of (b) transforming labor-power and material capital into material commodities and productive services which (c) can enter into a new cycle of production of the means of production or means of consumption.

   The distinction between productive and unproductive workers should not be taken to mean that only the former constitute the working class, the "proletariat," as opposed to the "capitalist class." The working class consists of all workers whose principal source of livelihood is the sale of their labor power, brain or brawn. This contrasts with the capitalist class whose principal source of income arises from the ownership of capital. True, most white collar workers may not know it, or be willing to admit it, and as a rule, identify their interests with those of the capitalists. They have occasion to learn to which side they belong in a depression, or when an electronic processing tape automates them out of a job, or when one general sales manager becomes a surplus when two companies merge into one.[5] The ownership of capital is the power to give or to withhold employment from those who depend on it for a living.

3. *Productive and Unproductive Expenditures.*—The distinction between productive and unproductive labor gives rise to the distinction between productive and unproductive expenditures. Elsewhere, in *The Falling Rate of Profit*, I have discussed the main types of unproductive expenditures, which include advertising and sales promotion expenses and all costs of war and preparations for war.

4: *Capitalist-Labor Relations.*—The obligation of capitalists to their workers is purely contractual. Capitalists hire workers and pay them wages and salaries only so long as they produce or help realize enough surplus-value to yield an acceptable rate of profit. If that not be the case, the workers will not be hired. They will be unemployed. For capitalists have only one aim in making use of their capital: the creation of surplus-value and its investment in the further expansion of their capital—in the continuing accumulation of capital.

The workers, likewise, have no other but a contractual obligation to the capitalists. The worker holds no fealty to his employer. He is a "free agent." He sells his labor-power for wages or a salary as a "free" laborer. His motivation is self-preservation. He has no other means of livelihood for himself and family except his labor-power. It is his only asset. In this sense he really is not free, but dependent. He depends on the willingness of a capitalist to hire him. Whereas the capitalist can live without hiring labor for a long time, the worker cannot live very long without being hired. In the end, though, the capitalist would cease being capitalist unless he had labor producing surplus-value for him.

And this brings us to the heart of the problem with which this book is primarily concerned, the problem of employment in a capitalist society.

24

3.
THE SOCIAL SURPLUS, "EXCESS. SAVINGS," AND UNPRODUCTIVE EXPENDITURES (A Historical Note)

It should now be noted that ideas about excess social surplus and unproductive expenditures, examined in the preceding chapters, are not altogether new in economic literature. We find them, in various undeveloped forms, as far back as the beginnings of economics, and down through Keynes in our own day. Excess savings and unproductive expenditures were the subject of one of the famous controversies in the early years of the 19th century between Malthus and Ricardo, two of the Founding Fathers of capitalist economics. With Keynes, the concept of excess saving forms the very starting point of his entire economic analysis. A brief review of the more important of these earlier concepts should help the reader to follow the application of our own ideas about them to the present-day problem of full employment.

1. *Malthus and Ricardo.*—During the years of the war with Napoleon, British farmers were induced by protective import duties and by rising prices to increase production. Several favorable harvests contributed to the resulting abundance of farm produce.

When Napoleon was finally defeated in 1815, a business slump developed in England, resulting in mass unemployment and great suffering among British workers. At one and the same time British farms were left with huge surpluses and falling prices of produce and British industry was left with bulging warehouses and falling prices of manufactured goods. As Malthus saw it, the country was suffering from a "glut." This he proceeded to explain on the ground that, since workers get less in wages than the value of what they produce, they cannot buy it all.[1]

To consume all that the workers produced above their own takings and so to avoid gluts and depressions, Malthus argued, "a country with great powers of production should possess a body of consumers who are not themselves engaged in production."[2] These "unproductive consumers" would take the excess off the market. The capitalists, he explained, cannot consume this excess because they have to do the saving.

Within the category of unproductive consumers, Malthus included the landowning class, menial servants, statesmen, soldiers, judges, lawyers, physicians, surgeons, and clergymen. Most of the nonmenials were either direct retainers of the landlords or were commonly supplied to the general community from the ranks of the landowning classes. Their labor, Malthus said, "does not terminate in the creation of material wealth." It is unproductive labor. But by consuming "material products" of "productive" labor they lessen gluts and so help maintain employment all around.[3]

To Ricardo, both Malthus' explanation of gluts and his remedies to prevent them were utter abominations in the eyes of the "true principles" of political economy. Following the dictum of Say's Law of Markets, shortly to be noted, he protested: How can there be a general glut of commodities when production automatically produces the purchasing power necessary to take the products off the market? So long as there is production there can be no limit to consumption. True, he conceded, wars, "bad" legislation, sudden shifts in public tastes may cause a temporary overabundance in some industries and shortages in others. But these in the course of time balance each other out. No *general* abundance and no *general* shortage of goods in relation to purchasing power is, therefore, possible.

As to Malthus' argument for the need of a class of unproductive consumers to take the surplus off the market, Richardo replied that such consumption, rather than improve conditions worsens them. Unproductive consumers, he declared, eat of the nation's substance without replenishing it. Unproductive consumption can be of no more benefit to the system than a fire would be.

Malthus even had gone so far as to advocate government spending (!) as a means of absorbing the excess output of the country. At this, Ricardo was truly outraged. "I could not have believed it possible," he wrote to Professor McCulluch in May 1820, after reading Malthus' *Principles*, "that so enlightened a man as Mr. Malthus should recommend taxation as a remedy to our present distress. He is not aware that the produce of a country is always consumed. . . ." Besides, he went on to argue, taxation means government spending, and government spending means competition for labor with private industry. That means rising wages and falling profits, diminishing and retarding capital accumulation.[4]

It is of interest to note that Malthus and Richardo debated an issue in the period of the infancy of capitalism which today confronts capitalism in its maturity. "Unproductive consumption" and "government spending" which Malthus put forth as means of easing a cyclical crisis, now seem to have become the props for the very maintenance of the continued viability of the system.

What was wrong with Malthus in this debate was his implied assumption that capitalist production is geared solely to consumer demand. He overemphasized the role of consumption as a propelling force of capitalist production and undervalued the demand for capital goods. But it is in the demand for capital goods, in capital investment, where capitalists' "saving" comes in. And it is precisely the failure of the potential savings of a community to find realization in investment, we will see, that sets up the conditions in which depresions and "gluts" materialize.

At the same time, Ricardo was wrong in his assumption that demand was always effective; that *all* the income a nation produces in any given time *always* comes back as consumer demand and as investment demand to continue full-employment production. The influence of Say was decisive in his thinking.[5] Later we will see how Keynes handled this question.

2. *Adam Smith.*—But already some 45 years before this Malthus-Ricardo debate, in 1776, to be exact, the first of the Founding Fathers of modern political economy discoursed on the question of unproductive labor and unproductive expenditures. That labor is productive, Smith had said, "which adds to the value of the subject upon which it is bestowed." Labor which has no such effect is unproductive. "Thus," he went on to explain, "the labour of a manufacturer [of a worker in a factory] adds, generally to the value of the materials which he works upon, that of his own maintenance and of his master's profit," coming close in the last phrase to Marx's concept of surplus-value.

The labor of those who do not add such value is unproductive labor and their consumption is unproductive consumption. They are maintained by the industry of the productive laborers.

> The labour of some of the most respectable orders of society [he wrote] is like that of menial servants, unproductive of any value . . . The sovereign, for example,

27

with all the officers both of justice and war who serve
under him, the whole army and navy, are unproductive
labourers. They are the servants of the public, and are
maintained by a part of the annual produce of industry
of other people. Their service, how honorable, how useful, or how necessary soever, produce nothing for which
an equal quantity of service can afterwards be procured.
The protection, security and defense of the commonwealth,
the effect of their labor this year will not purchase its
protection, security, and defense for the year to come.
In the same class must be ranked, some both of the
gravest and most important, and some of the most
frivolous professions: Churchmen, lawyers, physicians,
men of letters of all kinds; players, buffoons, musicians,
opera singers, opera dancers, etc.[6]

This is where Malthus got his definition of unproductive labor.
But it was not from Smith that he got his idea of the role of
unproductive consumption in capitalist production. For Malthus, unproductive consumption was a means of relieving gluts. For Smith
and, as we have seen, later for Ricardo, unproductive consumption
was a drag on capital accumulation. The public debt, for instance,
Smith argued, represented but "a certain portion of the annual
produce turned away from serving in the function of capital, to
serve in that of revenue; from maintaining productive labourers [and
adding to the wealth of the nation], to maintaining unproductive ones,
and to be spent and wasted, generally in the course of the year,
without even the hope of any further reproduction."[7] Government
spending was a wasting of resources. Hence, the *theory of Laissez-
Faire:* Let the government spend a minimum and interfere a minimum in the private accumulation of capital.

3. *Say's Law of Markets.*—After the Malthus-Ricardo debate,
more than a generation passed before, in 1848, John Stuart Mill
brought up the subject again, although from a different point of
view from either Malthus or Ricardo. Thereafter, excess social surplus and unproductive expenditures again cease to be subjects of
academic discussion for nearly a hundred years, except for two lone
voices in America (those of Veblen and Louis Boudin) to be cited
below, at the turn of the century.

The reason for the disappearance of these concepts for so long
may be traced to the seemingly endless potentials for capitalist growth
of the times. This made possible the dominance exerted on capitalist
economic theory those years by Say's Law of Markets which, as we

noted, was so influential with Ricardo in his debate with Malthus. According to this "Law," in Say's words:

> It is production which opens a demand for products. . . .
> A product is no sooner created than it, from that instant,
> affords a market for other products to the full extent of its
> value. Thus the mere circumstance of the creation of one
> product immediately opens a vent for other products.[8]

Thus the view became established that production equals consumption and consumption equals production. Supply created its own demand. The income generated in production equals the income paid out in that production. Consumption, therefore, equals production. Hence, a general surplus either of commodities or capital was impossible. Under this "law," indeed, even depressions were, theoretically, impossible. Demand is always effective; that is, it is always sufficient to clear the market. General overproduction, or general underconsumption is, therefore, impossible. General crises are impossible. Crises may come and go, but, in theory, there could be no crises!

So long, therefore, as that law held sway over the minds of economists, an uninvestible social surplus could not be conceived, nor could the idea of the need for unproductive expenditures à la Malthus appear. In an age when the labor supply appeared to be inexhaustible and continents lay open for exploitation, there could be no reservations about the endlessness of investment possibilities for all the potential savings of the community. It was not until 1936, when Keynes laid the ghost of this "law" through his own theory of the Effective Demand, that capitalist economists finally shed this dogma. Marx, to be sure, had exploded this law some seventy-five years earlier.[9] But capitalist economists have not been in the habit of reading Marx, and so the dogma persisted to dominate capitalist economic theory until the Great Depression of the 1930's shattered the economists' traditional complacency and paved the way for Keynes.*

4. *John Stuart Mill.*—In his conception of the role of unproductive consumption, Mill differed from both Malthus and Ricardo, as he did from Smith. With Mill, unproductive consumption was not, as with Malthus, aimed at bolstering consumer demand, but a means of retarding the accumulation of a capital excess which,

---

*A curious coincidence for economic astrologers to ponder is that Keynes was born in the year Marx died, in 1883.

as he saw it, tended to depress the rate of profit. And in this he differed also from Smith and Ricardo in that they were dead-set against any measure that would hold down the rate of capital accumulation.

In Mill's view, a declining rate of profit was the prime cause of the recurrent economic crisis—of "commercial revulsions." Following Adam Smith, Mill thought the rate of profit fell as a consequence of a redundancy of capital. Government expenditure, from tax revenue, was one of the means of reducing this redundancy. (What distance capitalism had traveled in the ¾ century since 1776, when the need for capital had seemed to Smith insatiable!) "When a country has long possessed a large production, and a large net income to make savings from," Mill wrote, "and when, therefore, the means have long existed of making a great annual addition to capital . . . it is one of the characteristics of such a country, that the rate of profit is habitually within, as it were, a hand's breadth of the minimum, and the country therefore on the very verge of the stationary state."[10]

Mill's concept of unproductive consumption was in the classical tradition, but it carried, in addition, moral and ethical overtones. Having been brought up in penury,[11] he understandably deemed as unproductive any expenditure "on pleasure or luxuries," even if incurred by productive workers. (We will find these ethical overtones a half-century later in Veblen's "conspicuously wasteful consumption," perhaps, in part, for similar reasons.) Mill's only "reservation" to this precept was "perhaps a certain quantum of enjoyment which may be classed among necessaries, since anything short of it would not be consistent with the greatest efficiency of labor."[12]

However, the existence of a class of unproductive consumers, Mill held, should not be a cause for regret. Rather, he thought, it should be a cause of self-congratulation. The phenomenon measured the ability of opulent societies to put aside, to "spare," a large portion of their annual produce for such consumption.[13]

5 *Karl Marx.*—Between Mill and Veblen, a half-century later, only Marx dealt seriously with the question of unproductive labor. However, he dealt rather sketchily with the collateral question of unproductive expenditures, both as related to the cyclical crisis and as related to the emergence of excess surplus-value.

"Let us suppose," he wrote, "that the whole society is composed only of industrial capitalists and wage workers . . . In that case," he argued, "a crisis could be explained only by" the disproportionate

30

outputs of the different branches of the economy "and by a disproportion between the consumption of the capitalists and the accumulation of their capitals. But as matters stand," he went on, "the reproduction of the capitals invested in production depends largely upon the consuming power of the *non-producing classes*." This is so, he said, because in a capitalist society the consuming power of the laborers is limited partly by the "laws of wages," and partly by the fact that they get wages only so long as they can be employed at a profit for the capitalist class. In other words, in order that some surplus-value be materialized in new net capital formation, the balance must be wasted in unproductive consumption. As Malthus had it, "no power of consumption on the part of the laboring classes can ever . . . alone furnish encouragement to the employment of capital."[14] The additional consumption of the "non-producing classes" is required for the re-investment of the accumulating surplus-value. If this consumption were not forthcoming, it would seem, not enough surplus-value could be invested and a crisis would ensue.[15]

With respect to the long-run, Marx saw that the increased output of surplus-value resulting from machine technology *makes possible* the maintenance of an increasing entourage of unproductive consumers. He does not yet see the *compelling necessity* for such consumption which would develop with the growth monopoly and capital-saving technology a hundred years later. "A larger portion of the produce of society," he wrote with respect to the effect of machinery on production, "is changed into surplus produce, and a larger part of the surplus produce is supplied for consumption in a multiplicity of refined shapes. In other words [seeing eye-to-eye with Mill], the production of luxuries increases." This "extraordinary productiveness of modern industry . . . *allows* of the unproductive employment of a larger and larger part of the working class," and the consequent multiplication of the servant classes, of the whole coterie of lackeys, government officials, priests, lawyers, soldiers, etc., etc., "who have no occupation but to consume the labor of others," that is, surplus-value.[16]

Note that the multiplication of surplus-value by the machine as yet only "allows" the multiplication of these unproductive classes. Marx does not see the time when instead of merely *allowing*, the multiplication of surplus-value will *compel* the multiplication of unproductive expenditures as a requirement for the very viability of the system.

6. *Thorstein Veblen.*—Veblen's treatment of unproductive expenditures at the turn of the century carries the strong moral overtones that characterized their treatment in the hands of John Stuart Mill.[17] But except for this similarity between him and Mill, Veblen develops his own theory more along the lines of Marx than along those of any other of his predecessor economists, although he did not associate himself with Marx's general theses. For Veblen, unproductive expenditures already assume a permanent and *necessary* place in the scheme of capitalist production, even though "conspicuously wasteful consumption" and other wasteful expenditures were also common in pre-capitalist societies. Now they become a fixed and inescapable characteristic of the system, along with the "parasitic" industries of advertising and war production (p. 64).

Veblen's idea of how unproductive expenditures affect prosperity and depression has two facets. On the one hand, he sees such wasteful expenditures as those for war, naval and military armaments as giving impetus to an era of prosperity (210-11, 251). On the other hand, "a persistent excess of parasitic and wasteful efforts over productive industry must bring a decline. The profit of the industries subsisting on wasteful consumption is deducted from the aggregate of the community" (64). Here Veblen is at one with Adam Smith in the assumed effects of the public debt on capital formation. Each industry, to be sure, produces its own profit, whether it produces beef or battleships. But the more of the nation's surplus-value is absorbed in building battleships, the less of the social surplus is available for real capital accumulation.

It is in this sense that unproductive expenditures can be said to be a drag on the system. Insofar as they are derived from surplus-value their deductions tend to reduce *real* capital accumulation as well as the *real* rate of profit, though not necessarily their money rates. This is so because so much of the unproductive expenditures give rise to paper profit and spurious accumulation. In the long run this threatens the viability of capitalism as the system of the private accumulation of real capital. But in the short run, in their effect on the cyclical phases of prosperity and depression, particularly in the emerging period of monopoly capitalism and capital-saving technology, the effect of unproductive expenditures is almost always salutary. As I have argued in *The Falling Rate of Profit* and shall argue in the present work, without the absorption of the excess social surplus in unproductive expenditures, an advanced capitalist economy would be subject to severe depressions.

In the development of this two-sided aspect of his theory Veblen was almost prophetic. The "extra-industrial" expenditures are "wasteful," he wrote, "simply because . . . in their first incidence [they] withdraw and dissipate wealth and work for the industrial process. . . ." Indirectly, they are good for trade; they increase the "vendibility" of the national product. It is when they cease to have this beneficent effect that the "disadvantageous business consequences come in view." (p. 252, n. 1).

This eventuality arises, he said, from the fact that there simply are not enough wasteful expenditures open to the system "on a scale adequate to offset the surplus productivity of modern industry . . . Private initiative cannot carry the waste of goods and services to nearly the point required by the business situation . . . Something more to the point can be done, and indeed is being done, by the civilized governments in the way of effectual waste. Armaments, public edifices, courtly and diplomatic establishments, and the like, are almost altogether wasteful . . . They have the additional advantage that the public securities which represent this waste serve as an attractive investment as securities for private savings, at the same time that, taken in the aggregate, the savings so invested are purely fictitious savings, and, therefore, do not lower profits or prices. [In *The Falling Rate of Profit* I have called these "spurious capital accumulation"]. . . . But, however extraordinary the public waste of substance . . . it is apparently altogether inadequate to offset the surplus. . . ."

"So long," therefore, Veblen went on, "as industry remains at its present level of efficiency, and especially so long as incomes continue to be distributed somewhat after the present scheme, waste cannot be expected to overtake production, and can therefore not check the untoward tendency to depression." (255-58). The wasteful, "extra-industrial" expenditures would have to go on in an increasing volume, if the nation is to avoid "a crisis of some severity." (252). And this is exactly what has been the case in the period of the Cold War: Ever-increasing unproductive expenditures, holding back crises "of some severity."

Veblen thus characterized a developing malady of modern capitalism which was to worsen in the course of time, yet which, two generations later, still lay outside the field of vision of prevailing economic theory in the capitalist world.

7. *Louis B. Boudin.*—With the much-neglected work of Louis Boudin,[18] we shed all the subjective and ethical overtones of John Stuart Mill and Thorstein Veblen in the treatment of excess savings

and unproductive expenditures. Boudin makes no reference to Mill or Veblen. The latter's work may have appeared when Boudin was already far advanced on his *Theoretical System*. In any case, it may be said that Boudin was the first economist (he was a lawyer by profession) to tighten up the argument—to bring out the intimate and objective dependence of the disposal of the "surplus product" of advanced capitalisms on unproductive expenditures, in particular, on wars. "While it is true," he wrote, "that under certain circumstances, the declaration of a war may hasten on an impending crisis . . .the usual and general effect of a war is just the reverse. A great war usually keeps a crisis out, for the reason that economically it has the same effect as a crisis and can take its place." It destroys uninvestible wealth. (pp. 250-51).

8. *John Maynard Keynes.*—More, probably, has been said and written about Keynes in the thirty years since his *General Theory* was published, than about any other economist, except Marx, in the past one hundred years. This has been so because for most capitalist economists, for most labor leaders in the capitalist world, for its disillusioned radicals, Keynes appears to have shown why capitalist economies tend toward depressions and how these might be contained. And all this stems, initially, from his special theory of the emergence of excess saving in a capitalist economy.

For all economists before Keynes who thought of it at all, saving was part of the capitalists' profit. The portion of their profit which the capitalists did not use for their personal expenditures were their savings, the "savings" of which Malthus spoke. These savings were the source of capitalist investment. What they could not invest could be called "excess saving." Some economists, like the Englishman John A. Hobson,[19] for example, saw this excess as emerging from the peculiar division of the national income between profits and wages, in that capitalists get too large a share of the total. The excess is a result of this inequitable distribution. Excess saving, thus, is identified with excessive profit. When these excessive profits are invested, more productive capacity is produced than the economy can take, leading to a contraction of production and employment, and a depression.

From all this, an obvious conclusion would appear to follow: If we are to avoid depressions, change the distribution of the national income so that the capitalists will not get as large a share as they now do. Since this would not suit the capitalists at all, the alternative, if we are to eliminate depressions, would be to change the system so that the emerging profit as social surplus would accrue to the people as a whole to invest as needed. In other words, change capitalism to socialism.

Keynes so defined excess saving that these socialist eventualities would not emerge. By his definition of savings it was possible to show how we could avoid depressions yet retain, even strengthen capitalism. True, capitalism tends to run into excessive saving, he said. But this does not arise principally from the inequitable distribution of the nation's income between capitalist and workers. It arises, he said, from the tendencies of all of us to spend less, relatively, on consumption and save more as our incomes rise. Not inequitable distribution, but the proclivity or "propensity" of man to save too much of what he gets—his thriftiness—said Keynes, is at the root of our trouble. It is a psychological law of human nature, he said, that when a man's income rises he tends to increase his savings. At full employment this tendency to increase savings conflicts with the emerging investment potentials. Investment falters and employment declines.

This relationship between saving, investment and employment, Keynes emphasized, was especially true in advanced capitalisms, where capital installations are already plentiful. Then, when at full employment, private investment falls short of consumers' saving potentials, the national income falls, and production and employment fall to such lower levels as are consistent with the emerging investment potentials. This, said Keynes, is why a fully-developed capitalist economy tends to operate not at full employment, but at various levels below full employment. All that is needed, therefore, to achieve full employment is to take such action as would increase the community's propensity to consume and such measures as would encourage investment.

Keynes, therefore, had no need for massive unproductive expenditures as a means of absorbing social surplus and provided for none in his schema. Least of all did he think of wars as an outlet for excess saving. Ancient Egypt, he said, built pyramids as a means of absorbing her surplus weath. "The Middle Ages built cathedrals and sang dirges. Two pyramids, two masses for the dead, are twice as good as one; but not so two railways from London to York." Today, "millionaires find their satisfaction in building mighty mansions to contain their bodies when alive and pyramids to shelter them after death, or, repenting their sins, erect cathedrals and endow monasteries or foreign missions . . . " when abundance of capital might interfere with abundance of output. We might even dig holes in the ground, "paid out of savings," and fill them up again to the same end. (*G. T.*, p. 131 and p. 220.) *

Later we will see how and why Keynes' economic analysis fell short of being sound economic theory and where it failed to square with capitalist political and economic realities. Here it is enough to add that Keynes' theory of how to make capitalism work without depressions was so novel (and its coming so timely) that it virtually revolutionized capitalist economic thought. Later his disciples would amend the grosser errors of his theory and would spell out and extend his policy recommendations.[20] But it was not long after the publication of the *General Theory* that everybody, it appears, had become a "Keynesian"—from Harvard University Professors to dues-paying members of the teamsters' union: Everybody—Republicans, Democrats, radicals, conservatives—all except a few die-hard cloistered fundamentalists in economic theory and standpat businessmen. To the majority, Keynes had revealed the secret of capitalist economic crises and showed the way for their containment, without sacrifice of any vital capitalist prerogatives.

Clearly, our search for an answer to the question: Is it possible to maintain peacetime full employment in capitalist America?, must begin in Keynesian economics. But before we go to Keynes, we must examine a theory of business cycles which leads up to him, namely, that dealing with underconsumption as a cause of economic depressions.

---

*For abbreviations, see Notes.

4.
UNDERCONSUMPTION AS A
CAUSE OF BUSINESS DEPRESSIONS

A. INSUFFICIENCY OF CONSUMER INCOME

1. *Origin and Significance.*—As first formulated by Malthus, we have seen, the underconsumption theory of depressions was no more than a statement of the observable fact that "productive" consumers did not get enough purchasing power to buy back their own products. Unless, out of the balance, purchasing power were supplied also to "unproductive" consumers—to the landlords, the clergy, the military and the like—Malthus argued, it is not possible to take the total output off the market. This is why we have gluts, he said. "It is indeed most important to observe," he wrote, "that no power of consumption on the part of the laboring classes can ever alone furnish an encouragement to the employment of capital."

The chief fault of such formulation of the theory of underconsumption lies in its failure to encompass in full the nature of the reproduction cycle of an industrial economy. In an industrial economy, whether capitalist or socialist, "consumption" is not only personal consumption, but also social and "productive" consumption. Production must generate not only consumer income, and not only replacement funds for the capital used up, but also funds for the expansion of capital and for the maintenance of the state. In Marx's terminology, it must provide not only for the "simple" but also for an "expanded" reproduction of capital, besides feeding, clothing, and sheltering the people. And it must provide for the social services of the modern state; that is, for the cost of government.

In 1875, in his *Critique of the Gotha Programme,* Marx severely castigated the Lassallean Socialists of Germany for their claim that under socialism the workers will get the "undiminished" or "full product of their labour." Not so, said Marx. Even under socialism funds must be deducted from the total national output for the expansion of the economy, for the maintenance of the state and for the social services.[1]

In a word, the underconsumption theory in its original formulation cannot answer this question: Suppose the workers got the full product of their labor, where would the money-capital come from to build the new facilities to employ the growing population and to raise their individual and social living standards?

The answer, of course, is, there would not be any. Society would be leading a pre-capitalist form of existence in which whatever man with his family produced he would himself, with his family, either directly or through exchange with similarly situated citizens, consume. The laborer would get the "full product of his labor." But it would be a small product indeed. There would be the wooden plow and the flail, instead of the tractor and the motor-driven thresher; there would be the ox cart, instead of the motor truck. It takes factories to make freight cars, and refrigerators and sewing machines. And factories are built with our "savings"—with the difference between what the laborer produces and what he gets for a living. Marx called this difference surplus-value; we call it social surplus. In his terms:

> . . . . The workers, can only consume an equivalent for
> their product so long as they produce more than this
> equivalent — surplus-value or surplus product. They must
> always be *over-producers*, must always produce over and
> above their needs, in order to be able to be consumers
> or buyers within the limits of their needs. [*Theories of
> Surplus Value,* p. 397-8. Marx's italics.]

Obviously, then, it is not a question that a difference exists between what the "productive consumer" produces and what he gets; but of what is done with this difference. And that depends upon the still more basic question: To whom does this difference accrue? Even in a socialist state this difference must exist. Else capital accumulation, the building up of the economy, would not be possible.

It is in this respect that capitalist underconsumption differs from the underconsumption that has been the lot of the masses throughout recorded history wherever exploiting and exploited classes existed. Before the advent of capitalism, the gap between production and consumption was for the most part filled by the luxurious living of the exploiters and by other wasteful expenditures—idle retinues, the Church, etc. Gradually, over the centuries, this excess went to build up the primitive capital accumulation which became the foundation for the development of capitalism. By absorbing that excess, developing capitalism precluded the precipitation of crises of overproduction. With the maturing of capitalist production, the gap tends to become ever wider, and the need for filling it with ever-increasing capital accumulation ever more pressing.

So, when underconsumptionists say that we have depressions because in a capitalist society production tends to exceed consumption, we say that if this were not the case we would have a continuous depression, and not alternate periods of prosperity and depression. For only so long as this gap exists is accumulation of capital possible, and only so long as capital may be accumulated can expansion continue and the economy progress.

Further, if it were true that the gap between production and consumption generates a crisis, why does it have this baneful effect only under capitalist conditions? A similar gap exists also in socialist societies. In the Soviet Union, for instance, under the program of accelerated industrialization, this gap has been considerably greater than in America in recent years, war years excepted. That is, in the Soviet Union a relatively greater proportion of the national income has been given to the production of capital goods than to consumption goods, than has been the case in America. Yet, "underconsumption" has not led to crises there. The underconsumption theory can have no case, unless it can explain this fact.

2. *The Effective Demand.*—The capitalist's profit, or that portion of it which he chooses not to spend for his own consumption, but to "save," then, is the source of funds used for the production of productive capacity and for the expansion of the economy, including the expansion of the social services. The problem, therefore, becomes that this "saving" must be continually spent if we are to avoid depressions and if we are to create the conditions for full employment on a continuing basis. For this we must know the nature of the aggregate demand for both consumer and producer goods, the social services, and their interdependence. And for this we must have a sound theory of the effective demand. We must have a theory which would explain why, under capitalist conditions, consumption *plus* private investment, *plus* expenditures for the social services repeatedly fail to create enough demand to keep the productive system in full operation, let alone preventing it from going into a recession.

Malthus, it will be remembered, failed to develop a theory of effective demand, although his theory of underconsumption clearly indicated the need for one, as all underconsumption theories must do. They all show that personal consumption alone cannot sustain full employment. Marx had a theory of total demand. But that remained *terra incognita* to the academic economists of the capitalist world. The attempt by Hobson in 1889, in collaboration with Mummery, to promulgate one cost him his job as lecturer of political economy with the London Extension Board.

> Saving [they had written] while it increases the existing aggregate of Capital, simultaneously reduces the quantity of utilities and conveniences [of goods and services, we now say] consumed; any undue exercise of this habit must, therefore, cause an accumulation of Capital in excess of that which is required for use, and this excess will consist in the form of *general over-production.* (2)

In other words, savings reduce consumer purchasing power and, if excessive, lead to over-investment, to over-production and to a depression.

To the established economic tradition of the time, this was rank heresy. As Hobson recorded it,[3] to the Professor who blocked his appointment, the proposition was "equivalent in rationality to an attempt to prove the flatness of the earth. How could there by any limit to the amount of useful saving when [according to established Ricardian-Sayan doctrine] every item of saving went to increase the capital structure and the fund for paying wages? Sound economists could not fail to view with horror an argument which sought to check the source of all industrial progress."

Only ten years previously, Professor Alfred Marshall had reasserted the "familiar economic axiom that a man purchases labour and commodities with that portion of his income which he saves just as much as he does with that he is said to spend." Saving is investment; and that was that. Crises of over-production, therefore, could not be.[4]

When, a half century later, the Great Depression exposed current academic business-cycle theory for the hollow shell that it was, bourgeois economists were still without a theory of effective demand. But mass unemployment, and the palpable mass poverty amidst the vast potentials for plenty, caused a recrudescence of the underconsumption theory. This opened a path back to Hobson's theory of over-saving, which Keynes used as a jumping-off point for a theory of effective demand, and from there to his *General Theory of Employment, Interest, and Money.*

". . . There exists at any given time," Hobson had written, "an economically sound ratio between spending and saving. Excessive spending encroaches on saved capital . . . Excessive savings" tend to induce the production of more capital goods than can be put "to full productive use."[5]

All we need to do, in order to maintain "full regular employment of the factors of production," is to find the "proper proportion between the production of consumable and that of capital goods."

Back of the tendency to over-save is the existing unequal distribution of the national income, he explained. The small, wealthy class cannot help saving. The more they save and invest, the greater their income; and the more they save. Investment increases employment and consumer income. But consumption does not rise proportionately to income. Consumers are conservative in their habits. Thus, proportionately to the larger output, consumption becomes even smaller. Before long, the outputs from these investments flood the market with goods that cannot be sold at a profit. In short,

> The current distribution of income throughout the industrial world [capitalist world, that is] tends normally to evoke a rate of saving and capital creation that is excessive, in this sense. [Ibid.]

Thus, it is "excessive" savings that bring on depressions. But nowhere does Hobson tell us what constitutes "excessive" savings. Apparently we cannot know that until after the event; and that is no help at all.

Hobson rejected the traditional notion that a fall of prices would automatically lead to an adjustment of the cycle. In his view, a fall of prices would make matters worse. Not because, as we might say, if prices fall profits fall, discouraging investment. But because, said Hobson, when prices fall, consumers increase savings! Consumers do not increase consumption in proportion to the fall in prices; they increase their savings instead. This at a time when savings had already proved to be excessive. (p. 55). Falling prices and increasing savings further "harden" the glut. (p. 56). Not until the depression is well under way and consumer income shrinks faster than prices fall does surplus saving entirely disappear. Now the reduced levels of consumption equate to or press upon the existing levels of production. The depression re-establishes workable proportions between spending, saving, and investment.

As for the cycle itself, said Hobson, "there can be no real remedy

except the removal of the surplus elements in large income [and] . . .
the disproportion between saving and spending" which they bring
about.

In a word, over-saving reduces the capacity to consume, on the
one hand, and on the other is the instrument which is used to increase the capacity to produce. The capacity to produce is increased
by the very means by which the capacity to consume is decreased.
The result is the periodic crisis of overproduction.

B. A BRIDGE TO KEYNES

1. *Are Savings Always Invested?*—A question presses for an
answer.

Hobson's reasoning proceeds from the unequal distribution of
income, to "excessive" savings, to excessive capital formation. The
assumption is that savings are forever invested in the renewal and
expansion of the capital plant, until halted by the limitations put on
consumption by the very act of saving. The question is: Is it true
that all the savings are always invested?

Suppose that all the savings are not always invested? In that
case the power to consume is reduced by the reduction of employment in the capital goods industries, while the power to produce is
no longer increased. Then indeed a depression is in the making.
Univested savings constitute a simultaneous withdrawal of consumption and of employment opportunities. Then production of capital
goods, or in general capital formation, declines, *before* consumption
expenditures do. The decline of investment in capital facilities, relative to savings, thus mark the onset of a crisis.

The question then becomes, what causes investment of savings
to decline?

After quoting the passage from Hobson we last cited, Keynes
wrote:

> In the last sentence . . . there appears the root of Hobson's
> mistake, namely, his supposing that it is a case of exces-
> sive saving causing the *actual* accumulation of capital in
> excess of what is required, which is, in fact, a secondary
> evil . . .; whereas the primary evil is a propensity to save
> in conditions of full employment more than the equivalent
> of the capital which is required . . .[6]

What Keynes was saying in this rather involved way is that
Hobson was in error when he believed that all savings are always
invested. What is true, said Keynes, is that we tend to increase our

rate of saving with the expansion of the boom when no more savings can profitably be invested.

As he subsequently put it (p. 370):

> . . . Mr. Hobson laid too much emphasis . . . on under-consumption leading to over-investment . . . instead of explaining that a relatively weak propensity to consume [and, therefore, a high rate of saving] helps to cause unemployment by requiring and *not* receiving the accompaniment of a compensating volume of new investment . . . .

". . . requiring and *not* receiving." The higher rate of saving requires a higher rate of investment; but further profitable investment opportunities are lacking.

Why investment opportunities may be lacking is the principal concern of Keynes' *General Theory*.

PART II

WHAT WE MAY LEARN FROM KEYNES

5.
KEYNES ON FULL EMPLOYMENT

Keynes' *General Theory* is difficult reading, as he himself knew. "This book," the Prefact begins, "is chiefly addressed to my fellow economists. I hope it will be intelligible to others." Well, it is not. It suffers from a confused and confusing style and from the use of a new, fuzzy and elusive terminology. In the view of one of his most admiring American disciples, the book is "badly written . . . poorly organized . . . [and] abounds in mares' nests of confusions."[1]

Since the *General Theory* serves as the foundation of present-day economics of the welfare state, which we wish to examine in detail, we must make its ideas intelligible to the nonspecialist reader before we can subject them to critical analysis.

A. MAIN THESES

1. *The Effective Demand.*—Before the publication of Keynes' *General Theory*, the view prevailed among economists that the productive forces of a capitalist economy always tended to produce conditions of full employment, so long as wages and prices were flexible. Keynes' most positive contribution toward an understanding of the problem of full employment was his demonstration that this prevailing view was untenable. He argued, on the contrary, that the normal tendency of capitalist production, irrespective of wage and price flexibility, was to operate at various levels of less than full employment. He derived this conclusion from his own theory of the effective demand, according to which the national income and the level of employment are ultimately determined by the interaction of businessmen's decisions to invest and the community's disposition to save. If businessmen tend to increase investment when the community's tendency to save is stationary or falling, we have the conditions for a business boom. When the businessmen's disposition to invest is stationary or falling, but the community's disposition to save is rising (and, therefore, the rate of consumption is falling), we have the conditions for a business recession. When the combined rates of consumption and investment are low, income and employ-

ment are low. When these combined rates are high, income and employment are high. The problem of full employment, then, arises from the interacting movements of saving and investment.

The levels of consumption, saving and investment in a capitalist economy, Keynes explained, are determined by three psychological propensities operating in the system. These were, he said: (1). The declining "propensity to consume," by which he meant that consumers on the average tend to spend a decreasing portion of their income and save an increasing portion as that income rises. (2). The declining "marginal efficiency of capital," by which he meant that capitalists expect to realize a lower rate of return per unit of capital, as new investment is added to the existing productive stock. (3). "Liquidity-preference." By this Keynes meant that moneyholders tend to hold on to their cash until the interest rate rises high enough to overcome this natural reluctance to part with any of it.

2. *Saving and Investment.*—In general, Keynes argued, full employment is not achievable in a capitalist economy on a continuing basis because the large savings which tend to be generated at high levels of employment tend to exceed the investment potentials at those levels of employment. At high levels of employment, productive capital assets tend to become "less scarce." Profit expectations (the marginal efficiency of capital) then tend to fall and the rate of investment is slowed.

Now, a slow-down in the rate of investment means that the income taken out as savings from the total income stream does not all flow back into production. The employment level at which this income was produced then falls to a level consistent with the lower level of investment.

Here is how Keynes reasoned this out:

When a person "saves" he does not "spend," and when one does not spend he deprives another person of a sale and a third person of a job. If what was saved were invested, an offsetting job would be created. Saving would equal investment. Put it this way:

Consumer expenditures + consumers' saving = National income
Consumer expenditures + investment   = National income
Therefore, saving = investment.

By "investment," then, is meant expenditures for the production of capital goods; by "consumption" is meant expenditures for the production of labor-power and the personal expenditures by capitalists. The difference is the "saving" which equates to, or must be "offset" by, "investment."

If investment is available to offset savings at a high level of employment and income, that high level would be achieved. If only a low level of investment is available to match the emerging savings, then income and employment must fall to the level at which the emerging savings find investment outlets. If, then, any portion of what is currently saved, granted a normal lag, is not currently invested, it is lost to the income stream of the community. The community's total income is reduced to the extent of the uninvested savings and by even more as production and employment decline. An attempt has been made to take money out of the national income as savings, without supplying an offsetting investment to replace it. Total income then falls. An individual saver may have his money. He may put it under the mattress, or in the bank, or even buy an existing bond. But the economy as a system of production does not have it. A saving has to be put to productive use by way of buying a new productive asset; it must be made available to the community if it is to be counted as a part of its total income. My "money in the bank," therefore, is not a saving in this sense, unless and until a businessman borrows it to invest, say, in putting in additional shelves in his store.

My "investment" in an *existing* bond is not a saving. My money becomes a saving only when as payment for a *new* bond it is used to buy a new productive capital asset. Unless my "saving" is thus converted into new productive assets, it is lost to the community. From the community's viewpoint the saving not thus invested ceases to exist; it is "nowhere," as Mrs. Robinson has expressed the idea. The end result of "uninvested" savings is a lessened total national income, lessened *total* consumption, *and* lessened saving equal to the lessened volume of the current investment. (pp. 83-4, 210-11).*

Now, said Keynes, as a community's aggregate income rises, the *marginal* propensity to consume "weakens"—the increments of consumption do not rise in proportion to the increments of income. The tendency to save increases. Since, by his reckoning as we have just seen, for any aggregate income, in any given period, the emerging savings must equal the emerging investments, the increased savings from the increased income must be invested if that total income, and its corresponding volume of employment, are not to fall. But since, according to the law of the declining marginal efficiency of capital, continued new investment must mean a decline in profit expectations, as capital assets become "less scarce," new investment

---

*Unless otherwise indicated, page references in parentheses in these chapters are to the *General Theory*.

cannot be added to new investment indefinitely. Before long, as we approach an income corresponding to a condition of full employment, the increased savings potential falls out of balance with new investment opportunities. The savings become abortive, in the sense that if they do not emerge as investment, they do not emerge as a portion of the community's total income either. Savings not invested spell a reduction of employment and a decline of savings.

This decline of total income, employment and savings continues until the rate of attempted savings again equals the rate of emerging investments at a lower level of employment. On the surface, consumer expenditures and capital investments constitute the effective (total) demand, which equals national income (output) and the volume of employment entrepreneurs may deem profitable to create. (pp. 23-25; 29; 55.) Beneath the surface the level of the national income is determined as the resultant of the complex balance of the psychological forces or propensities described earlier.

Consumer expenditures cannot supply enough demand to create full employment or anything near it. In accordance with the psychological law of the propensity to consume, consumers leave a widening gap between their income and their expenditures as employment and the aggregate income increase.

It follows that profitable employment, and income, can be maintained only if government expenditures are added to current investment so as to absorb all the emerging savings. We need the jobs created by consumer purchases, government expenditures *and* new investment from current savings, *above mere capital replacement*, to absorb the output of existing plants; otherwise employment would be contracted. As one economist has put it: "In order to make full use of the factories already in existence, we must always be building new factories."[2] We must continually be investing our savings in the expansion of our productive assets and in social or collective consumption (government spending) if production and employment are not to fall from the levels at which these savings are generated. Only at the bottom of a depression, when large portions of the existing productive capacity are idle, may consumption alone equal current output. But then a considerable portion of the consumer demand originates not from current employment, but from other sources, such as past and future savings (borrowing), public relief, social security benefit payments, and so on. By then, also, profits and savings have about vanished.

3. *The "Employment Multiplier."*—Furthermore, said Keynes, although consumption bears a fairly predictable relation to income—

48

is a "stable function" of income—investment is extremely unstable. People change their habits of consumption and of saving only over a long period of time or under unusual circumstances, he argued. Investment, on the other hand, is subject to the uncertainties of profit expectations, which often fall short of the mark, and is changed accordingly. Also, according to Keynes, investment exerts an "employment multiplier" effect. As it percolates through the economy it creates additional income-producing employment beyond its own primary outlay. The new employment of a thousand workers, say, in building a new bridge, creates the secondary work and income for hundreds in the fabrication of steel bars, shapes and plates, wire and girders, lumber and cement. The combined new earnings of all these workers create a tertiary demand for the employment of more candy makers, garment workers, truck drivers, and so on. Thus, investment must "lead to a total increase of employment which is a multiple of the primary employment required by the investment itself."[3]

Therefore, said Keynes, the amount of employment which employers as a whole find it just profitable to create will for the most part depend upon the amount of the current investment. This he called, "the equilibrium level of employment." (p. 27.) With a given propensity to consume and the multiplier effect of investment, different equilibrium levels of employment become possible, depending on the level of income at which the emerging savings will equal the level of emerging investment. Since, as we have seen, the investment and saving potentials begin to diverge as we approach a national income corresponding to full employment, equilibrium employment tends to settle at levels below full employment. "Chronic unemployment" becomes the rule. Full-employment equilibrium can obtain only "by accident or design," as when current investment just equals the current saving resulting from the propensity to consume at a full-employment level of income. (pp. 27 and 28.)

4: *Preliminary Critical Observations.*—We have gone into detail to explain Keynes' theory of the relation between saving and investment because that is crucial to our own theory of the growing dependence of capitalist economies on unproductive expenditures to maintain viability. Later (p.78) I will show just why Keynes' definition of saving was too narrow to account for an excess above investment potentials. Capitalist savings are much greater than the mere difference between consumer income and consumer expenditures defined by Keynes. Capitalist savings originate in a far richer source than the satiety of individual consumers. They originate in the social surplus which capitalist production creates, regardless of con-

49

sumer propensities. This social surplus is much greater, we will see, than the total of consumers' savings, and requires much larger investment offsets than do the consumers' savings. Lacking such investment potentials, the economy would suffer from a chronic depression if the excess social surplus were not absorbed in unproductive expenditures.

Keynes' explanation of the decline of the rate of investment as due to a superfluity of capital is also faulty. The rate of investment declines not so much because capital becomes "less scarce," as because it becomes more efficient. One must multiply capital assets by their productivity to arrive at their abundance or scarcity. But Keynes argued for his thesis by assuming a stationary technology (p. 245). And there are many other faults in Keynes' theoretical system which need to and will be examined as the book progresses.

None of these faults, however, detract from the usefulness of the powerful tool for economic analysis which Keynes forged with his theory of effective demand. His concept of the saving-investment relation makes it possible, for the first time in the history of *capitalist* economic thought, to treat rationally of the capitalist tendency to fall into depressions and ultimately into secular stagnation. Keynes' own use of this tool may have been defective, but the tool is there. The problem of full employment is now treated everywhere in terms of consumption and saving and of saving and investment, as components and determinants of the total national income, levels of employment and rates of economic growth.

B. A KEYNESIAN DILEMMA

The contradictory movements of saving and investment as components of the national income create a dilemma: Always, as Keynes saw it, capitalist entrepreneurs, in search of profit, are engaged in producing for current consumption and, through investment in new capital equipment, in providing for the production of consumer goods and services in the future. But as with an increase in the supply of the physical capital, prospective profits on the new capital additions become less promising—the marginal efficiency of capital tends to decline—investment is curtailed. If, under the circumstances, consumer expenditures do not increase to offset the curtailed investment, the effective demand declines and drags employment down with it. But, "under the circumstances," we are told, consumer expenditures do not increase. They rise more slowly than the rise in income. On the rise, consumers increase savings at the very time when opportunities to invest those savings are diminishing.

"So," said Keynes, "failing some novel expedient, there is . . . no answer to the riddle, except that there must be sufficient unemployment to keep us so poor" that consumers will not save more than can be absorbed by profitable investment (p. 105). Should we say that the recurrent depressions, by averaging out the good years with the bad, perform this unique function in a capitalist society?

C. Keynes' "Novel Expedient"

Let us recall that besides the consumption-saving-investment relation just noted, there is also a profits-interest-investment relation. The "inducement to invest," Keynes tells us, "will be found to depend on the relation between the schedule of the marginal efficiency of capital and the complex of rates of interest on loans of various maturities and risks" (pp. 27-28).

With the aid of the state, therefore, Keynes would (1) increase the community's propensity to consume, and thereby reduce the rate of saving, at the same time that he would (2) have the entrepreneur accept a low marginal efficiency of capital and (3) the investor accept a still lower rate of interest. The latter he would have the state drive down to zero. By these means it might be possible to achieve and maintain conditions for full employment.

For the short run, for the requirements to control the business cycle, the state would raise the community's propensity to consume by extracting savings through taxes and loans and dispensing them on public relief and social security benefits, and by reducing the high personal incomes where the marginal propensity to consume is low and saving is high. The latter he would accomplish through imposing higher "death duties" (high estate and inheritance taxes, in America) and higher tax rates on the higher personal income brackets. These measures should not, he warned, be allowed seriously to disturb the existing basis for the distribution of the nation's wealth and income. Only the "large disparities" should be so removed. "There are valuable human activities," he argued, "which require the motive of money-making and the environment of private wealth-ownership for their full fruition." "There is," therefore, "social and psychological justification for significant inequalities of incomes and wealth, [although] not for such large disparities as exist today." (p. 374.)

51

Besides the short-time business fluctuations that need to be put under control, there is the long-run tendency of capitalism toward secular stagnation as investment tends to slow down with the accumulation of a nation's productive capital. To retard this downward trend Keynes would have the state render capital "less scarce" to the end of reducing the marginal efficiency of capital (the expected rate of profit) and eliminating the rentier who fattens on exploiting the scarcity-value of capital. This the state would accomplish through organizing and socializing investment, and by reducing the interest rate through a variety of monetary and fiscal measures. The lowered interest rate would serve to maintain a viable differential between the falling tendency of the marginal efficiency of capital and prevailing interest rates (pp. 375-77).

Keynes did not spell out in any form of detail how the state would go about "organizing" and "socializing" investment, except to say that it would determine the aggregate amount and the "basic rate of reward." This basic rate would be very low, indeed. It would "just cover" their labour costs of production, "plus an allowance for risk and the cost of skill and supervision." Through its own investments, whenever private investment faltered, and through inducements to capitalists to increase private investments, the nation's capital assets would be made "less scarce" and the marginal efficiency of capital, profit expectations, would progressively decline "approximately to zero within a single generation." The long-run tendency of the rate of profit to fall would be given official recognition, and officially it would be made to persist in that falling direction.

At the same time, liquidity-preference would be eased and the interest rate driven down toward zero, by the operations of the central banking system, by management of the public debt, and by other fiscal measures available to the modern state. This, of course, would mean the progressive elimination, the "euthanasia," of the rentier, of the money-lender. But that, Keynes assured us, is a historical inevitability in any case. "Communal saving through the agency of the state," such as social-security taxes, corporate reserves for depreciation, and institutional savings—bank savings, insurance premiums, etc.—have long since made his services obsolete. He has long since become a "functionless investor." This rentier "capitalist," who for generations has been exacting tribute from the economy in the form of interest because he was able to keep capital scarce, must lose his place and power in the economy as the proposed state action rendered capital abundant. (pp. 220-21; 372-78.)

Two questions now press for an answer. First, can the state achieve a lowering of the profit rate to a mere payment for investment "risk" and a zero interest rate, without producing a veritable revolution in the structure of the "economic system in which we live?" To some followers of Keynes this "stationary" state "of zero net profit" is not only conceivable, but is conceivable also as a viable form of capitalism. But capitalism and the stationary state are wholly contradictory terms. It is precisely from a stationary state that capitalism as a *dynamic* system of social production took its departure. Capitalism can remain capitalism only when it is advancing—growing and expanding. This advancing, growing and expanding are predicated on profits above mere risk returns on investment. A zero net return capitalism means a zero net investment capitalism, and a zero net investment capitalism means an atrophying capitalism.

The second question is this: Can we expect a capitalist government to transform capitalism into a profitless economy without itself having first been vitally transformed? Surely, when capitalist governments "intervene" in the affairs of private business enterprise, it is not for the purpose of driving profits down, but of safeguarding them and even to advance them. Capitalist governments go to war to protect and advance the foreign investments and profits of their citizens. They raise tariffs to protect home investments against foreign competition. They permit rapid tax write-offs to *enhance* profits from new investments. They buy and stockpile "strategic" raw materials to maintain high prices and high profits of producers. (This scandal finally came to the surface in early 1962.)

It would need to be a wholly new form of government that would reverse all these profit-guaranteeing policies and institute profit-depressing policies. It could not be a capitalistically-oriented government.

Keynes' answer to the first question was no more than a specious evasion. He wrote:

> Whilst ... the enlargement of the functions of government, involved in the task of adjusting to one another the propensity to consume and the inducement to invest, would seem to a nineteenth-century publicist or to a contemporary American financier to be a terrific encroachment on individualism, I defend it, on the contrary, both as the only practical means of avoiding the destruction of existing economic forms in their entirety and as the successful functioning of individual initiative. (p. 380.)

53

He provided no answer to the second question at all; it does not seem even to have occurred to him.

E. THE TRADE CYCLE

The *General Theory* was Keynes' economic analysis aimed at establishing a theory of employment. His major tool in that analysis, we saw, was his theory of the effective demand. A theory of the business cycle, of the "trade cycle" as the British call it, was incidental with him. He devoted to it only one chapter of "Notes" some 20 pages in all, toward the end of the book of near-400 pages. While a theory of the business cycle is incidental also with us— we too are primarily interested in a theory of long-run tendencies of capitalist production—we give a summary of these "Notes" of Keynes' to round out his contribution to capitalist economics. We do this especially because he conceived of the business cycle in terms of the fluctuations of profit expectations, or what he called the marginal efficiency of capital, and his ideas of what determines these fluctuations are extremely vulnerable, as we will show in the next chapter.

1. *Boom and Collapse.*—". . . I suggest," Keynes wrote (p. 313), "that the essential character of the Trade Cycle . . . is mainly due to the way in which the marginal efficiency of capital fluctuates. The Trade Cycle is best regarded . . . as being occasioned by a cyclical change in the marginal efficiency of capital." How does this come about?

This comes about, he said, as a result of the fact that the marginal efficiency of capital depends in large measure "on current expectations as to the future yield of capital goods. . . . But . . . the basis for such expectations is very precarious. Being based on shifting and unreliable evidence, they are subject to sudden and violent changes." (p. 315.) On the highly institutionalized stock exchanges, investment is "under the influence of purchasers largely ignorant of what they are buying and of speculators who are more concerned with forecasting the next shift of market sentiment than with a reasonable estimate of the future yield of capital assets. . . ." At the later stage of the boom, further, investors are imbued with optimistic profit expectations and are prone to discount the rising cost, including a rising interest rate, and the growing abundance of capital. When doubts arise concerning the reliability of these expectations, they come suddenly. In an "over-optimistic and over-bought market" the disillusion may fall with "catastrophic force," which spreads from the investors to the entrepreneurs. The marginal efficiency of capital has collapsed. Investment stops. Employment is cut. The slump is on.

A collapse of profit expectations creates a sharp increase in the fear of parting with cash, in liquidity-preference, and a rise in the interest rate. Now there is no easy way of reversing the trend. While a lowering of the interest rate might have permitted the boom to continue a while longer, a reduction, now that the crisis has broken out, cannot be of help. The rate cannot be made to fall fast enough nor low enough to restore a working relation with the falling marginal efficiency of capital, determined as that is now "by the uncontrollable and disobedient psychology of the business world" (p. 317).[4]

Keynes based this theory of the effect of stock-market psychology on real business investment on a separation between investors and entrepreneurs, that is, between the people with money to invest and the people who would use money in running a real business enterprise. "In former times," he wrote, when the investor was also the entrepreneur, the speculative element rested on the entrepreneur's foresight as to risk and in his ability to manage a business successfully. Today, "with the separation between ownership and management" and "the development of organized investment markets," the continuing revaluations of existing investment by stock market speculators "inevitably exert a decisive influence on the rate of current [real] investment." (pp. 150-151.) And later (p. 316, n. 1) he reasserted the idea: ". . . Although the private investor is seldom himself directly responsible for new investment, nevertheless the entrepreneurs, who are directly responsible, will find it financially advantageous, and often unavoidable, to fall in line with the idea of the [stock] market, even though they themselves are better instructed."

Clearly, Keynes here greatly overstated the case. Unquestionably, a violent stock market crash, such as occurred in 1929, will affect real investment decision, will scare businessmen into pulling in their horns, so to speak. Even if some entrepreneurs occasionally time new issues with a rising stock market, that is not the way most real investment is financed. Most real investment is financed from depreciation reserves and retained corporate profits, even though under certain circumstances they resort in part to external financing. (See n*, p. 67 below.) The modern corporation embodies within itself both the saving and the investing functions precisely as did the individual capitalist-entrepreneur of "former tmes." In brief, Keynes here premises a separation of functioners where no such

55

separation exists, except as corporate *operating* efficiency dictates the need for separate management and finance committees. The answer to the question of full employment will not be found on the Stock Exchange.

Keynes had to have the "ignorant" stock purchasers and fly-by-night speculators influence the rate of investment for the development of his central thesis. He wished to advance the thesis that it was insufficient investment rather than the inadequacy of consumer income, that triggered the onset of depressions. For that, he created the rentier-investor and made him the villain of the piece. To set him up, Keynes made a sharp demarcation between the "rentier" and the "entrepreneur," that is, between ownership and the business-man, carrying us back to the money-lender, money-user relationships of pre-Victorian days.

2. *How a Depression Ends.*—The propensity to consume, we know, works both ways; it works on the up- as well as on the down-grade. On the down-grade consumption comes closer and closer to the declining total income and may even exceed it in the end: the ratio of consumption to income rises very high. On the down-grade, then, the declining total consumption, although it exerts a downward pressure on production and employment, holds both back from going down to zero.

Meanwhile, during the depression a portion of the existing stock of capital assets becomes obsolete or shopworn, requiring replacement. At the same time, the surplus raw materials accumulated in the boom and the goods left unfinished when the boom collapsed are gradually worked off. Inventory carrying-costs are brought down, as are also interest rates and other costs of production, such as wages. On the down-grade, money-wage rigidities at first hold up costs and so depress profits and employment. Now prices move ahead of wages, improving the profit outlook.[5] The marginal efficiency of capital is beginning to show tendencies to rise. New investment again appears profitable. Conditions are ripe for a business recovery. (pp. 318; 331-32.)

F. CLOSING THE FRAME OF REFERENCE

The frame within which Keynes enclosed his theory of employment is now complete: The interest rate, in relation to the marginal efficiency of capital, governs the volume of investment. The higher the volume of investment in any given period, the lower is the marginal efficiency of capital. When the marginal efficiency of the increased investment falls to the level of the prevailing interest rate, the rate of investment levels off.

The volume of investment, through the multiplier, determines the volumes of income and employment. At each level of income the amount of savings available for investment and the size of the multiplier are determined by the propensity to consume.

Thus, the propensity to consume, a psychological law, and the marginal efficiency of capital, another psychological law, together with the rate of interest which is determined by still a third psychological law, namely, liquidity-preference operating with reference to the quantity of money, all in their interaction with one another, determine the volume of income and employment.

In his *Means to Prosperity*[6] Keynes had written that "poverty comes from some failure of the *immaterial* devices of the mind, in the working of the motives which should lead to the decisions and *acts of the will*, necessary to put in movement the resources and technical means we already have."

This can hardly be the case. The operational psychologies of the business world, the "immaterial devices of the mind," are not autonomous or initiating. They are derived from the exigencies of capitalist production and the production relations between different capitalists and between them and workers. The operational psychologies which Keynes developed in the *General Theory* would close all avenues of amelioration of capitalist tendency to economic crises, short of a successful mass psycho-therapy of businessmen or, alternately, as he would have it, by the intervention of the state. Viewed as derived from objective forces operating in capitalist economies, these psychologies cannot be treated as independent, causative agents in the formation of the business cycle. They are socially determined by the irrationalities of the system. The conditions of capitalist production which generate the periodic crisis, as Marx had it, are independent of the good or bad will of the capitalists. These are the conditions which determine also the "psychology" of the business community, rentier and entrepreneur, as well as the role of the state.

That the conditions of capitalist production, against which Keynes wrote the *General Theory* (in 1936) required government intervention if the economy was not to dissolve into chaos, may also be true. But, in the *General Theory* Keynes failed to uncover the true nature of these conditions or the forms of government intervention required for their amelioration. He smothered both in the obscurities of his pseudo-psychologies and in the fancied "propensities" of consumers and investors.

6.
CRITIQUE OF KEYNES' THEORIES*

A. REASONS FOR THE CRITIQUE

In the bare outline of Keynes' principal theses given in the preceding chapter, we considered three of the "ultimate-independent variables" of his system: the propensity to consume, liquidity-preference, and the marginal efficiency of capital. These "three fundamental psychological factors," together with "the wage unit as determined by the bargains reached between employers and employed" and "the quantity of money as determined by the action of the central bank," constituted for him the "determinants of the economic system." Not, to be sure, in an absolute sense, but as the most meaningful factors for purposes of economic analysis. In their interaction, these seemed to him to determine the volume of employment and the national income (245-247). By implication, the political factor too might be included in this system of determinants. Keynes' state appears in his pages as self-made and self-acting, independent of the economic and psychological factors operating in the system on which it would exert a controlling power. In all this he assumed existing production relations and production forces to be constant.

Now we ask, what determines the determinants? What determines the quantity of money released by the central bank? What determines the propensity to consume?, the marginal efficiency of capital?, liquidity-preference? We need to know what manner of state is that which in a class society would reshape the interests of the dominant class without, in the process, itself first having been reshaped? How sound are the postulates on which he built his theoretical system? How well do the elements of his theoretical system square with observable facts?

We want to know all this because the soundness of Keynes' policy recommendations depend on the soundness of his theoretical principles, and because his theoretical principles and his policy recom-

---

*For an earlier, condensed critical statement on Keynes, see my article, "An Evaluation of John Maynard Keynes." *Science and Society*, Spring 1955.

mendations today dominate the economic thinking of most capitalist economists and of capitalist states. For it can be said, paraphrasing Keynes' evaluation of Ricardo's influence, that Keynes, with an assist from the Great Depression, conquered the capitalist academic mind and the minds of practical capitalist politicians, as no other economist since Ricardo did over a century before him. When Americans read the debates in Congress and the advice of economists on balancing the budget, on raising or lowering the interest rate and on increasing or contracting the money supply of the nation; when they read about raising or lowering taxes, about deficit spending, about inflation, and of the so many other measures advocated to stimulate production and combat unemployment, they read Keynesian economics in the raw.

We must, therefore, know how far, if at all, Keynes uncovered the causes of capitalist tendencies to depressions and how valid is his practical program for achieving an economy of full employment in a capitalist society? How cut through the confusion in Washington and how untangle the contradictory advice emanating from the experts? This and the chapters that follow are designed to help us do that. In the present and in the next chapter we check his theories. The rest of the book tests the policy recommendations derived from his theories. Throughout, we shall bear in mind that we are confronted with two forms of capitalist tendencies to depression. One, the tendency toward the secular decline of the system which was Keynes' main concern. The other, the tendency toward the cyclical, the periodic breakdown, which is forever the "present danger" and with which economists and politicians are mainly concerned today, even though the question of "economic growth" is beginning to push to the fore.

B. The Interest Rate

1. *"Liquidity-Preference."*—We begin with the interest rate. In the Keynesian schema the interest rate, after all, is the ultimate barrier to continuous investment and so to continuous high-level employment. The "interest rate," also, has become an almost daily topic for newspaper comment on the ways and means of controlling inflation and retarding recessions. Keynes, we have noticed, would go so far as to eliminate the rentier as a means of removing this barrier. What determines the interest rate? And is it the potent force in the business world that Keynes' theory would lead us to believe it is?

Two things, said Keynes, determine the interest rate: "Liquidity-preference" and the quantity of money. Liquidity-preference, Keynes defined as the natural tendency of man to hold on to cash in the absence of sufficient inducement to part with it.

The quantity of money which an individual will want to hold, Keynes explained, is fixed by the amount which he has to begin with, by the degree of his current tendency toward liquidity-preference, and by the power of the counteracting pull of the current rate of interest. (pp. 167-168). For reasons of certain business as well as psychological considerations, Keynes argued, an individual will prefer to hold on to his cash. But hoards do not earn interest. He will, therefore, part with some of his money in the form of loans if the interest rate is sufficiently attractive. This is the "quantity of money" which an individual will prefer *not* to hold in the form of cash. In a word, the interest rate is the "reward for parting with liquidity for a specified period." It is, therefore, determined at the point where the desire to hold a certain amount of cash is just offset by the pull of the interest rate offered for that quantity of cash. (pp. 166-168).

Thus, we can take Keynes' word for it that the rate of interest is "a highly psychological phenomenon." (p. 202). It is not a payment for *waiting*, as the neo-classical economists had argued, but for *not hoarding*, for *parting* with liquidity. (p. 182).

Two questions may now be raised.

(1). Liquidity-preference is a psychological phenomenon and so also, said Keynes, is the interest rate which is largely determined by it. If that is the case, both the interest rate and liquidity-preference must be greatly affected by the psychology of the business world which varies with the ups and downs of business, which in turn, he has told us, vary with the psychology of investment. It would seem, therefore, that it is the rate of investment that ultimately determines the interest rate and liquidity-preference, rather than the other way around as Keynes had it.

This is not to accuse Keynes of seemingly circular reasoning. He argued for a dynamic phenomenon from a static base, even though a degree of interdependence of the movements of the interest rate and the rate of investment is undoubtedly present in his reasoning.

(2). Interest, according to Keynes, is the "price" which A pays to B to acquire the liquidity B gives up. If neither values liquidity highly the interest rate will be low. If both value it highly, the interest rate will be high. If their valuations of liquidity differ from each other, the interest rate will represent some sort of an average price of their respective liquidity-preference.

Now we ask, since interest is a part of the national income, where does the wherewithal to pay it come from? Is liquidity a productive service like labor? Does liquidity itself breed interest? Does money?

The *General Theory* does not provide an answer to any of these questions. Neither the role which Keynes assigned to the interest rate in effecting the volume of investment, nor his explanation as to its origin, is in accord with the realities of the business world.

In treating of the interest rate, Keynes became so obsessed with the parasitism of the "functionless investor" that he neglected to observe that interest is a return on money capital of the same nature and origin as the return on all capital used in capitalist production; that it is a form and a part of capitalist gross profit. Interest is a payment made out of this profit, earned on the entire capital, for the use of a particular portion thereof, even though this portion may be nothing more than a bank credit advanced on production in process. One capitalist (say, a business firm) shares his profit with another capitalist (an individual, a bank, another business firm) in return for a loan in order to make more profit, or even only to maintain the present rate of profit. He would not borrow if it did not "pay him" to do so.

Let us take a capitalist with a given sum of money M and start him in a business. (Where he got this money is of no consequence for the moment; we'll assume he inherited it.) Now, a capitalist does not engage in a business venture and risk his capital for the fun of it, nor to provide work for the jobless, nor for the purpose of seeing his money go through a process of reproduction only to come back intact in the original amount. He wants his money to "make" money. He wants his money M to come back to him enlarged to the extent of M^1.

To achieve this end our capitalist must do several things. To begin with, he must part with his liquid capital M—he must *part with liquidity*—in the form of "investment" in labor-power, materials, land, plant and production equipment. He then must put these production commodities through a production process which will result in their transformation into new commodities, C, which he will sell at a profit. His original M will have been "metamorphosed," as Marx described it, into M^1.

In other words, in order for interest to emerge at all there must first take place a transformation of money capital into labor-power and production materials, and finished products, and from these back again into money capital. M must be converted to C and C to M¹, for profit and, therefore, for interest to emerge. Thus interest is created as part of the surplus value of the capitalist in the course of production. It then emerges in capitalist bookkeeping as a separate accounting item, incidentally, deductible for tax purposes *from* the gross profit. Interest is charged as a cost in the net profit account.

Keynes treated money and interest as if they were independent of this production process. He seems to have ignored the fact that it is production that in large part provides both the basis for money creation (credit) and the demand for credit-money and that it is production which produces the surplus-value out of which alone interest can be paid, and by which alone its maximum rate can be determined.

Keynes would have it the other way around: That money generates production and that interest is paid for that money for other reasons than those arising from production. Thus, in Keynes' view, money breeds money. This is a fallacy which Marx exposed generations ago. According to this conception, in Marx's words, "capital appears as a mysterious and self-creating source of interest, a thing creating itself. . . . The use-value of money . . . becomes a faculty of money to generate value and yield interest, just as it is the faculty of a pear tree to bear pears."[1]

This is not all, said Marx, as if addressing himself to a future Keynes: "Still something else becomes perverted. While interest is only a portion of the profit, that is, of surplus-value . . . it looks now on the contrary as though the interest were the typical fruit of capital, the primal thing, and profit, in the shape of profit of enterprise, a mere accessory and by-product of the process of reproduction."[2]

If, then, we are to understand the phenomenon of interest in capitalist society, we must understand the phenomenon of profit in such society. For that, we must know the economic and *social* forces in which profit originates and how it is apportioned among the various forms of capital—money capital, merchant capital, industrial capital. There is nothing "psychological" in any of these determinations, except as the businessman's acts reflect these external forces.

Except in times of crisis, when all money and credit relations may be violently disrupted, the rate of interest depends primarily on the prospective profitability of the loan to the borrower, given the normal reluctance of lenders to part with cash. In other words, on the demand side it is the rate of profit that determines the rate of interest which borrowers will be willing to pay. On the supply side, the rate will depend upon the degree of reluctance of individuals to part with cash, that is, on liquidity-preference.

A hundred and fifty years before the *General Theory*, Adam Smith had written:

> It may be laid down as a maxim, that wherever a great deal can be made by the use of money, a great deal will commonly be given for the use of it; and that wherever little can be made by it, less will commonly be given for it . . . The progress of interest, therefore, may lead us to form some notion of the progress of profit. [3]

In a word, interest can be nothing more than a segment of profit, or of surplus-value, to use the Marxist terminology. Where the capitalist has his own money resources he receives his full profit. (The first Henry Ford did essentially that.) If he has to borrow from others, he must share it with them. When profits are low, then interest rates will tend to be low. When profits are high interest rates will tend to be high, in part because lenders will then hold back on investment in anticipation of still higher profits and still higher interest rates.

It is only in times of a developing crisis—and then it becomes one of the symptoms of the coming crisis—that the interest rate tends to move in the opposite direction from profits, and violently so. It is then, when profits fall drastically, that the interest rate may rise by leaps. There is then a universal rush for liquidity—to "conserve" resources and to meet contractual obligations. As the pressure for cash becomes general—everybody trying to avoid bankruptcy—"liquidity-preference" stiffens, a "money shortage" develops and the rate of interest rises sharply as the value of disposable assets sharply falls. Obligations cannot be met and an epidemic of bankruptcies ensues. Under these conditions, "liquidity-preference" becomes so marked as to create the illusion that it has an independent existence. "On the eve of the crisis," wrote Marx, "the bourgeois, with the self-sufficiency that springs from intoxicating prosperity, declares money to be a vain imagination. Commodities alone are money. But now [in a crisis] the cry is everywhere: money alone is a commodity! As the hart pants after fresh water, so pants his soul after money, [as if this were] the only wealth."[4]

In treating liquidity-preference as a basic determinant of the interest rate, Keynes was led to postulate an independence for the rate of interest in relation to the rate of profit (his "marginal efficiency of capital"). To maintain that thesis he created the rentier whom he endowed with the psychology of liquidity-preference and placed upon him the chief responsibility for determining the interest rate. For his pains he decreed his euthanasia, together with his interest rate.

What Keynes was clearly talking about was a stage of capitalist development long since gone by, when most savings did originate in individual "thrift." For that period of money-lenders and individual entrepreneurs it is, perhaps, possible to speak of a consumption-saving-investment relationship in the Keynesian sense. But no longer. Increasingly, as industrial capitalism has developed, and the corporate form of business organization with it, financing investment has been taken over by the banks, by the industrial corporations themselves, and by such saving institutions as insurance companies, as Keynes himself was not unaware. (pp. 373 and 376). More than a half century before Keynes wrote the *General Theory*, Marx had observed that:

> . . . with the development of large scale industry money capital, so far as it appears on the market, is not represented by some individual capitalist . . . but assumes more and more the character of an organized mass which is far more directly subject to the control of the representatives of social capital, the bankers.[5]

And, in our own day, Professor Schumpeter, in his contribution to the *New Economics*, wrote that Keynes

> displayed a curious reluctance to recognize a very simple and obvious fact and to express it by the no less simple and obvious phrase, that typically industry is financed by banks.[6]

Even these characterizations of the mode of investment financing are largely dated. Self-financing—financing from internal resources—and private placements have increasingly tended to supersede financing through banks in recent decades, except for short-term borrowings. Indeed, corporate self-financing provided the major form of capital investment already in Keynes' day. The individual financier, Keynes' rentier, now lives mainly in the pages of the *General Theory* and in the rantings of political demagogues. The "euthanasia" of the individual rentier, which Keynes proclaimed as the salvation of a faltering capitalism, has long been a faded epitaph on the weatherbeaten tombstones of the "robber barons" of the 19th century, although the functions of the rentier still are with us, even if he himself is not. Banks, too, charge interest for their loans, and so also do insurance companies, etc. Instead of the individual rentier we now have the collective rentier. Would Keynes have wished the euthanasia of this collective rentier, as well? Perhaps. An official zero interest rate would accomplish that feat, but interest would not thereby be abolished. It would only be concealed as a portion of profits, where it originates in the first place, as, except under certain circumstances (see n* p. 67, below), industry divests itself of funded debt and converts its assets into equity capital. "Over the past several decades," reads a United States Department of Commerce report,[7] "interest-bearing debt declined relatively to corporate assets and interest rates fell relatively to rates of return on such assets. As a result, a shift from interest to profits occurred within the property income flow." The conclusion was pointed up with the accompanying Chart I. By the early 1960's net interest originating in corporations amounted to no more than 0.3 per cent of the value of the corporate output. (S. C. B., November 1962, p. 25.) Interest paid in 1962 by the 100 largest manufacturing corporations amounted to less than 1 per cent (0.7) of total receipts and in 1963 to 0.5 per cent. (F. N. C. B. of N. Y., June 1963 and August 1964.)

CHART I

Profits and Property Income as Percent of Income Originating in U. S. Corporations

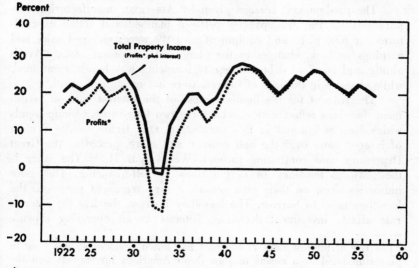

* Before tax, and including inventory valuation adjustment

2. *Interest and Investment.*—In the Keynesian theory of the interest-investment relationship, a decline in the rate of interest increases the inducement to invest, while a rise reduces that inclination. This theory, long and loudly proclaimed by Keynesians, has become the gospel of trade journals, trade unions and of all economic fiction writers. In the official economics of both London and Washington the interest rate has been treated in the postwar period as the antibiotic to both the inflationary and deflationary bacteria. But all scholarly studies have shown that normally the rate of interest does not vitally affect the rate of investment, except, to an extent, in the case of such long range investment as housing and public utilities.[8]

Furthermore, even if it were true that low interest rates are a stimulant to business investment, the argument itself would have no relevance to present-day capitalist viability and growth, whatever may have been the case a half century and more ago. Advanced capitalism is not suffering from inadequate productive capacity requiring stimulation, but from a tendency to excess capacity in need of adequate outlets for its output. Undoubtedly, a sudden and very sharp rise of the official interest rate may serve as a psychologically constricting force in an expansionary phase of the business cycle and may even precipitate a deflation in the small-business segment of the economy. But a corresponding fall in the official interest rate will hardly exert the opposite, that is, an expansionary effect. (More of this, later.)

The predominant reasons given by American manufacturing corporations for the discrepancies between planned and actual expenditures for new plant and equipment in 1949 were: changed sales and earnings outlook, changes in the plant and equipment costs. "Availability and cost" of debt and equity financing was barely mentioned, while changes in the rate of interest were not mentioned at all.[9]

The reasons for the ineffectiveness of the interest rate on investment decisions reflect with special force two long-run economic trends which Keynes ignored in this connection. One is the secular decline of interest rates over the half century and more, preceding the Great Depression and continuing through World War II.*[10] The other is the growing tendency of corporations to self-financing. The more industries draw on their own resources for investment purposes, the less they need to borrow. The less they borrow, the less the interest rate affects investment decisions. Interest as an operating expense

---

*The rise of interest rates in the past half-dozen years or so has been in part stimulated as a means to slow down American investments and the flow of gold abroad. In part it was due to a general price rise.

has been a declining fraction of capitalist enterprise. A United States Department of Commerce study of the "Financial Experience" of a representative sample of large and medium size American manufacturing firms, covering the years 1927-1951, showed that the proportion of firms whose interest payments amounted to 10 per cent or more of profits before taxes and interest had declined from the 40 per cent for 1927 to less than 6 per cent for 1951. For all American corporations, that is, including public utilities, etc., as well as the manufacturing industries, interest payments are shown to have amounted to 8 per cent of earnings before taxes and interest in 1952, in contrast to 12 per cent just before World War II, and to the 30 per cent in the late 1920's.[11] See again remarks on net interest originating in corporations two pages back and accompanying Chart 1.

It would seem, then, that the role of the interest rate as one of the principal determinants of the rate of investment—the role that Keynes assigned to it—has been descending to relative insignificance as the rate has gone down and as corporations, in any event, have been drawing less and less on outside sources to finance their investment needs.*

3. *Sources of Investment Funds.*—The rapid growth of corporate self-financing has disposed of Keynes' individual rentier as decisively as it has of the interest rate as a controlling factor in business investment decision making. The individual financier now exercises his talents in such speculative ventures as are afforded in the bond and stock exchanges, for example. Almost all stock and bond market transactions are now dealings in *existing* securities. In 1958, for example, the *daily* turnover of stock dealings ran to 10-12½ billion dollars. The volume of *new* stock offerings for the entire year ran up to no more than $11.6 billion. New financing is nowadays mostly done, and has been done for a long time, directly by banks, by

---

*The survey of Current Business, November 1952, pp. 7-13. The inflationary expectations in the later 1950's stimulated new corporate borrowing, as did also the availability of interest on bonds as a tax-reducing cost. The relatively high tax rates on corporate income continued from the war years led to an increase of corporate funded debt and to an increase in debt payments. In 1957 these payments stood at 14 per cent of total corporate profits before taxes and interest, whereas in 1952, we have just seen, they amounted to 8 per cent. The earlier contrast with prewar rates, however, is still valid. Just prior to the war they averaged 22 per cent and in 1929, 34 per cent.

See: *U. S. Income and Output, op. cit.*, p. 12.

insurance companies and by the investing corporation out of their undistributed earnings and, increasingly, from depreciation reserves. This last form of financing has increasingly become the principal source of corporate investment funds.

In a word, investment capital is not a stock, a fixed fund which is attracted or repelled in the market place by a magnet called the interest rate. Investment capital is a flow which varies with the rate of production and is created in production. The rate of interest is determined by the rate of that flow, not the other way around, as Keynes would have it.

So for example, in the 8½ years from the end of 1945 through mid-1954, the manufacturing corporations of the United States used $115 billion in various forms of capital investment. Less than $4 billion, or a little over 3 per cent of this sum came from stock issues and only about $15 billion, or some 13 per cent came from long-term obligations. Close to 68 per cent came from internal funds— from retained earnings and from depreciation allowances. The remainder came from short-term obligations, including bank loans, trade and other current liabilities and Federal tax accruals,[12] all of which would be liquidated from future earnings. And this has been the general trend since. (See, for example, S.C.B., November 1962, p. 2.)

A news item in the *New York Times* of June 30, 1952, carried the information that by the end of that year the oil companies of America will have invested $20 billion in expansion and development since the end of World War II, of which new financing was "negligible": "Program Carried Out by Companies Plowing Back Large Part of Earnings."

C. The Marginal Efficiency of Capital

1. *"Expectations."*—Investment is slowed, said Keynes, when net profit expectations—the marginal efficiency of capital—decline. The marginal efficiency of capital declines as investment makes capital less scarce. What determines the rate of investment?

"The state of confidence," said Keynes, determines the rate of investment. (p. 149.) The state of confidence is one of the major factors which determines the marginal efficiency of capital, and that, as related to the interest rate, is the ultimate determinant of the rate of investment. (pp. 148 and 149.) Thus, like liquidity-preference, Keynes' "expectations" are a purely psychological phenomenon. They are born, as he said, of "animal spirits" and are nurtured on the "nerves and hysteria" of stock market speculators. It is a "characteristic of human nature," Keynes tells us, "that a large proportion of our positive activities depend on spontaneous optimism rather than on a mathematical expectation. . . . Most, probably, of our decisions to do something positive . . . can only be taken as a result of animal spirits . . . and not as the outcome of a weighted average of quantitative benefits multiplied by quantitative probabilities."

"In estimating the prospects of investment," Keynes concluded, "we must have regard, therefore, to the nerves and hysteria and even the digestions and reactions to the weather of those upon whose spontaneous activity it largely depends." (pp. 161; 162.)

This precariousness of business expectations is aggravated, he contended, by the fact that under the corporate system of business enterprise, ownership or the investment function, has become increasingly separated from the entrepreneurial function. These owner-investors are imbued with a stock market psychology, which is subject to violent swings between speculative over-optimism and speculative over-pessimism. In the end, these feelings spill over into the psychologies of entrepreneurs and thus into their profit expectations.

As such, therefore, Keynes' "expectations" lack the tangible qualities required for analytical purposes. As Professor Schumpeter phrased it:

> Expectation acquires explanatory value only if we are made to understand *why* people expect *what* they expect. Otherwise . . . expectation conceals problems instead of solving them.[13]

After all, we need to go but a short step beyond the "science of business forecasting" to discover that the "animal spirits" which call forth the day-to-day gyrations of stock prices do not determine the next phase of the business cycle. It is not the rise or fall of stock prices which determines the rise or fall of corporate profits and corporate investment, but, as a normal proposition, it is the other way around. Undoubtedly, "animal spirits" do give rise to speculative moods which feed upon themselves and do stimulate entrepreneurial confidence. But in the end, these must come face to face with the objective realities of the business world—face to face with profit spectrums. It is when corporate profits and corporate investments are expected to rise or fall that stock prices tend to rise or fall. Occasionally, we get the peculiar phenomenon, such as occurred in the late 1920's, when an excess flow of savings is absorbed in luxury expenditures generated by the illusory capital gains of a rising stock market. This is another form of unproductive use of savings. The last observation goes a long way in explaining the apparently paradoxical phenomenon of a booming stock market in the face of recession rates of production that was the case in 1957-58 and again in the Fall and Winter of 1960-61.[14] Of course, the inflationary expectations of the times and the inflow of institutional savings, pension funds, for example, have had their effects in the direction of raising and sustaining stock market prices.

To quote Professor Schumpeter again:

> . . . those ups and downs of . . . investment expenditure are themselves only a surface phenomenon and . . . we must try to see what there is behind it . . . Unless we do this, investment . . . is a mere label for a blank space and if we fill this blank space by some such thing as expectations, we are filling a blank space with another blank.[15]

As "expectations" the marginal efficiency of capital has no scientific significance unless it is measured against actual profit trends, as, for instance, if it were a reflection of the fact that, in Keynes' words, "the current yield shows signs of falling off." But then the question would arise, why should the yield be falling off? Keynes' answer is equivocal. When speaking of the short-run, he seems to think in terms of a theory of diminishing returns. (pp. 289; 302-03; 305-06.) Less profits are produced with each increment of capital and labor in relation to each other. When speaking of the long run, it is the supply and demand of the physical capital that dominates his thinking: "The current yield shows signs of falling off, as the stock of newly produced durable goods steadily increases."

And the latter seems to be his governing theory. "The only reason," he wrote, why an asset, in the course of its use, yields a return greater than its own cost, that is, a profit "is because it is scarce . . . If capital becomes less scarce the excess yield will diminish, *without its having become less productive*—at least in the physical sense." (p. 213, italics supplied.) In other words, as Marx mocked, "capital appears as a mysterious and self-creating source" of interest and profit, of surplus value.

The flaw of this theory of capital is that it does not allow for the technical progress in capitalist production and increased productivity of labor. It is a technologically static theory. The commodity capital remains of the same productive quality and labor productivity is held constant for the years under consideration. In fact, Keynes was

70

quite explicit in this regard when he wrote (p. 245):

> We take as given the existing skill and quantity of available labor, the existing quality and quantity of available equipment, the existing technique, the degree of competition, the tastes and habits of the consumer . . .

In a word, the model he constructed for the capitalist system is a static model. Everything moves by standing still. But "skill" and size of the working force constantly undergo change and tastes and habits of consumers change, if not always spontaneously, then by the effect of the billions of annual sales promotion dollars and advertising conditioning. And not only may all the new capital that is continually brought into production be an improvement over the old— it generally is—it may also revolutionize the efficiency of the old capital, thereby decreasing unit costs and increasing profits. Capital additions, or even mere replacements, are for the most part aimed at "capital-saving" as well as at labor saving, the traditional role assigned to the introduction of a new machine. The continuous technological revolutions which capital investment produces are a basic feature of capitalism. They are, in fact, the very mechanics of the dynamism of the system. To assume that capitalism may grow, yet operate on the basis of technological constancy is to project motion upon an assumption of no motion. Yet this is essentially what Keynes' scarcity theory of capital asserts to be the case.

Incidentally, this technological dynamism of capitalism offers a basis for at least part of an explanation of the decline of investment opportunities, which concerned Keynes so much. From purely a technological point of view, it may be said that it is capital-saving investment which leads to a decrease in investment potentials, rather than a growing abundance of capital and a consequent falling rate of profit. If in a particular industry a decrease of investment occurs, this may be due not to the abundance of its physical assets and a consequent fall in the rate of profit, but to the greater output achieved with a relatively lesser volume of capital. Investment opportunities diminish not because capital becomes abundant, but because the new capital makes labor more productive. This, as I have shown in *The Falling Rate of Profit* (from Chapter 6 on), has indeed been the striking characteristic of 20th century capitalism: a rising labor productivity without a corresponding rise in the value of the material capital relative to wage payments. A measure of this phenomenon is the finding that since 1929 the rate of growth of the total gross capital stock of the country has been about one-half that of the total national output. (*S.C.B.*, November 1962, p. 14.) The per cent increase in the stock of the fixed capital per employed person was 5.4 in the years 1947-57 and only 1.3 per cent in the years 1957-62. (*Manpower Report of the President, 1964*, p. 51.) In 1962 investment amounted to 14 per cent of the total national output, compared with 15 per cent in 1959 and 16 per cent in 1955. This lag in business outlays for new plant and equipment shows itself also in their decline as a per cent of the G.N.P. At 9 per cent for 1962 it compares with 11 per cent for 1956 and 1957. Only in the commercial and service areas has investment grown, testifying in part to the growing importance of services—unproductive expenditures largely—in the American economy. (S.C.B., January 1963, pp. 5-6.)

Finally, it should be noted that Keynes' scarcity theory of capital leads to a theory of secular stagnation and away from a theory of continued capitalist progress. This, indeed, served American Keynesians as the guiding star in their theorizing until the run of postwar prosperity changed their minds (see p. 113ff). As the system develops and capital assets grow, he argued, progress becomes more difficult: As a nation's invetment and income rise, more tends to be saved and, unless investment outlets are stimulated by a new external force, a new invention, for example, the system of capitalist production must unwind into a secular depression. Since, however, according to the *General Theory*, investment is limited by the marginal efficiency of capital; and since the marginal efficiency of capital tends to fall as with the progress of industry "capital becomes less scarce," the "progress of industry" leads to its own retrogression. True, further investment would be possible if the interest rate were depressed low enough to raise the marginal efficiency of capital; but too low an interest rate meets with the barrier of liquidity-preference of the money lenders, and the principal source of investment funds dries up. So, again, we meet up with the limitations imposed upon progress by the psychological law of the propensity to consume, the law which states that as income rises, less relatively is consumed and more is saved—more tends to be saved than is good for the system.

Once more, then, we must examine the meaning and import of Keynes' concept of the propensity to consume. Before doing that, however, we should remember that if pertinent at all, this concept applies only to the relation between individual consumer income and individual consumer saving. It cannot by any stretch of the imagination apply to corporate income and corporate saving—increasingly the fuel that propels capitalist production.

7.
CRITIQUE OF KEYNES' THEORIES: Concluded

D. THE PROPENSITY TO CONSUME

1. *Consumption and Investment.*—The place which Keynes assigned to consumption in his theory of employment was based on two complementary assumptions. The first is that consumption is a declining proportion of a growing national income; that is, the marginal propensity to consume tends to decline or, to put it in another way, the increments of consumption do not rise proportionately with the spendable income. The second is that investment is largely independent of the current volume of consumption. "The scale of investment," he stated, "depends on the relation between the rate of interest and the schedule of the marginal efficiency of capital corresponding to different scales of current investment." It is, he added, only with regard to the prospective profit rates that consumer demand may play a part in the determination of the current scale of investment. Profit expectations are based, in part, on the volume of the existing stock of capital assets and, in part, on the extent to which the current consumer demand requires an increase in the productive investment (p. 147).

Neither of the two initial assumptions corresponds adequately to the realities of the capitalist world. As will be shown, for the mass of consumers consumption is not a declining proportion of a growing national income either in the short or in the long run. Since the beginning of the present century, in fact, consumption has risen as a proportion of national income, while the portion going into capital formation has tended to decline. (See *F.R.P.*, p. 157 and p. 159n.) Employe compensation tends to keep pace with the national output. (*S.C.B.*, November 1962, p. 24 and March 1963, pp. 12-14; also n.4, below.)

Keynes erred, similarly, in relegating consumption to a subordinate place in determining the rate of investment. In large part he did so as a reaction against both the underconsumptionists and against Say. The position of the most economically literate underconsumptionists, such as Hobson, was that under the existing maldistribution of income both savings and the automatically associated investment are so high as to produce periodically a critical imbalance between productive capacity and consumption potentials. Say, too, assumed an automatic association between savings and investment, but for him an imbalance between productive capacity and consumption was inconceivable. With Keynes, the maldistribution of income plays a relatively minor part in the consumption-investment relation, except as it may affect total savings through the low propensity to consume of the rich. But for him there is no automatic investment of all the emerging savings. Investment and savings potentials are independent of each other. They are fundamentally determined by different sets of forces. No matter how low consumption is, the problem of maintaining high levels of income and employment is one of finding investment outlets for the emerging savings. His analysis almost ignores the connection between the investment potential and consumption potential.

Marx, in his criticism of Say, was at pains to demonstrate why the relation between production and consumption could not be treated either in the one-sided manner of the underconsumptionists or in the manner of Say. Capitalist economy, Marx argued, is an exploitative economy. In the employment of wage-labor the capitalist constantly strives for an increasing divergence between the output of the worker and his consumption power which he gets in the form of wages. This is how the capitalist increases his profit. With an increasing capital investment per worker—with the "progress of industry"—the individual worker must receive a decreasing portion of the output if the rate of profit on the invested capital is not to fall. That is, an increasing ratio of the value of the material capital to wages requires an increase in the rate of surplus-value.

But capitalist economy is also a market economy. The commodities produced must be *sold* at a profit, and only such commodities are produced and only in such quantities as can so be sold. In a market economy, therefore, total production and total consumption must in the long run be held in fairly close proportionality to each other. This becomes possible, for example, in the recovery phase of the business cycle, when employment is on the increase. Then investment of new capital can take place without increasing the capital invested per worker. The rate of profit can be maintained without having to decrease the workers' portion of the output. Hence, in this period we can have a continuous expansion of total wage payments as employment increases, a corresponding expansion of consumer demand, and an increasing capital stock which remains in fair proportion to both wage payments and consumer demand. All this can take place without a decline in the rate of profit.

Note that both of these conditions, namely, the maintenance of the rate of profit and the maintenance of a rough proportionality between investment and consumption, are essential to the continued operation of the system. The one, because capitalist profit is the *raison d'être* of the system; the other, because, in the last analysis, investment cannot blindly disregard the trends in ultimate consumption. You cannot just build factories to build factories for their own sake. You build factories that will produce goods for people to buy.

Say's Law postulated such strong bonds of unity between production and consumption as to preclude the emergence of any consumer market problems and, hence, the possibility of a general "glut." Keynes, observing the rupture between investment and consumption which occurs as a result of a crisis, treated it as if it were a normal feature of capitalism. He did the same, we noted, with the crisis phenomenon of liquidity-preference and with the crisis phenomenon of an over-abundance of capital. He failed to see that the normal relation between investment, production and consumption requires that they bear a workable relation to one another. He, threfore, over-emphasized their degree of mutual independence. He postulated, instead, as his law of the formation of the national income the proposition that consumer consumption decreased and investment increased (relatively) as production and income increased, until an equality was reached between a falling marginal efficiency of capital and a sticky interest rate. The incongruity of the assumption of a continued divergence between consumption and investment as a normal feature of a market economy seems to have escaped him.

2. *Consumption and Income.*—Keynes derived his "fundamental psychological law" of the propensity to consume "with great confidence both *a priori* from our knowledge of human nature and from detailed facts of experience." Human nature is so constituted, he argued, that when an individual discovers that his income is greater than what he needs to satisfy his "habitual standard of life," "he is apt to save the difference." Also, the higher the income the wider relatively is "the gap between income and expenditure." (pp. 96; 97.) He called all this a stable function of consumption and asserted that this relationship between consumption and income becomes impaired only under unusual and revolutionary circumstances. This gave him his origin of saving and his theory of the effective demand.

Actually, for the vast mass of consumers the relationship between consumption and saving is highly unstable. Numerous studies

75

have shown that it varies not only according to Keynes' conception of the propensity to consume (as a schedule of demands), but also in response to changing price levels, to earning prospects, to past incomes, and to the *source* of income—whether it is derived from wages or from profits, etc.[1] For the middle-income families, according to one observer, "expenditures on a number of items increase faster than income, and total expenditures press hard on the total income." Basing herself on American experience, this observer concluded that

> There is no clear evidence that the 'psychological law'
> [of the propensity to consume] is a fundamental law of
> human nature . . . Mr. Keynes seems to have propounded
> a theorem which may be applicable to a particular group
> at particular times, not a general psychological law which
> may be relied upon to describe the action of all men (or
> even most men) at all times.[2]

We all have witnessed the experience of the postwar years when consumer expenditures not only rose with a rising income, but at times exceeded it. Less was saved from the current income, past savings were used up and future savings were mortgaged in purchases on the installment plan to make up for wartime shortages or to advance living standards. So, for example, between 1946 and 1947 disposable personal income (that is, personal income less income taxes) increased by less than $10 billion. At the same time personal consumption expenditures increased by more than $18 billion. Personal savings thereby fell by $8½ billion. On a smaller scale this pattern has been repeated since then.[3] It should be noted that these figures are for all American consumers taken together, for the rich who never have to borrow and for the poor who seldom save.

In the *U.S. Income and Output* (pp. 3 and 4), cited before, we are told that in the 7 years 1951-57 the spending-income ratio did not differ from the average by as much as one percentage point. This despite the enormous rise in personal income over these years. Further, in the postwar decade, we read, ". . . individuals . . . spent and saved roughly the same proportions of their after-tax incomes as they did in the prewar era." And this has held true since.[4]

Had Keynes lived among working-class families, who make up the bulk of consumers in capitalist society (Keynes was a rich man),[5] he would have learned two things which would have improved his vision. One, that the income of the masses never rises suddenly

76

high enough to put them into a category of savers of importance. Second, when their income is raised, say, through a raise in wages, *their* "human nature" is such that they are likely not only to expand consumption, but even expand it beyond the level warranted by the raise. They will spend their newly-won additional earnings on *improving* their habitually *low* standard of life. They will buy necessities previously denied them. And they will "splurge." They will go from hamburger to chuck, to sirloin.

They will go further than that; and this applies to middle-income as well as to low-income families. In anticipation of "continued good wages"—all this assuming that prices have not simultaneously, or even previously, advanced ahead of the wage increase—they will buy a television set, they will replace badly worn household furnishings, perhaps buy a car, on *installment*. Not only will little of investment savings come out of the wage increase, but also future wage increases will be mortgaged away. As Sir William Beveridge saw it, the savings of most people are relatively insignificant and are made for future personal consumption rather than for purposes of investment. "They merely postpone consumption." At any moment of time, "while some are saving for future security, others are spending what they had saved in the past for this purpose and the two cancel out."

The savings that call for offsets in investments, for Britain and the United States alike—"the savings that tend to produce depression" Sir William added, "are the undistributed profits" of corporations and "the large surpluses of a very limited class of owners of great wealth."[6]

Keynes' consumer was an image of himself, the well-to-do British aristocrat. He did not really consult "the detailed facts of experience."

What is undeniably true is that for the wealthy classes consumption expenditures lag behind their rising income. As *their* income rises the portion they save rises. It is not a matter of "human nature," or a "psychological law." They cannot possibly consume much more than is "habitual" with them. Even the rich cannot sleep in more than one bed at a time.

A more serious defect in Keynes' psychological law of the propensity to consume, as it relates to saving and investment, is its presumed application to the business community as well as to individuals. Can one seriously talk of a "psychological law," when the A.T. & T. or General Motors pays only half of its earnings in dividends, "saving" the other half? Can one seriously say that corporations, by withholding half of their earnings from their wealthy individual stockholders or from other corporations, "withhold income from consumption?" Yet it is business saving, rather than personal saving that dominates the resources for investment. In all the years since 1929, when the statistics begin, personal savings never amounted to more than $\frac{1}{2}$ of the business savings, and these personal savings include all the savings of the rich—really the other half of the business "saving" paid out in dividends, and other payments to property.

3. *Consumption and Saving.*—Finally, as already noted in an earlier connection (p. 49), Keynes' entire analysis suffers from his faulty definition of savings. His division of the national income into the two components of consumer expenditures and saving (hence, into consumption and investment, since by definition saving equals investment) is too restricted to reveal fully the operating forces which determine the level of employment in a captalist economy. The definition fails to reveal the full magnitude of the social surplus which must flow back into production if full employment is to be achieved, and maintained, in a capitalist economy. Recall how the social surplus emerges from capitalist production: let c stand for capital consumption, that is, for the amount of depreciation of the nation's fixed capital in one year; v for the wages of productive workers, and s for surplus-value. Then $c + v + s =$ the value of all the goods and services a nation produces in any given period of time, say one year.

In current parlance of economists the same total value is called the Gross National Product, GNP for short. $GNP = c + v + s$. Thus, the GNP stands for the goods and services produced in a given time as well as for the payments made for their production: the payment to the capitalist for the fixed capital used up, wages of the production workers, and the surplus-value appropriated by the capitalists. It is out of the latter that the capitalists are fed, unproductive workers are supported, the state maintained and savings derived for investment in the expansion of their capitals.

Now, Keynes defined saving as the amount left of the national income after deduction for consumer expenditures. But to be useful for a full employment analysis, the concept of saving must be broadened to the equivalence of the entire social surplus produced in a capitalist society, and the concept of consumption broken up into the amount of personal consumption expenditures of productive workers and the capitalists and the amount of consumption expenditures of unproductive workers, including those working for the war machine. The condition for full employment, then, obtains only when what is left of the national income after deductions for the personal consumption of the productive workers and the capitalists, at full employment, is absorbed (1) by private investment + (2) by unproductive consumption, including in the latter most government "investment." When Keynes equates the national income to "consumption" plus saving (private investment) he conceals the portion of consumption of the unproductive classes and the portion which is unproductive investment.

Again Keynes treated savings as an attribute of sated individuals, as flowing from the "propensities" of individuals to increase their saving as their income rises. As we see it, savings are the total social surplus which a capitalist economy creates through its unique division of the net national income between capitalists and productive workers; i.e., through the division of the national income between surplus-value and wages.

These distinctions are not "mere theory." They bear vitally on the question of the continued, long-run viability of capitalism as a system of social production, and they bear as vitally on the practicality of the measures being put forth by economists and politicians for containing the short-run, cyclical depressions.

E. The State and Investment

1. *"Socializing Investment."*—Keynes was never clear on what he meant by organizing and socializing investment. In places he seems merely to say that the state, being in a position to see things from the viewpoint of the needs of the economy as a whole, would take measures to direct private investment into the most nationally fruitful channels. In other places he seems to advocate active state intervention with its own investment, with the aim of supplementing and encouraging private investments.

But he nowhere fully defines "government investment." If it is an increase in government expenditures for social insurance and for the social services that he means by the phrase, then it is no more than an addition to consumer expenditures, when not derived from consumer taxes. If it is real investment that he had in mind, then he failed to note the conflicts which that would engender in the system *vis à vis* private enterprise. If injected into productive, self-liquidating enterprise, such government investment would tend to become a substitute and would further curtail the outlets for private investment. Consumers would prefer to buy government-built homes, which would not carry profit in their price, to buying the houses on which private real estate companies make a profit; and would prefer to buy shoes, or refrigerators, produced in government-owned plants to the higher-price products of privately-owned plants. Private real estate would lose a market for profitable investment, and orders for shoes and refrigerators in the private plants would gradually dwindle to zero. Government "investment" would then become not a stimulant to, but a depressant upon private enterprise. This essentially would seem to be the inevitable outcome, at least in the long run.[7]

The necessity for socializing investment, which follows upon the Keynesian analysis, is not alone conditioned by the exigencies of the business cycle. It is essentially a secular phenomenon, since with the progress of industry capital assets become "less scarce" and the rate of private investment falls. It is not, therefore, a case of the state's entering into and withdrawing from the economy with the changing phases of the cycle. Socializing investment, on Keynes' premises, would become a long-run and cumulative program of government. What, however, has actually been happening in America since soon after the end of World War II, is that "government investments" have taken the form not of a productive, and thereby of a competitive nature, but of an unproductive nature. Investments in the cold war— building aircraft carriers, nuclear weapons, foreign military bases; stock-piling "strategic" war materials, etc.—do not come into conflict with private investment and do not "glut" the market. In these, indeed, we have stimulants to private investment. On the side of "organizing" investment the government has devised the privilege of rapid amortization of capital construction at home and "tax encouragements" for investments abroad.

What all such "investments" of government do to the economy by way of "maintaining full employment" is another matter, to be taken up in some detail in a later connection (see Chapter 12, below). Here it is enough to observe that, after World War II, these investments have stimulated private capital formation beyond any magnitude which a peacetime economy dominated by monopoly capital could absorb even with the continuously concurrent expansion of such government expenditures of an unproductive nature. (See Chart II, for example; also *J.A.S.A.*, June 1964, p. 548.)

If there is no Third World War and world peace becomes a realizable possibility, all these unproductive government expenditures must gradually be greatly reduced. In that case, if full employment is to be maintained on the basis of the Keynesian premises, government expenditures will have to take the form of productive investment. And once that is admitted, once the need is admitted for the state to "supplement" genuinely private investment, it must also be admitted that the state is there to stay. The state would then be not a means for saving capitalism, as Keynes assumed, but of gradually transforming it, first into a "mixed" economy and finally into socialism. Is capitalism ready and willing to get itself "socialized" out of

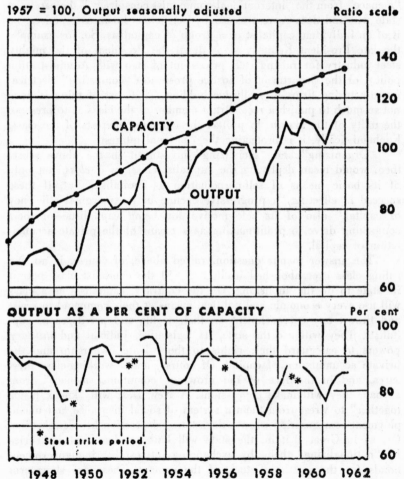

CHART II

CAPACITY AND OUTPUT, MANUFACTURING

1957 = 100, Output seasonally adjusted   Ratio scale

CAPACITY

OUTPUT

140

120

100

80

60

OUTPUT AS A PER CENT OF CAPACITY   Per cent

100

80

60

* Steel strike period.

1948   1950   1952   1954   1956   1958   1960   1962

*From *Measures of Productive Capacity*, Joint Economic Committee Print. Hearings, May 1962, p. 129.

existence? Keynes, we will recall, treated this whole question rather cavalierly. He never followed through his own premises. But there is a prior question, the question of the class nature of the state, which must and can be answered and which Keynes also ignored: Can we expect the state, which in any class society can do no more than act in the general interests of its ruling class, to undertake economic policies which in the end must contravene these interests?

To be sure, under present-day world tensions, in the face of the "menace" from the "international communist conspiracy," the capitalist state will and does repress especially pernicious business practices, be it of an individual capitalist or a group of capitalists. So, for example, the late President Kennedy slaps down the President of the mighty steel industry for raising steel prices out of step with Administration policy, or the Department of Justice prosecutes "competing" electrical manufacturing firms for collusive bidding. That sort of thing is done not so much to punish a recalcitrant member of the class as to preserve the unity of the *system*, to protect the common interests of the class. Euphemistically, it is protecting the "national interest."

"Organizing" and "socializing" investment in the above sense, then, would mean depriving the capitalist class, *as a class*, not only of its basic means of self-perpetuation as capitalists, but, if these succeed in effecting "a progressive decline in the marginal efficiency of capital," also of its sole motive for being capitalists—of their compelling drive to profit-making as a means of the private accumulation of capital.

The answer to our question, raised above, of course, is no. No ruling class ever abolished itself, nor will the capitalist class permit its state to do the abolishing. On the contrary, capitalists as a class will use every economic and political means at their command to resist and thwart any encroachment on their rights and privileges as capitalists. They will *use* the state, its legislative, judicial and *military* powers to safeguard their rights to the private ownership and the private accumulation of capital. Of course, under working-class pressures, and in the face of the growing "communist menace" from abroad, they will make concessions. A New Deal will "knock heads together" to wrest from them a system of social insurance and unemployment compensation when a devastating depression breeds rebellion. Or, as in Great Britain, the state will bail out bankrupt industries by "nationalizing" them, by exchanging interest bearing government bonds for the worthless stock of the owners. These are short-term "sacrifices" which in no way abrogate or even seriously infringe upon the long-term capitalist domination over the production and distribu-

82

tion of the national income, which is the essence of capitalism and of its tendency to the periodic breakdown.

The trouble is that all Keynesian policy recommendations are rooted in the Keynesian conception of the state as an independent ruling force, existing in and by itself outside the system which creates it. But as Schumpeter has put it (*Essays*, pp. 291-2):

> There is no scientific sense whatever in creating for one's self some metaphysical entity to be called, 'The Common Good' and a not less metaphysical 'State' that, sailing high in the clouds and exempt from and above human struggles and group interests, worships at the shrine of that Common Good. But economists of all times have done precisely this . . . It was a major scientific merit of Marx that he hauled down this state from the clouds and into the sphere of realistic analysis.

2. *Appeal to the Capitalists.*—The alternative is to say with Dr. Lawrence Klein, an American Keynesian, that the capitalists can be brought "to look upon the entire system and their social responsibilities" to correct its faults.[8] But in this Dr. Klein is guilty of a triple delusion:

(1) that the capitalists as a class recognize any social responsibilities except such as may redound to their own benefit.

(2) that they could "correct" the basic faults of capitalism without ceasing to be capitalists.

(3) that they would do so if appealed to on moral grounds as Keynes and Klein would appeal.

Professor Harrod recounts an instance of the public-be-damned attitude of the ruling class elicited by none other than Keynes himself at a hearing of the Macmillan Comitee on Finance and Industry (1930) of which Keynes was a member. Mr. Montagu Norman, Governor of the Bank of England, was the witness, Keynes interrogating:

Mr. Keynes: "So it is of the essence of the case that the Bank Rate should have an important effect; that when it is raised it should have an effect in the direction of unemployment. That is what you want. Am I right?"

Mr. Norman: "Yes, I should think it was. . . ."

Professor Harrod adds:

> There was a certain aloofness in the answers and an
> implication that this long effect was not his business.

Further, Professor Harrod testifies, the examination of the wit-
nesses was a "dreary business." "It was not only," he informs us,
"that these eminent practical men could not debate Keynes' latest
theories; they seemed to be unaware of elementary text-book doctrines
about banking which had been current for decades and were familiar
to the merest tyro in economics and journalism. They took a narrow
view of their duties and had no conception of their relation to wider
questions of economic policy."[9]

Keynes made his greatest contribution to bourgeois economics
by shattering the belief in the classical doctrine of the harmonious
working of capitalist economy. It is from here that the Keynesians
take off. *Laissez-Faire* capitalism is dead; the Great Depression of the
1930's buried it. A managed capitalism, the argument now runs, is
the order of the day, and here the state steps in. How, in what
manner and with what ultimate success, are the subjects of the
remaining chapters of this book.

84

8.
WHY KEYNES WAS ACCEPTED

A. THE LACK OF A THEORY OF EMPLOYMENT
FOR MONOPOLY CAPITALISM

In view of the demonstrable failures of the *General Theory* to establish a sound theory of employment, the question naturally arises, how is it that Keynes had become the virtual oracle of leading capitalist economists and publicists? The answer, I submit, is two-fold: Keynes was accepted (1) because of the lack of a theory of effective demand and so of a theory of employment at the time, 1936, when his *General Theory* was published; (2) because when the *General Theory* appeared, the capitalist world was mired in a depression that had by then lasted six years, and existing business cycle theories could offer no way out, any more than they could explain its causes.

Keynes seemed to answer both these questions. He presented plausible explanations why post *laissez-faire* capitalist economies tended to operate at less than full employment and he appeared to show how this tendency might be arrested, or at least mitigated by state action.

Keynes did not identify his work as a theory of capitalist viability in its monopoly stage of development. He mentioned "monopoly" only once in his entire book, in connection with a remark on administered prices (p. 268). It is capitalism in its monopoly stage that requires for its continued viability ever-increasing state involvement in wage and price stabilization; in tamping down business fluctuations; in mitigating the effects of unemployment; in putting a check on labor demands; in holding back a runaway tendency to extremes in the distribution of the national income. Keynes' *General Theory* justifies this direct extension of state power in the affairs of the market place. He thus betrayed a "false consciousness," as Marx would say. He built for himself a world of psychological propensities for which he prescribed controls, and which, in a roundabout way apply to the realities of monopoly capitalism. In this process monopoly capitalism becomes state monopoly capitalism, wherein the state takes measures to safeguard and strengthen monopoly power and big business interests in general.

85

1. *Keynes vs. the Classical Tradition.*[1]—The classical economic theory, said Keynes, suffered from too many damaging faults for an understanding of capitalist tendencies to depression, and these he set out to expose and eliminate. Thus he laid the ghost of Say's Law and substituted for it a theory of the effective demand. Consumption, saving and investment do not automatically relate to one another so as to effect a tendency for the economy to operate at full employment. Supply (production) does not create its own demand, as Say's Law had it, nor is demand always sufficient to call forth the full productive resources of a nation. Production creates a nation's income. But that income does not automatically nor always flow back into the production stream to continue the level of production that generated that income.

What is more, said Keynes, an equality between demand and supply does not necessarily signify a condition of full utilization of resources—a fundamental tenet of the classical economists. Supply and demand might be equal at different levels of production and at less than full employment. For example, the supply of and the demand for savings (investment) (as he defines these terms), are equal at different levels of resource use, and as a rule are so at levels below that of full employment. (See pp. 46-9, above).

Again, he argued, it is not the interest rate that equates saving and investment, as the classicists believed it did; saving equals investment whatever the interest rate. Nor does the volume of saving determine the interest rate, or the interest rate the volume of saving, as they had asserted. The rate of saving, he said, is determined by the independent psychological law of the propensity to consume, and the interest rate, basically by the equally independent psychological law of liquidity-preference, as that may be affected by the money-supply. Together, the rate of interest and the marginal efficiency of capital determine the rate of investment and, through the multiplier effect, the rate of employment and the national income. It is, therefore, within our power to control the rate of employment through affecting the rate of saving and the rate of interest. By appropriate tax measures we can raise the propensity to consume and decrease the rate of saving, and by increasing the supply of money in circulation we can reduce liquidity-preference and so the rate of interest. That would raise the rate of investment so that it becomes equal to the rate of the emerging savings.

As a matter of fact, said Keynes, the whole classical notion of the role of saving in capitalist society was an archaic concept. The full savings potential of the community, the classicists had held, would always be invested, thereby automatically leading to a state of full employment. Hence, they had declared, the virtue of individual thrift. Individual thrift, in their belief, was a public blessing.

This would be so said Keynes, if the aggregate individual attempts at saving were matched by the aggregate of individual plans for investment. But this, as a rule, is not the case. For one thing, the people who do the saving may not be the people who do the investing. For another the propensity to save and the propensity to invest are determined by diverse forces. The first is determined by the independent psychological law of the propensity to consume; the second, by the marginal efficiency of capital and by the interest rate. It is for this reason, for the most part, that we have such proneness to depressions.

Rather than a public blessing, individual saving often becomes a public curse. Individual saving may enrich the individual. But if not invested, it impoverishes the nation. An act of saving is an act of *not-spending*. Not-spending depresses prices of consumption goods and probably also the marginal efficiency of capital. The demand for new investment then declines. The national income declines and savings decline. Uninvested individual savings spell the long-run capitalist tendency to depressions and to the negation of savings.

It should be remembered that even your "savings in the bank" can be a loss to the economy if the bank cannot find someone who would borrow it for business use. The same is true if you "invest" your savings by buying an existing bond or existing shares of stock. Your purchases on the stock exchange may raise the prices of the securities you buy. But such "investment" of your savings does not necessarily increase the productive assets of the community.

When depression threatens, said the classicists, cut wages in line with the increased competition for jobs among the unemployed. That will reduce costs and encourage entrepreneurs to resume production, increasing employment.

If you cut wages when depression threatens, said Keynes, you cut consumer income. That lowers demand, which cuts production of consumer goods, which cuts the demand for production goods, both accelerating the decline and leading to a deepening of the depression. Wages are not only a cost; they are also an income. You may, in fact you should, cut wages, he said, only after the depression had turned the corner. You should do that by raising prices. That will raise profit expectations, encourage investment and speed recovery.

Keynes' special contribution to bourgeois economic analysis, therefore, lies in his demonstration that, left alone, the free forces of capitalist economy do not tend to create a state of full employment, as the classical tradition had assumed. The tendency to save more than can be profitably invested, as capital assets accumulate, pulls the volume of employment down below the full employment level. Under-employment rather than full employment is the norm toward which a mature capitalist economy, possessing large capital assets, tends when left alone. When a capitalist nation reaches maturity it gradually ceases to grow and may even begin to decline. A "secular stagnation" sets in.

To reverse, or even only to arrest this tendency toward a condition of under-employment and secular stagnation, the Government of a mature capitalism must set up controls over the free interplay of economic forces, especially those which affect savings and investment. The excess of concentrated wealth and income must be sheared off by high taxes. The interest rate must be driven down even to a point where the rentier class itself might be eliminated. Investment must be socialized—". . . the duty of ordering the current volume of investment cannot safely be left in private hands," Keynes contended. (*General Theory*, p. 320.)

Both critics and disciples have argued that all these strictures against the clasical economists were neither novel nor essential as a point of departure for Keynes' analysis. So Professor Samuelson, a disciple, wrote, in commenting on "the old latent belief in Say's Law of Markets," "Events of the years following 1929 destroyed the previous economic synthesis. The economists' belief in the orthodox synthesis was not overthrown, but had simply atrophied . . ."[2]

"In my judgment," wrote Professor Harrod in "Keynes and Traditional Theory," his article in *The New Economics*, "Mr. Keynes has not affected [*sic*] a revolution in fundamental economic theory but a readjustment and a shift of emphasis."[3]

Be that as it may, all this seems to have been kept "top secret" by the "top" economists. To the commonalty of the profession Keynes' repudiation of Say's Law came as a revelation. Referring to this achievement, Paul Sweezy wrote:

> It is almost impossible to exaggerate either the hold
> which Say's Law exercised on professional economists
> or its importance as an obstacle to realistic analysis.
> . . . Historians fifty years from now may record that
> Keynes' greatest achievement was the liberation of Anglo-
> American economics from a tyrannical dogma. He opened
> up new vistas and new pathways to a whole generation
> of economists.[4]

2. Keynes' vs. Predecessor Theories.

—Keynes thus made a two-pronged dent in the consciousness of his contemporaries, initiate and novitiate alike. He gave them what seemed to be a definitive theory of employment which, as a by-product, also demolished the foundations on which most predecessor bourgeois business-cycle theories had rested. And he gave them the hope of mitigating the worst features of the business cycle as well as of the general tendency of the system towards secular stagnation. As Professor Schumpeter summed it up:

> Before the appearance of the *General Theory*, economics
> had been growing increasingly complex and increasingly
> incapable of giving straightforward answers to straight-
> forward questions. The *General Theory* seemed to reduce
> it once more to simplicity, and to enable the economists
> once more to give simple advice that everybody could
> understand. But exactly as in the case of Ricardian eco-
> nomics, there was enough to attract, to inspire even,
> the sophisticated. The same system that linked up so well
> with the notions of the untutored mind proved satisfactory
> to the best brains of the rising generation of theorists.[5]

Until the appearance of the *General Theory*, explanations of the business cycle were, for the most part, of a unitary character. In each case one or another specific economic factor was singled out as *the* cause of business fluctuations. (We ignore here the complaisant notions of some that cosmic forces condescend to turn the wheels of our business fortunes.) The interest rate, bank reserves, inventory accumulation and decumulation, waves of big and little innovators and of innovations, over-saving, capital shortage, over-production, under-consumption etc., etc., each was put up by one economist or another as ending in a bottleneck which choked off a business expansion, precipitating a crisis. Each individual factor was assumed to cumulate crisis-provoking disturbances in an otherwise harmoniously functioning, self-correcting economy.

The student of pre-Keynesian economics could only be bewildered by this multiplicity of explanations which he confronted, each apparently a rival explanation, each apparently unrelated to and independent of the others.

Keynes made the conspicuous advance in that he seemingly showed that all these factors must be interrelated in an analysis of capitalist production. Furthermore, he did that not as an eclectic, but as a synthesizer. His was an attempt at distillation and integration rather than of reconciliation and amalgamation. Thus he tried to show how the volume of investment capital (savings) was related to the rate of consumption; the rate of consumption, to the national income; the national income, to the volume of investment; the volume of investment to the rate of profit—to the marginal efficiency of capital; the marginal efficiency of capital to the rate of interest; and all of them to one another.

A correlative weakness of pre-Keynesian bourgeois business-cycle theories was that they placed each cycle in a self-enclosed sphere. After each crisis the economy would just unwind into a lower rate of production (capital investment "topping off" is the new economic vulgarism), until it reached a turning point in a depression. After each depression, the economy just spiraled up, "bottoming up," another economic vulgarism of the 1950's, until it reached a turning point in a boom. An exogenous force, say, a new invention or innovation, lifts the economy out of a depression. A bottleneck chokes off the boom. The economy cannot break through the cycle in a secular advance, nor forever uncoil into a continuing depression. At each end of the cycle, at the peak and at the trough, there is a "turning point" from which the cycle repeats itself in endless oscillation. There was neither growth nor decline for the economy in these theories. Capitalism just cycled on, so to speak.

What concerned all these economists was the explanation of the sequence of business events which constitute the elements of a cycle—the sequences which occur between the upper and lower turning points. The title which Professor Mitchell gave to his last work—"What Happens *During* Business Cycles" (our italics)—characterizes that preoccupation of these economists.

The problem, however, is not only, nor even primarily, the sequential development of the elements of a cycle. It is not enough to know, for instance, that the rise or fall of the interest rate precedes or follows the fall or rise of the money supply; or that, say, the rise or fall of the rate of production of consumer goods precedes or follows the rise or fall of the rate of production of capital goods, etc., etc. Such information may throw light on the *inner* sequences of capitalist production. It does not explain why capitalist economies *move* in *cycles*. In other words, the problem is not initially the *intra-cyclical* relations of business factors, but the cyclical development of capitalism. These intra-cyclical relations take on meaning only when we learn to recognize the forces which propel the economy to move in cycles as a characteristic of its growth and development—when we move from a static to a dynamic analysis of the capitalist process of production.

To an extent this static conception of the business cycle is found also in Keynes. But he does not isolate it from the dynamics of capitalist tendencies. As we saw in Chapter 5, Keynes had but a rudimentary theory of the business cycle. A downturn in production and employment, he asserted simply, comes as a result of a periodic collapse of profit expectations (of the marginal efficiency of capital) and that comes as a consequence of a sudden collapse of business confidence. Conditions become ripe for a recovery when wage rates and interest rates have been shaken down to where investments again become profitable; when raw materials and consumer goods inventories, left over from the boom, have been used up and new orders are at hand; when capital assets have become obsolete or shopworn, calling for replacements. Prices then tend to rise and the schedule of the marginal efficiency of capital moves upward, to the next boom. In all this he was within the tradition of intra-cyclical analysis.

But, and here he made the advance over his predecessors, he placed these intra-cyclical tendencies within a dynamics of capitalist development. As capitalist ecnomies mature and capital assets become less scarce the long-run tendency of the schedule of the marginal efficiency of capital is to move downward, leading to the secular decline of the system. As we will see in the next chapter, the first *application* of the *General Theory* by Keynes' disciples was cast within the framework of this theory of secular stagnation. It served them as the jumping off platform for the advocacy of all those remedial economic policies which have come to be known as Keynesianism, including the theory of the Welfare State.

It is here that the break with his predecessors was most complete, and it is here that one will find the source of his greatest impact on his contemporaries. Keynes sounded the alarm, and the multitude heard.

B. The Needs of the Times

1. *The Need for an Answer to Depressions.*—Keynes' theory of secular stagnation helped to explode the belief of generations that the free play of economic forces tended always to bring about conditions for full employment, and the *facts* of the times seemed to bear him out. One by one, the *postulates* of his theory might be shown to be wanting.[6] But there was no denying in 1936, when the *General Theory* was published, that under-employment had apparently become the permanent condition of the capitalist world. (It had been the rule in Great Britain since the end of World War I.) The reasons Keynes gave for that condition might be incorrect. But the condition was there.

Keynes' basic break with his predecessors and the greatest impact on his contemporaries, thus, stem precisely from his demonstration of the falsity of Say's Law and from his consequent emphasis on the role of the effective demand. *All* of the income paid out of production, Keynes pointed out, *must* flow back into production as investment *and* as consumer demand if employment is to be sustained, whereas Say's Law *assumed* that it did so flow. That the propensity to consume, the marginal efficiency of capital, the interest rate are not the independent variables Keynes asserted them to be, was beside the point. In their interaction Keynes appeared to have located the causes of the periodic breakdowns of the system as well as of its tendency to a secular stagnation, and to provide a neat package of remedies for both these tendencies. That Keynes' account of the determinants of consumption and investment fails to fit the realities of the business world, was beside the point. After Keynes we *know* that it takes both investment and consumption to maintain a given level of employment and that if either declined, but the other did not effect a compensating rise, the government must fill the gap if employment is not to fall from that level. That the unequal distribution of wealth and income is not the *cause* of excessive saving, but that both are the result of the class nature of a capitalist economy—its division into capitalists and wage earners—was beside the point. We now *know* that the rich have a "low" propensity to consume, and that something should be done about it! Or we would have depressions of increased severity.

It was this urgency "to do something," at the time the *General Theory* was published, that explains the speed and completeness with which Keynes inspired his contemporaries. By 1936 the depression had lasted more than six years, the whole capitalist world was engulfed by it, and the end was not in sight. Keynes seemed to explain why it had come, as well as, by invoking the aid of the state, to show a way out. Further, he seemingly charted a method of preventing future depressions. And all that within the boundaries of a viable capitalism.

And, as we have seen, there was the special reason for Keynes' conquest of the academic mind in capitalist countries in that prevailing business-cycle theory utterly failed to explain the why of business cycles in general and the why and the whither, in particular, of the cycle which was ushered in by the collapse of the stock market in summer and fall of 1929.

As is well known, when first the crisis and then the depression of that time hit the capitalist world, its economists stood as bewildered and intellectually as helpless as tribal medicine men before the ravages of a plague. None of the bourgeois economists, including Keynes, had foreseen that turn of events. In 1928, the Englishman, R. G. Hawtrey, thought the trade cycle was probably becoming "a thing of purely historical interest." Keynes, in May 1929, wrote of the British scene (Britain, we remember, never had fully recovered from the 1921 depression):

> In three to five years we should be able to employ every one without the aid of special schemes. . . . We must lift ourselves out of the rut. Once we have succeeded in doing that, our business men will be able to run things for themselves.[7]

The failure to anticipate the crisis and the failure to find a way out of the depression were, this time, a challenge not only to the academic economist, but to the practical politician as well. Five thousand miles from Washington and less than half that distance from London a new economic system had come into being which knew no economic crises and which precluded cyclical unemployment. It was a monstrous system from the point of view of official economic doctrine and of established economic institutions in America and in England. But when millions hunger, with no let-up in sight, thoughts and feelings transcend distances, doctrines, and institutions. Keynes sensed the danger inherent in chronic mass unemployment and proclaimed a solution. "It is certain," he wrote in his "Concluding Notes" of the *General Theory* (p. 381), "that the world will not much longer tolerate the unemployment which, apart from brief intervals of excitement, is associated—and, in my opinion, inevitably associated—with present-day capitalistic individualism.* But it may be possible by a right analysis of the problem to cure the disease whilst preserving efficiency and freedom." [!]

The utter sterility of the known body of business-cycle theory was a vacuum which any logically consistent doctrine, such as Keynes' seemed to be, would readily fill. The postulates were not questioned; only the conclusions mattered. The obscurities and the new esoteric terminology of the *General Theory* were accepted as profundities. This held especially true for American and, in particular, for the younger generation of American economists. Their learning in economic theory

---

*As noted at the beginning of this chapter, nowhere in the *General Theory* does Keynes relate his thinking to the impact of monopoly on the capitalist drift of his time. For our own treatment of this question see pp. 148 ff and 208 ff, also *The Falling Rate of Profit, passim.*

had ended, for the most part, with the antiquated ideas of Professor Marshall of England and of the American Professor Taussig, and their knowledge of the business cycle had been derived from the "descriptive analysis" of Professor Wesley C. Mitchell and from the leads and lags of the "A," "B," and "C" curves published by the Harvard University Bureau of Business Research. Marx was unknown to them except, perhaps, as the false prophet of a false economics who preached the abolition of capitalism as a way of abolishing capitalist crises—throwing out the baby with the bath water! Could we not have a theory for abolishing crises without abolishing the system which produces them? Could we not have Socialism *within* Capitalism?

Keynes seemed to say, Yes, we could, and to say it with enough ambiguity to convince the student and the layman alike. He would "socialize" investment to reduce profits to a minimum; he would drive the interest rate down to zero and eliminate the parasitic rentier; he would reduce the inequalities of wealth and income. He would do all that—to make capitalism work! Thus Keynes provided the restive young American economists with "Marxist" concepts without a threat of Marxist consequences. A "Peoples Capitalism" and the Welfare State would replace Keynes' "decadent international but individualistic capitalism" and forestall the need for socialism. As one American economist viewed it twenty-two years later, "by drawing to himself the enthusiasm of the young and the restless, he [Keynes] kept an intellectual generation from going Communist."[8]

2. *Keynes' Radicalism.*—Keynes had always talked radical, and this prepared the ground for the acceptance of his "radical" proposals for saving capitalism. As far back as 1917 (December 24) he said in a letter to his mother from Paris (things were then going badly for the Allies on the war fronts):

> My Christmas thoughts are that a further prolongation of the war . . . probably means the disappearance of the social order we have known hitherto. With some regrets I think I am on the whole not sorry. The abolition of the rich will be rather a comfort and serve them right anyhow. . . .

> Well, the only course open to me is to be buoyantly bolshevik; and as I lie in bed in the morning, [9] I reflect with a good deal of satisfaction that, because our rulers are as incompetent as they are mad and wicked, one particular era of a particular kind of civilization is very nearly over.[10]

To the radicals of the economics profession such phrases as "socializing" investment and the "euthanasia" of the rentier made an especial appeal. To sacrifice the rentier as a burnt offering at the altar of a surviving capitalism satisfied their need for a scapegoat as well as assuaged their fear of a socialist solution to capitalist crises. And after all, few young American Ph.D. economists, especially the "radical" ones, are of the rentier class.

The depression did not last long enough after the publication of the *General Theory* to test the validity of Keynes' policy recommendations. The war came along and erased the unemployment rolls. To some ardent Keynesians that fact proved Keynes' central thesis: Government stimulation of and supplements to private investment provide jobs for all. But one does not need a Keynes to tell us that when the unemployed are given jobs unemployment disappears. It is one thing, however, to have full employment as a result of production for war; it is another to achieve full employment when the swords are beaten into plowshares.

The dilemma for Keynes was how in a *private-profit* economy to employ the rapidly accumulating wealth without by that act destroying the system. The Ancients, we saw him say, had a solution: They built pyramids with their excess wealth and mined precious metals which would never glut the consumers' market. In the Middle Ages the wealthy "built cathedrals and sang dirges." Malthus' theory of unproductive consumption as a means of mitigating "gluts" comes into its own.

Yet what Keynes failed to see, but which the orthodox economists fear despite his reassurances, is that in his policy recommendations he was involved in a basic contradiction, the contradiction of grafting onto a private accumulation economy a process of social control over investment. Can that contradiction be resolved in favor of continued capitalist viability?

PART III

FROM CAPITALIST STAGNATION TO THE WELFARE STATE

9.
INTRODUCTION TO THE WELFARE STATE

A. The "Three D's"

For generations before the onset of the Great Depression, relief of the victims of unemployment in America, as of the "poor" in general, was the concern almost entirely of private charity and philanthropy. Only to a very small extent was it the concern of public agencies, and that largely of a local character. In the larger American cities there were the "United Hebrew Charities," the "Catholic Charities" and the Protestant philanthropic federations, besides the numerous church, fraternal and neighborhood bodies that ministered to the poor. All had staffs of social workers whose jobs it was to investigate the needs of applicants for "relief"—for food, clothing, shelter and medical care—and recommend allocations. Village, town and county, and municipal "outdoor relief" offices supplied baskets of food, fuel and clothing and hospital care on a small, non-sectarian basis. For the homeless poor they provided "flop houses." For the "indigent poor" they provided "almshouses," "poor houses" and other "eleemosynary" care. In the dread winter of 1914-15, one recalls, the churches were thrown open to give shelter to the homeless unemployed. In the depression of the 1930's, towns and cities set up "soup kitchens" for the long lines of hungry men, women and youths. Always "vagabonds" and "tramps" and "hoboes" were jailed for a night and escorted beyond the town limits the next morning with a stern warning of more severe punishment if they returned. "Each town should care for its own poor," was the theory.*

And all those years Professors of Sociology gave courses in "Social Pathology" and in "Charities and Corrections" (the present writer gave such a course), describing the Dependents, the Defectives

---

*The Legal Aid Society of Hartford, Connecticut, recently challenged the constitutionality of a State law under which a person of another State who becomes an object of public charity is subject to deportation to his place of origin. The case at issue was that of a woman from South Carolina who had lived in Hartford 28 months, was employed 22 months and then became a recipient of municipal welfare. See the *New York Times*, September 18, 1960.

and the Delinquents — the "Three D's" — as the unfortunate ex-crescences of an otherwise healthy churning economic system. In large measure, it was explained, these "pathologies" were self-inflict-ed — were due to improvidence and shiftlessness — or, most charit-ably, to acts of God. Their alleviation was the natural duty of the provident, of the "better" classes of the community.

In America these "Three D's" were to be found largely in the newest immigrant populations, while the organizers and dispensers of the private charities came from among the immediately preceding generations of immigrants.

B. What America and Keynes Learned From the Great Depression

Then came the cataclysm of 1930-33, with millions of workers of all races and nationalities, natives as well as "foreigners," thrown out of work and deprived of their means of livelihood. "Even Wall Street brokers," the grim saying went the rounds, lost their jobs.

This disaster was clearly not self-inflicted nor, surely, decreed by God, although some learned men there were, who blamed it all on sunspots and on other influences from Above. Furthermore, all existing remedial institutions proved utterly inadequate to keep many of these millions from starving or from freezing to death.

And the millions became restive. There were the soldiers' "bonus" marches and the marches of unemployed thousands des-cending on Washington demanding bread. Workers, who never be-fore would have talked to a union man, began organizing into trade unions. They defied court injunctions, tore up "yellow-dog" contracts and staged sit-down strikes. They even used firearms in resisting private vigilantes and State militiamen, and the municipal police that were assigned to maintain "law and order." Farmers thwarted sher-iffs' foreclosure sales of neighbor homesteads, sometimes with bogus bids, sometimes with force.

The families of 15 million jobless Americans were in need of the merest necessities of life. As we have seen Professor Samuelson say, "the economists' belief in the orthodox synthesis [Say's Law] . . . had simply atrophied. . ."

The times called for action, desperate and quick, and the action to be taken was clearly indicated if mass starvation, perhaps rebel-lion, were to be prevented: First, it was necessary to feed the starving — to organize relief measures on all fronts on a national scale, to be paid for from the National Treasury; second, to provide a stand-by system of mass relief for future contingencies of involuntary unem-ployment; third, to provide for the present and future "impecunious" aged — the "superannuated" they were euphemistically called — for the impoverished sick and for destitute widows and orphans; and, finally, to take such measures through long-range legislation as might serve to mitigate the tendencies of the economic system to break down into periodic depressions. In the future, the people would not again be expected to take the dole as an answer to the loss of a job.*

To meet the immediate needs of the jobless multitudes and their dependents, there came the Federal Emergency Relief Adminis-tration (F.E.R.A.), the Works Progress Administration (W.P.A.), the Public Works Adminstration (P.W.A.), the Civilian Conservation Corps (C.C.C.), and the National Youth Administration (N.Y.A.) to give bread and jobs to city jobless. And then came the Resettle-ment Administration (the R.A.) and the Agricultural Adjustment Ad-ministration (A.A.A.) to help the bankrupt farmers. In the years 1933-42 close to $25 billion in Federal, State and local funds were dispensed by these agencies to relieve the ravages of the depression. Social-Security legislation was enacted to mitigate the contingencies of future mass unemployment. The Securities Exchange Commission (S.E.C.), the Federal Deposit Insurance Corporation (F.D.I.C.) were aimed to protect the innocent investor and to stave off future finan-cial panics. The National Labor Relations Act (N.L.R.A.) provided protection for trade unions against the risk of being declared by the courts "conspiracies in restraint of trade" under the Sherman Anti-Trust Act. There was the dubious talk of regulating the rate of private investment through the National Industrial Recovery Act, and even of placing a moratorium on new "inventions." A third of the

---

*That the poor are still with us and that millions still depend on the dole for subsistence, may be deduced from the following paragraph in the 1962 *Economic Report of the President*, p. 109:

Per capita disposable personal income, measured in 1961 dollars, ... surpassed $2,000 a year in the last quarter of 1961. Nevertheless, about 30 per cent of all families and unrelated persons have less than $1,000 of money income per person, and are now below the level that the average American achieved a quarter century ago.

In this connection, see also: Michael Harrington: *The Other America*: *Poverty in the United States*, and Conference on Economic Progress: *Poverty and Deprivation in the United States*: *The Plight of Two-Fifths of a Nation*.

President Johnson's declaration of "war on poverty" points up this condition.

farm output was to be "plowed under." The country was taken off the gold standard, and the dollar was devalued to increase the quantity of money and reduce the interest rate as inducements to private investment. The Federal Housing Agency (F.H.A.), the Home Owners' Loan Corporation (H.O.L.C.) and a revived R.F.C. (Reconstruction Finance Corporation) were aimed in the same direction

A list of the agencies that were set up to ease credit facilities and lower interest rates alone would cover a quarter of a printed page. The sheer multiplicity of these and the other New Deal agencies testifies to the urgency of the moment, as well as to the backward status of social legislation in America. In England and on the Continent, social-security legislation, for example, dated decades back of the 1930's.

Above all, the country was taken off the fifty-hour work week and the forty-hour work week enacted in its place. The commonsense rationale for this action was the "share-the-work" slogan, but fundamentally the effect was to reduce the excess surplus-value which a fifty-hour work week was then capable of producing. The alternative was to keep twelve to fifteen million workers from producing surplus-value. Cyclical unemployment had always been a means of halting the accumulation of uninvestible social surplus, but at the unemployment rate precipitated in the 1930's, this traditional means had become *politically* intolerable. A reduction of work hours had become imperative if capitalism was to be saved from the Midas curse of its potentially overwhelming riches.

To be sure, even these half-way concessions in social legislation met with the fiercest resistance from organized reaction — from the America Firsters, from the Social Justice fascists, from the Liberty League standpatters, from the American Bund. But saner counsels prevailed and "that man" in the White House became the by-word of hatred among the American rulers of high finance.

Now go back for a moment to the *General Theory*. All the New Deal measures, except the reduction of work hours, to mitigate the effects of the raging depression and forestall future depressions can be shown to have been promulgated there in the language of the theoretical economist, couched, to be sure, in a new and esoteric terminology. The F.E.R.A., W.P.A., P.W.A., the minimum wage law, higher personal income tax rates, higher corporation income tax rates, the N.L.R.A., the A.A.A. — were all measures aimed at increasing mass consumption, "raising the propensity to consume." The N.I.R.A., R.E.A., S.E.C., R.F.C., F.H.A., H.O.L.C. were aimed at "organizing," if not quite at "socializing" investment. Going off

100

the gold standard and devaluing the dollar, and all the other measures to ease credit facilities were to increase the money supply, lower "liquidity-preference" and the interest rate, raise prices and stimulate private investment. Higher tax rates on corporation earnings, primarily aimed to finance the increased government expenditures, tended also to lower the "marginal efficiency of capital." Public works (P.W.A., T.V.A.) were to serve as government investment supplementing private investment.

Of course, there is no intention here to assert that Keynes' *General Theory* was a mere rationalization of President Roosevelt's *ad hoc* measures to bail American capitalism out of palpable bankruptcy. Nor, definitely, can it be said that President Roosevelt instituted the New Deal, holding a copy of the *General Theory* on his lap while delivering a "fire-side chat." (The *General Theory*, it will be remembered, was published in 1936, after most of the New Deal legislation had been enacted.) While working on his book, Keynes had several talks with the President and some correspondence with him and New Deal policy makers. There was a certain amount of give-and-take here between "theory" and "practice," but on the whole, both were dictated by the necessities of the times. In one considered view, for example, the fiscal policy of the New Deal "was forced into service as compensatory device more by accident than by design."[1] Further, we have the word of the most vociferous of American Keynesians that Keynes' influence on the President was incidental rather than profound. All that can be said of their relationship, according to this Keynesian, is that Keynes "approved of many of the New Deal policies: the monetary expansion and the reduced rates of interest; programs to raise farm incomes; the encouragement of collective bargaining; higher taxes on the well-to-do; the devaluation of the dollar; relief and investment policies." Only on one major front did he not approve. That was the encouragement of foreign investment. Here Keynes was, perhaps, "concerned over the loss of European and particular British markets."[2]

Keynes' *General Theory* was thus an economics of depressions, even as Roosevelt's pragmatism was dictated by the urgency generated by a Great Depression. Both dipped their pens in the same ink. But the ink was there first, and the New Deal acts came before the *General Theory* was published. First came the demands of masses in destitution, rumbling rebellion. Then came the New Deal; and *then* came Keynes.

The New Deal, we know, did not end the depression; nor could it. It did not reach for basic causes. At best, it could mitigate its severest effects. It was war orders that finally ended it. Thus Dr. Leonard P. Ayres, leading American commentator on the current economic drift, wrote in late 1940:

> American business is now surging into a period which promises to become in time one of the most active in its history . . . .
> This expansion of business activity has all the outward appearances of the beginning of a period of self-sustained prosperity, but of course in reality it is nothing of the sort. This expansion of production, and this calling back of the unemployed to places on the payrolls, does not result from free enterprise competing for business in open markets. It comes instead from a situation in which two great customers, the United States and Great Britain, are demanding huge volumes of special goods and paying what they must to get them in the shortest possible time.

A chart on defense expenditures reproduced below punctuated this observation.[3]

It was now necessary to explain why the depression had been so severe and so prolonged. And it was necessary to find in this explanation guides to a program for preventing future depressions or, if that prove unfeasible, to blunt their severest impacts on the people. That explanation came in the form of the theory of "secular stagnation." And that gave rise to the "Keynesians" and to their doctrine of government action to contain the business cycle and stimulate economic growth, under the slogan of "building the Welfare State."

C. THE THEORY OF SECULAR STAGNATION

The theory of secular stagnation had its first full articulation in America. In 1938, two years after the publication of the *General Theory* and when the American economy was experiencing a sharp sinking spell in the midst of a slow recovery, Professor Alvin Hansen put it forth in his book, *Full Recovery or Stagnation?* It was developed later in England,[4] in his own later works[5] and by several other economists in America and elsewhere.*

---

*In the following paragraphs the theory of secular stagnation is presented in the form developed by these economists. Later (pp. 147ff) we will show how this formulation is a purely mechanistic description of manifestations, rather than an analysis of underlying forces.

CHART III

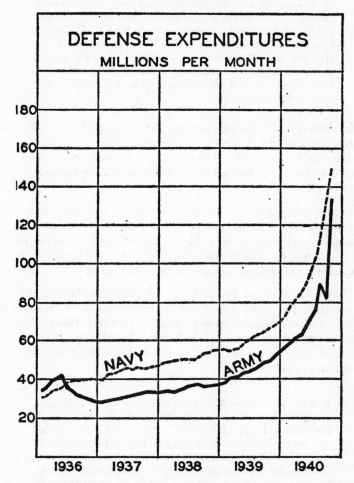

DEFENSE EXPENDITURES
MILLIONS PER MONTH

In his *Full Recovery or Stagnation?* Hansen was seeking to explain the sudden turn in the depression for the worse after the faltering recovery from 1933 to 1937. He reasoned that both the slowness of the recovery and the sudden relapse were due to the fact that the recovery measures thus far taken had been aimed largely at stimulating consumption. But rising consumption, he argued, is not a sufficient force to stimulate full or continuing recovery. That force, he said, lay in net new investment, in investment beyond mere capital replacement. "I think," he wrote (p. 279), a consensus can be reached on the proposition that former recoveries have typically been carried forward on a wave of new investment which was *not* narrowly gauged by the current and immediate level of consumption purchases. Large bold projects, looking far into the future, have typically been undertaken in the upswing period . . . Had the rate of investment always been narrowly geared to the current rate of consumer demand, we should never have witnessed the material progress achieved in the nineteenth century.

Investment in upswing periods, he continued (p. 280), has typically led and not followed consumption. "The industrial revolution, the waves of railway construction, the boom based on electricity and automotive power had no relation whatever to the current volume of consumption."

In the years 1933-37, no such net new investment had arisen to give permanence to the recovery. When in 1937, in addition, the consumption supports were suddenly slowed and in some respects even countered by withdrawals (by the new social-security taxes), he explained, the ensuing collapse became inevitable.

"But," he went on (p. 288), as if talking to himself, "I must not overstate the case. For there is one other consideration that troubles me and raises uneasy doubts whether, though we had managed our affairs ever so wisely, we should even so have been safely and securely on the road to full and sustained recovery. For, he went on to say,

it is not true, as is sometimes alleged, that technological conditions have been uniformly and at all times equally favorable for new investment outlets. Not every period can be characterized as a kind of new industrial revolution. The introduction of power-driven machinery was followed by a prolonged period of difficult readjustment. In a later age, as the curve of railway construction eventually flattened out, it was discovered that there was no adequate ground for the easy optomism that plenty of promising investment possibilities would surely appear to fill the gap. In point of fact they did not appear in adequate volume, and so there ensued toward the close of the century a prolonged period of *secular stagnation*. It is true that in the course of time technology gave birth to the electrical and automobile age and with it a new

era of highway construction. Altogether these developments swallowed up vast sums of capital: but it is not
difficult to see that this latter episode is nearing comple-
tion and, as has happened before, nothing else of equal
magnitude has so far [1938] appeared above the horizon.
(Italics supplied.)

This, together with the "wholly new fact of a rapidly approach-
ing cessation of population growth" and, as he later argued, together
with the growing tendency of investment to become capital-saving
rather than capital-absorbing, and the closing of territorial expansion
possibilities, put limits on the possibility that enough new *private*
net capital investment can be expected to emerge to assure us of an
economy of continuous full employment. The conclusion thus became
inescapable that:

From being purely a cyclical compensatory device,
designed to stimulate consumption, *public* expenditures
may come to be used increasingly as a means of directing
the flow of savings into real investment. [p. 289. Italics
supplied.]

Here, then, we have both the theory of secular stagnation and the
reason why, henceforth, the maintenance of full employment would
require not only government stimulation of mass consumption, but
also government real investment.

Now we want to know, in greater detail, three things: (1). Why
consumption alone cannot supply the motive power to sustain full
employment. (2). How meaningful is the theory of secular stagnation
in its bearing on the severity of depressions and what are its im-
plications to the continued viability of capitalism? (3). The role of
government. How Hansen, and the Keynesians, would have the
government stimulate private consumption and direct "the flow of
savings into real investment" as a means of assuring an economy
of continued full employment. Item (1) and, in part, item (2) are
the subject of the remaining part of this chapter. More of item (2)
and item (3) are treated as the book develops.

D. Consumption and Investment

Consumption alone cannot maintain an economy of full employment, according to Hansen, because, however high, it does not call for
more capital investment than is enough to maintain the current rate

of output; that is, for no more than to maintain the existing capital stock. It does not call for more investment than is required to replace the capital used up in the current production cycle. More than that will be required only if there is an increase in consumer demand due either to an increase in real wages or to an increase in employment, or both, and that will happen only when the system is operating at full capacity production.* Otherwise no new additional investment capital may be required. At any given time the value of the output of the consumption goods is matched by the expenditures for that output. The cost of the capital used up, and paid for by the depreciation allowance, is covered in the price of the consumption goods produced with that capital.

But in a capitalist society the *income* produced at any given time is greater than the *cost*, including labor cost, of the output produced. It is greater than the value of the capital used up plus the amount paid out as consumer (workers') income. Marx called this excess value surplus-value. What is left of the surplus-value after deduction by capitalists for their own personal consumption is the community's total savings — what we here call social surplus. It is this social surplus that must find new net investment, if full employment is to be achieved and sustained on a continuing basis.

Professor Hansen did not analyze these facts in quite this way. He contented himself with half an answer, so to speak. But that was enough to give him his lead to the stagnation thesis. With reference to the fact that in the course of the Great Depression replacement investment kept up fully with capital consumption, he wrote (*ibid.*, p. 294):

> But why did not replacement stimulate consumption and consumption in turn stimulate new investment until full recovery was achieved? The answer, in part at least [he explained] — is that the cumulative process theory has severe limits. Without fresh supports from outside this process quickly peters out.

For, as he later developed this thought:[6] "Replacement investment expenditures are obviously not to be counted at all as a constituent element in the size of the national income, since it is already

---

*In accordance with the acceleration principle, under these conditions the demand for capital goods will increase at even a greater rate than the increase in the demand for consumption goods.

incorporated in the consumption figures . . . the level of consumption determines the volume of replacement investment expenditures." But it does not determine the volume of the long run net investment; that is, the investment additional to replacements.

True, one can conceive of a society in which all investment is geared to consumption. But that would not be a capitalist society. That could be true only of a pre-capitalist society, in what Marx called an economy of simple commodity production and reproduction and what present-day economists call an economy of zero net investment and we called an atrophying capitalism. It will be true in post-capitalist society — in a fully-developed socialist economy, in which planned investment will be a function of planned consumption, individual and social.

In the unplanned and private-profit economy which is capitalism the drive to maximize profits tends to minimize consumption, both personal and social, relative to the total output. On the one hand, capital accumulation would be impossible without this gap. On the other, it creates a tendency for capital accumulation to outrun consumption potentials. This creates a tendency for national savings to exceed the potentials for investment derived from the stimulus of increased consumption. But unlike the investment-consumption relationship dictated for a socialist economy, investment in a capitalist economy is only loosely and indirectly linked to consumption. In the early stages of recovery from a cyclical depression the link is based on speculative expectations of future increased rates of consumption. In the later stages of the boom, that link tends to reflect more closely the actual or induced growth of consumer demand. The prospect of a leveling off of consumer demand as full employment is reached, and when no new net additions to the employed labor force are at hand, becomes a key factor in the collapse of the boom.

In the pre-capitalist era the production process took the form of C-M-C. The independent artisan, using his own labor, produced a commodity, C, which he sold for money, M, which he used to replenish the C — the capital stock and his labor power used up in the first cycle of production, repeating the process. Production then was production for consumption. And consumption absorbed all the community's output and so equalled the community's total income. (Say's error, we can see, was that he assumed for capitalism these pre-capitalist production relations.) There were no excesses in the form of a social surplus or savings derived from profits, and no *new* capital investment. It was a consumption economy and a stationary state.

107

Once, however, the production process is changed from a system in which independent artisans work for their own account into a system in which the worker works for the account of others, for a capitalist, he no longer gets "the full product of his labor." Production does not equal consumption, as Say had it. The capitalist gets a share of the worker's output, and the simple equivalence between production and consumption no longer obtains. True, capitalists also eat. But individual capitalists, to remain capitalists under the categorical imperative "expand or die," must each save the larger portion of his share of the output. It is the aggregate of these individual capitalist savings, the class savings, that must be invested in new additional capital if the system is to be in a dynamic balance. It is this new *net* investment out of capitalist savings that provides for the *expansion* of the economy: for the continued creation of ever-more consumption goods, for ever-rising consumption expenditures and savings, transforming the pre-capitalist state into a dynamic capitalist state.

In a dynamic capitalism, then, where part of the national income is privately saved, full employment cannot be maintained unless new net investments are constantly being made out of these private savings. In the 1930's no such new investment was forthcoming either for past or for current savings, and, as Professor Hansen explained it, such new investment is predicated upon the "continuous development of new investment outlets such as are created by technological progress, the rise of new industries, the discovery of new resources, the opening up of new territory, and the growth of population. [But, as he saw it], these 'external' forces collapsed in 1928, and a year later the boom was over."[7]

We have seen in our earlier analysis of the dynamics of capitalist expansion (p. 47, above), unless the emerging or potential social surplus is immediately channeled into *new* capital investments, it perishes abortively. It ceases to be. It disappears from the total national income. In a word, if the "savings" from the current output are not currently invested or otherwise disposed of into the economy, through unproductive expenditures, for example, the system not only fails to expand, but, because of the operation of the multiplier effect (see pp.48-9, above), fails also to maintain existing levels of production and employment. In the past and until World War II these contingentcies determined the depth and duration of depressions. *Since the depression of the 1930's, expenditures for the military and other large unproductive expenditures have lifted the bottom of depressions by the employment of large masses of unproductive workers.* This is the essence of secular stagnation of advanced capitalism.

E. The Keynesian Answer to Secular Stagnation

Professor Hansen, thus, conceived of secular stagnation as a condition when a long trend of economic growth flattens out and no new long-term industrial developments are in sight. In such a condition, he said,[8] business recoveries tend to be "weak" and "anemic" and depressions long and deep. The "essence of secular stagnation," then manifests itself in "sick recoveries which die in their infancy and depressions which feed on themslves and leave a hard and seemingly immovable core of unemployment."

In the past, he explained, all long-term upward business trends had been propelled by one or another major industrial innovation or a cluster of such major innovations. Railroad building in the second half of the nineteenth century was such a major innovation. Electrification in the first thirty years of the twentieth century was such another. This first period of the twentieth century was further "buoyed up" by the "four giants" — street railways, telephone, electric power, and automobile industries. These in turn stimulated the rapid growth of a number of subsidiary industries requiring large investment funds — iron and steel, plate glass, rubber, copper, petroleum, road construction, etc., and their subsidiaries. Together, such long-term innovations create waves of prosperity which lift booms to new peaks and shorten and cushion cyclical depressions.

But then, always, he argued, the "new" industrial complex sooner or later reaches maturity and ceases to grow, "as all industries finally must." The whole economy then experiences "a profound stagnation," unless a new industry supplies a new stimulus to economic expansion. For, as he went on to explain, "it is not enough that a mature industry continues its activity at a high level on a horizontal plane . . . It is the *cessation of growth* which is disastrous."[9]

Indeed, Professor Hansen thought, by the end of 1900-29 only electric power remained with large prospects for further growth, and "the great era of expansion was over." Even automobile production had " gradually reached an asympotic level [had flattened out on a plateau] after 1923, and the curve of the construction of roads similarly flattened out toward the end of the twenties and thereafter declined."

"Thus," he concluded, "the decade of the thirties resembles the conditions of the nineties [following the decline in the rate of new railway building]." Technological development making for expansion had temporarily spent their force.[10]

And now (in 1938 and 1941), Hansen argued, even if technological progress created a new wave of innovation, as it well may, it cannot on its own, as was the case in the past, lift the economy to a new secular, long-term, advance. Certain structural changes have meanwhile occurred in capitalist countries which retard the effects of technological innovation on economic growth of the long wave variety. Among these are the cessation of population growth and the limitation of new terrtoral expansion.

Hansen estimated that the growth of population and the opening up of new territory, and the discovery of new resources accounted for half of the investment outlets in the nineteenth century. About 25 per cent of the capital accumulation in England and about 14 per cent in France had been invested abroad by 1914.[11]

But, now, the population of the major European countries has long since virtually come to a standstill and the rate of growth of the American population has been strikingly declining since after World War I. True, Russia and the Orient are still growing. But (this was written in 1941, before Pearl Harbor), "foreign capital is not likely to play any significant role" in the industrialization of Russia and "China and the Orient generally [including India] offer, in view of the present and prospective turmoil in that area, relatively meager investment opportunities. At all events [he was sure], no one is likely to challenge the statement that foreign investment will, in the next fifty years, play an incomparably smaller role than was the case in the nineteenth century."[12]

"Thus the outlets for new investment are rapidly narrowing down to those created by the progress of technology." (*Readings*, p. 378.)

Here, too, the outlook is not very encouraging, for two reasons. One, we cannot assume (in 1941) "that we can take for granted the rapid emergence of new industries as rich in investment opportunities as the railroad, or more recently the automobile, together with all related developments . . . to which it gave rise." (*F.P. and B.C.*, p. 362.) Second, the new technologies tend to be capital-saving, rather than capital-absorbing. (*Readings*, pp. 374 and 375.) Both these new factors tend further to limit investment outlets for savings.

To cap it all, Professor Hansen, in line with prevailing theories. argued that monopolies tend to retard the rate of innovation. Where in former years price competition compelled firms to seek advantage in cost-reducing innovations, the argument ran, under monopoly conditions profits tend to be safeguarded through price maintainance rather than through cost-reducing capital expansion. Under the one, investment would be accelerated; under the other, retarded. The automatic forces of the price mechanism no longer operate to stimulate innovation. (*F.P. and B.C.*, pp. 46-7 and 363-365; also *Readings*, p. 380.) Hence, again, the tendency to secular stagnation.

Steindl, (see n. 4, p. 102) went so far as to assign to monopoly the major role, if not virtually the sole role, in the decline in the rate of capital formation; but not by way of retarding innovation. Rather, monopoly does so by investing excessively! The gradual elimination by monopoly of price competition since about the turn of the century, he argued, tends to enhance profit margins in the monopolized industries. This enlarges their internal investment funds which of themselves stimulate investment. "The mere fact that business concerns accumulate savings is sufficient to induce them . . . to invest." But this "self-perpetuating" growth of capital tends also to produce an excess of productive capacity. And that exerts a retarding influence on further investment (*op. cit.*, pp. 191-93 and 2-5). (The reader will recall Hobson's argument in this general vein.)

Steindl, thus, had no need for the pressures of Hansen's four other "external" forces to explain the assumed tendency toward secular stagnation in America. The rise there of monopoly does it. Indeed, his theory would seem to link up more closely with observable facts than Hansen's does. For Steindl could show that the rate of capital formation (pp. 156-161) and the rate of population growth (p. 168) started declining years before the 1930's, paralleling the growth of monopoly. In Hansen's explanation they seem to have emerged as positive phenomena not much before that fateful decade.

Be that as it may, the consequences and the action required to counteract them are the same for both Steindl and Hansen. Steindl wrote (p. 175):

> If the [U. S.] government had not borrowed the greater part of the outside savings in the 1930's, then — as business was not willing to borrow them for the purpose of investment — the system would almost certainly have been driven rapidly into strong decumulation of capital — with increasingly negative profit rates.

That the government must take measures to slow down capitalism's tendency to secular stagnation — the tendency to a "strong decumulation of capital" — to prevent depressions and to blunt their effects, should they nevertheless occur, is now the doctrine of most capitalist economists, including the Keynesians.[13] They differ among themselves only as regards the measures to be taken, in what doses, and the extent to which Government should "interfere" in the private operations of the economy in order to achieve economic stability and economic growth. Most all, however, are agreed that, henceforth, the safety of the people's livelihood, as well as the continued viability of capitalism itself are now the responsibility of the state. With the Keynesians it is a question of taking steps for ensuring "the security and stability of the social structure," as Hansen has put it,[14] or for "saving capitalism," as Seymour Harris has it.[15] And for this, one must have a general long-range plan in the form of building the Welfare State.

To preserve the security and stability of the existing social order — to save capitalism — the government is asked to proceed along three broad fronts: Monetary, Fiscal and Spending. As Harris sees it: "In a period of deficient demand it is necessary [for the government] to pump money into the system, reduce taxes, and raise public expenditures; and in periods of excess demand, to withdraw money, raise taxes, and reduce public expenditures."[16] These would be the regulative, or control devices. In addition, the country already has certain "built-in stabilizers," such as old-age pensions and unemployment insurance, which Hansen has defined as "social mechanisms so constructed that they automatically operate to offset unbalancing tendencies and exert pulls on the economy tending toward stability."[17]

What Professor Hansen and Keynesians generally mean by "The Welfare State," how specifically they would go about achieving it, and what building a genuine Welfare State would mean to the viability of a capitalist economy, an economy of the private accumulation of capital, are the subjects to which we now turn.

THE BUILT-IN STABILIZERS

For most of the capitalist economists who would have the state take action to prevent business depressions, the automatic, or "built-in" stabilizers are endowed with near-talismanic power. In the late Professor Slichter's judgment, the very age-old capitalist tendency to periodic crisis is vanishing under the impact of this seeming magic — the business cycle is being "broken up" under it.[1] For Professor Hansen, we have just seen, they are "social mechanisms so constructed that they automatically operate to offset unbalancing tendencies and exert pulls on the economy toward stabilization." In the prosperous years preceding the recession which began in the second half of 1957, this doctrine was proclaimed with so much certainty that most Americans, including many erstwhile critics of capitalism, began to believe with Slichter that the system was becoming depression-free.

Economists can now list any number of so-called built-in economic stabilizers as operating for the stability of the system. Principally, these fall into two broad categories: Social Security and the graduated personal income tax.

In the case of Social Security, the idea is that in periods of high employment payroll taxes automatically rise, while benefit payments then automatically decline. There are fewer unemployment claims then and many retired persons go back to work. The rise in total payroll taxes and the decline in benefit payments lessen consumer purchasing power and, therefore, inflationary consumer demand.

In the case of underemployment, it is asserted, the opposite effects take place. Less is withdrawn in payroll taxes and more benefits are paid out as unemployment claims rise and as the old folks go into retirement. The deflationary fall of consumer purchasing power is thereby lessened; consumer demand is stabilized, and so is the economy as a whole.

Similarly, with the personal income tax. The collection of this tax rises with prosperity and declines in depressions with tax rates remaining the same. In prosperity the effect is to lessen the rise of consumer purchasing power; in a depression to retard the decline.

In a word, the elasticity of Social Security taxes and benefits and of the personal income tax is seen as exerting a stabilizing influence on the economy by affecting the size of consumer income.[2]

An examination of the nature and function of these institutions reveals that they have been, and can be, only minor factors in economic stabilization. Let us begin with Social Security.

A. Social Security as a Business Stabilizer

1. *Unemployment Insurance.* — The first thing that can be said about Social Security as a business stabilizer is that its effects on total consumer demand have been greatly overstated. This is aside from the fact that changes in the magnitude of consumer demand cannot be the initiating causes of significant changes in business, except when production presses on productive capacity. (See pp. 105-06, above.) Take the case of unemployment insurance. The benefit payments which a worker gets during the eligible weeks of unemployment do hold back *his* ,consumer demand from falling to zero. But total benefits may amount to no more than about 30 cents for every dollar lost in wages of the covered unemployed. When all the jobless, covered and not covered are counted, the total benefits amount to no more than about 20 per cent of the total lost payrolls and to 15 per cent when the wage loss due to increased part-time employment is included in the reckoning.[3] This in no way compensates for the concurrent loss in wages *and salaries* in the affected industries. We stress the *and salaries* because these may actually increase in a recession insofar as the service industries then become most active (in "pushing sales", etc.). In any case, the largest concentration of joblessness is in the commodity-producing industries, particularly in manufacture and mining, where workers earn *wages*. The white-collar workers, the "salariat," suffers less unemployment.

So we find that in the 1949 recession, for example, unemployment benefits rose by not quite $1 billion over the preceding year, while total wages *and* salaries (we have no statistical breakdown for the two) fell by about the same amount. But this total fall was the algebraic sum of a fall of $3.4 billion in the commodity-producing industries and a rise in the distributive and service industries and particularly in government — Federal, State and local.[4]

In the 1954 recession, unemployment benefits rose by a little over $1 bilion compared with 1953. This time total wages and salaries fell by nearly twice as much (by $1.8 billion). But once more, a sharp decline ($4.0 billion) in the commodity-producing industries was offset to more than half by the concurrent increases in the white collar industries and government.

The story repeated itself, with interesting variations, in the 1958 recession. This time, while benefits rose by $2.2 billion over the preceding year and wages and salaries in the commodity-producing industries fell by twice as much, *total* wages and salaries actually rose—by $2.4 billion in the distributive and service industries and by over $3.0 billion in government payrolls.

Similar relationships obtained in the 1960-61 recession. Between the first quarter of 1960 and the corresponding quarter of 1961, unemployment benefits were increased by $1.4 billion and Old Age and Survivors' Insurance by $1.1 billion. At the same time wages and salaries in the commodity-producing industries fell $5.4 billion and gross private domestic investment fell $19 billion! (*Economic Report* of the President, January 1963, pp. 188; 189, and 184.)

At all times, it should be remembered further, simultaneously with benefit payments the system continues to withdraw consumer buying power by way of the payroll tax, accumulating social security and unemployment compensation reserves. The tax on payrolls is a deduction from the worker's wages and is entered in the employer's books as a wage cost in figuring prices and profits. A hundred-dollar-a-week factory worker gets only $97 when the 3 per cent unemployment tax is sent on to the government. The "wage cost," though, is figured at $100.

Obviously, then, the net effect of unemployment insurance benefits has been and can be but very partial where consumer incomes and consumer demand are most vitally involved.

2. *Old Age Pensions.*—And this holds true for the Social-Security System as a whole, that is, including old-age and survivors' insurance, along with unemployment insurance, except that now we must also reckon with "contributions to the Social Insurance Fund" as well as with the Unemployment Insurance Tax, namely, the payroll tax, which is a deduction from consumer income. In periods of "over employment" the increase in wage payments far outweighs the increased payroll deductions and lessened benefit payments in their possible effects on the rise of consumer demand. Contrariwise, when unemployment sets in, much more is lost in wages than is offset by the reduction in the collection of payroll taxes and by the increase in benefit payments. The idea that in a period of underemployment less is withdrawn in payroll taxes is largely a fancy when the magnitudes involved are

taken into consideration. Between 1947 and 1948, for example, unemployment insurance taxes dropped a mere $63 million from a total of $1,274 million. Contributions to the Social Insurance Fund dropped $528 million from a total of $5,562 million. This Fund has never since declined again. The subsequent declines in unemployment tax receipts have been as inconsequential as in the first instance. In the recession of 1957-58, they fell $20 million from a total of $1,859 million and in the 1960-61 recession, they actually rose by some $300 million.

The notion that the aged move in and out of retirement as business falls or rises is wholly a figment of the imagination of people who had never worked in private industry. The aged retirees are not normally rehirable. Older workers of less than retirement age now find it increasingly hard to hold down, let alone find a new job in industry as age creeps up on them. (See, for example, *Manpower Report of the President*, p. 8.)

None of this, of course, is to deny that Social-Security benefits and unemployment compensation blunt the hardships of the unemployed, of the aged and of widows and orphans, who have no other source of livelihood than these benefits. Surely, they are socially and morally more desirable means of sustaining life than were the charities doled out in pre-New Deal days. They do help sustain the consumer demand of the unemployed, even if only to the extent of a fraction of its full employment levels and only for a limited number of weeks. Nevertheless, it must be remembered that the *movements* in payroll taxes and in benefits payments cannot seriously affect the *movements* of the business cycle. This is so because of the relatively smaller replacements of lost consumer income, compared with the vastly greater losses in investment and payrolls in the production industries, and to the weakness of the stimulus which changes in consumer demand exert on the movements of the business cycle, in any case, except when the economy operates at full capacity production. They are even less effective in stimulating economic growth or in arresting the capitalist trend to secular stagnation. An altogether differently conceived social security system is required for that, as we shall presently see.

To claim that this social leislation exerts a significant stabilizing effect on the economy is, to say the least, grossly misleading, as the four post-war recessions to date since the end of the war testify. It lulls the people into a belief that the cause and cure of capitalist crises lie in juggling a few hundred million dollars of consumer demand in an economy where the Gross National Product may fall a near $19 *billions* in a matter of 12 months of recession, as happened

116

in America in 1960-61. Unemployment insurance benefits will help keep the unemployed workers' body and soul together—for the period of eligible weeks, but they cannot stem or reverse the forces that bring on unemployment. Old-age and survivors' insurance is even less pertinent in this respect. This is an expanding system, benefits increasing annually with the increase of the aging population and coverage, and from time to time with the increase in rates. Never since the beginning of the system (essentially in 1940) has the number of beneficiaries ceased to rise, despite repeated bursts of business prosperity over these years. And in no year have total benefit payments declined.

The phenomenon of an *increase* of total wages and salaries in times of recession deserves notice at this point. It bears on the tendency of increasing unproductive employment in a mature capitalism, both absolutely and relatively to the employment of productive labor. In January 1957, for example, production workers in the manufacturing industries of the United States numbered 13,238,000. That number declined continually thereafter until, in May 1958, it had fallen to 11,415,000, the low for the recession, or 10 per cent. During the same period their payroll index fell from 165.5 to 140.9 for a loss of over 20 per cent. For all manufacturing employees the annual total of wages and salaries fell by nearly $4 billion between 1957 and 1958. Yet for all employees of the country, wages and salaries were by more than a billion dollars higher in 1958 than in 1957.

The explanation for these divergencies, as already partly noted, lies in the words "employees" and "salaries." The number of nonproduction workers, for the most part "employees," has been increasing and so have "salaries." These increases have come in government employment, in the service industries and in the other unproductive occupations. (See Chart IV following.) In the decade 1953-63 employment of white collar workers increased 6.5 per cent; of service workers 2.1 per cent; *zero* for blue collar workers and a loss of 1.5 per cent for farm workers. (*S.C.B.*, January 1964, p. 17.) The ratio of nonproduction workers to total employment in manufacturing increased from 16.4 in 1947 to 26.1 in 1963. (*Manpower Report of the President,* p. 228.) Between 1956 and 1958 wages *and* salaries in the manufacturing industries fell by over one billion dollars. But they rose by over $3 billion in wholesale and retail trade; by $1¼ billion in finance, insurance and real estate; by over $4 billion in the "service" industries; and by over $5 billion in government, Federal, State and local.[5] When Americans read in their newspapers that "personal income" has been the sustaining force in the recession these figures

117

should tell them where this personal income comes from, and to these figures should be added, "personal interest income and dividends." These were maintained at a rising annual rate, increasing from the $30.7 billion in January 1957 to the $32.9 billion in May 1958.[6] A rising output of social surplus by a decreasing number of productive workers makes possible increasing employment and payrolls of unproductive workers. In fact, in all nonagricultural industries the number of full-time jobs of production workers continually declined in the five years 1957-62. The only rise was in contract construction. The major source of the job growth these years has been the public sector of the economy, both directly and in the jobs generated in the private economy by government expenditures. Indeed, between 1957 and 1962 the number of full-time jobs resulting from private demand actually declined. (*Manpower Report*, p. 22.)

B. THE PERSONAL INCOME TAX AS A STABILIZER

1. *Definitions.*—The concept of the personal income tax as a built-in stabilizer falls in the Keynesians's schema into the category of "fiscal policy." This policy encompasses two aspects of government budgetary operations aiming at stabilizing the economy. One concerns the relation of taxes to government spending and to the rate of private investment. The other concerns the relation between taxes and consumer purchasing power and consumer demand.

In its first aspect, fiscal policy dictates that in a period of declining business and sluggish economic growth the government raises consumer demand by spending more than it collects in taxes—by "deficit spending." In the event of an inflationary boom, the government is advised to spend less than it collects in taxes and thus run up a budgetary surplus. Government spending above its receipts, it is argued, will prevent a developing recession from turning into a large-scale depression, while lowering taxes will stimulate investment, production, employment and economic growth. On the other hand, the government by withdrawing more from the national income stream in taxes than is returned to it in expenditures, is expected to dampen and hold down the inflationary presures of the boom.

Since the first aspect of fiscal policy relates to the question of the budget, it is not treated in detail at this point. It is treated later, along with the broader question of government spending and the effect

CHART IV

NAGRICULTURAL EMPLOYMENT, BY INDUSTRY, 1947-63

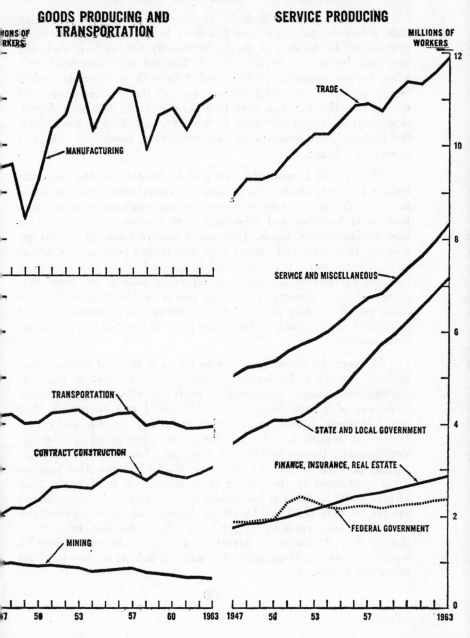

GOODS PRODUCING AND TRANSPORTATION

SERVICE PRODUCING

MILLIONS OF WORKERS

MANUFACTURING

TRADE

SERVICE AND MISCELLANEOUS

TRANSPORTATION

STATE AND LOCAL GOVERNMENT

CONTRACT CONSTRUCTION

FINANCE, INSURANCE, REAL ESTATE

FEDERAL GOVERNMENT

MINING

of taxation on the rate of private investment. In the remainder of this chapter we treat of the second aspect of fiscal policy, namely, of taxation in its bearing on consumer demand.

2. *The Proposals.*—Basically, taxation is conceived as possessing both automatic and regulative functions in the control of business fluctuations. In the case of the Social-Security tax, we have seen, the automatic function is largely stressed. This tax rises with prosperity, when benefit payments decline, and falls with a depression when benefit payments rise. This is also true of the graduated personal income tax. This tax, too, rises with prosperity and falls in a depression, rates remaining the same. In this way, according to Keynesians, the business cycle provides its own correctives, insofar as consumer demand is a factor.

The thought is now advanced that in addition to this automatic built-in feature of the tax, the government should take conscious action to reduce this tax, as well as the out-and-out consumption taxes when business is declining, and raise them when business threatens to turn into an inflationary boom. This would involve reducing federal excise and sales taxes and cutting rates and raising personal exemptions in the federal personal income tax.[7] In Hansen's view, adjustments in the personal income tax rates are especially suitable for these purposes. When the personal income tax rate is cut, he contended, "take-home pay is at once affected and so consumption expenditures are stimulated. When raised, an immediate check is imposed on inflationary developments."[8]

However, he advised, changes in tax rates to offset business fluctuations are not to be applied to the corporation income tax. The contemplated changes are aimed at short run effects, at the cyclical tendencies of a capitalist economy. If applied to corporations, they would seriously disturb long-run commitments as to costs and prices. Instead, as regards tax changes that would affect long-run economic developments, Hansen looked with favor to a "modified" corporation-income tax such as that advocated by Michal Kalecki. This involves a tax forgiveness on the income to be invested in fixed assets. Such income would be taxed at lower rates than the rest of the corporation's income, or even not taxed at all. In America we have practised this sort of tax forgiveness by way, for example, of the accelerated amortization plan: Corporations have been allowed to depreciate their investment in capital construction for war and defense in five years out of current profits.

Several other forms of tax-abatement incentives to capital investment are in common practice in America. Depletion allowance in the oil industry comes to mind here; tax-free land offered by many towns and States to attract new industries is another example.

Presumably, tax inducements would be withheld if capital construction threatened to generate an inflation. But Hansen saw another, an automatic deterrent to inflationary investment. If investment were pushed too far, he thought (following Keynes) its marginal efficiency would fall to the level of prevailing interest rates and put a halt to further investment.[9]

3. *Question of Timing.*—Assuming the effects of tax adjustments to be as claimed by their advocates, two problems must be solved before the adjustments are attempted. First is the problem of timing: at what conjunctures of cyclical events should taxes be raised or lowered? Second is the problem posed for America by the peculiar structure of its tax system.

As regards the timing element, it is clear that to be effective the tax adjustments must be put in operation before and not after an undesired turn of the business cycle had taken place. When the turn had been made the cumulative economic processes set in motion by it may already be too strong to be reversed, or even halted, by any such adjustments. It might become a case of the tortoise chasing the hare.

Theoretically it is all well to say with Hansen that the tax on payrolls, for instance, would be raised progressively with the approach of the peak of a boom and that "As soon as it is evident that a turning point has been reached, the tax collections should cease entirely."[10] But, in practice, how is one to know when and how call the turn? "Business forecasting" is, of course, out of the question when the determination of national policy is concerned. Our business cycle analyses have been wrong even when made years *after* the event, as witness the failure of our economists to date to arrive at a sound theory of the business cycle after 150 years of trying. We still remember the dismal failure of our economists to anticipate, or even appreciate, the turn of events in 1929-32 and, more recently, that which followed the close of World War II.[11]

It has been suggested that Congress and the Administration arbitrarily select an index in the turn of the cycle when to implement given tax adjustments. Such, for instance, might be a rise of a certain magnitude in the amount of unemployment over a period of say, three consecutive months, or of a maximum amount in any one month.[12] Even so, the observed recession may then already be on the way

121

toward a depression and lie beyond the presumed remedial effects of a change in tax burdens.*

4. *Question of the Tax Structure.*—But all these, after all, are preliminaries, addressed to the assumption that appropriate tax measures will reverse or, at least, halt an unwanted economic trend. The prior question is: to what extent can such measures be effected? The idea, we will remember, is for government to raise taxes on consumers to slow down consumer demand when inflation threatens and to lower such taxes to raise consumer demand when deflation and unemployment threaten. Obviously, the extent to which this might be accomplished, if at all, depends on the magnitude of these taxes susceptible to Federal control. For all these policies are addressed to the Federal government. Yet the Federal government has relatively small leeway in the matter of the collection of consumption taxes.

For the present purpose we identify as consumption taxes all taxes raised on the basis of *income spent.* These would include all excises, customs duties, the real estate tax, and all avowedly sales taxes. Except for the out-and-out sales taxes which everybody can see, most consumption taxes may also be called indirect or *hidden* taxes—they are hidden in the price consumers pay for the goods and services they buy.

By the same token all non-consumption taxes may be called direct or open levies: They are imposed on the basis of *income earned* and do not (theoretically speaking) enter into consumer prices. (Actually they do, for the most part, as we will see later.) They are imposed on incomes remaining after all sales transactions have been consummated. The payroll tax, though a tax measured by income imposed before the sale of the commodities, nevertheless enters into the final price. The payroll tax, therefore, is included with the consumption taxes. Among the nonconsumption taxes we include the personal income tax, the corporation profits tax, inheritance and estates taxes and the capital gains tax.

The list of consumption taxes is virtually unending. We pay them with the food we eat and the liquor we drink, and the tobacco we smoke. We pay them with the clothes we wear, with the house we live in and when we go to see a baseball game. We pay them with the heat and light bills, with our telephone calls and with the bithday greetings we send by wire. All sales taxes are consumption taxes. The "business" taxes which shopkeepers, farmers, manufacturers

---

*Recently, the Department of Commerce, in cooperation with the National Bureau of Economic Research, began publishing a bulletin called *Economic Indicators*, aimed at showing the lead and lag statistics within a cycle.

pay they pass on to consumers in the price of the goods and services they offer for sale so long as the levy applies industry-wide.

These are the taxes, together with the income taxes on the lower-income brackets, that it is proposed the government manipulate as a means of raising and lowering consumer demand.

Now, it does not take us far into the facts of the case to make us doubtful of the use of the proposed tax adjustments as devices for seriously damping business fluctuations:

(1) By far the larger proportion of America's consumption taxes lie outside the reach of the Federal government, although it is the Federal government that is called upon to manipulate them in this regard. The major portion of these taxes are collected by State and local tax bodies, for which they are, indeed, the principal source of revenue. A federal tax policy aimed at increasing (or decreasing) consumer purchasing power by way of adjustments of consumption taxes would, at best, be only fractionally effective, unless they could be made to spill over into State and local tax jurisdictions. This it is wholly impossible to do without first completely breaking up a tax structure which has been in existence since the birth of the Republic.

Not only that, but also all major governmental functions on State and local levels would have to be radically changed. For example, the real estate tax, the principal consumption tax of local governments, is also the principal source of funds for the public schools. Both the tax and the function have been the prerogatives of local school boards since the free public school system was established in America over a century ago. Each local "school district" exercises virtual sovereignty over both the taxing and the educational policies in its bailiwick. It would take more than a "Professor's theory" to induce the more than forty thousand autonomous school boards as well as various State and local government units concerned with education to admit the Federal government into their patch of taxing authority. For that, they fear, would inevitably mean also "government meddling" in their educational policies. And that would never do! It might tend to raise school standards in areas where, for peculiarly American sectional and sectarian reasons, the local power elite would rather keep low. (On the other hand, suppose Dixiecrats in Congress get control of the Committee on Public Education!)

(2) The personal income tax falling on the lower-income classes, on the masses of consumers, constitutes no more than about one-quarter of the total personal income tax raised by the Federal government. And it constitutes but a minor fraction of total consumer expenditures. Any adjustments in the federal portion of the country's consumption

123

taxes and in its lower-bracket personal income tax would have to be drastic, indeed, to have a telling effect on total consumer demand.

A few "statistics" will not be amiss here.

Table 1
Amount and Per Cent of Federal, State and Local Consumption Taxes
(Average five years, 1958-1962) [13]

Tax Jurisdiction	Million Dollars	Per Cent of Total
Federal	13,656	29.6
State and local[14]	32,439	70.4
Total	46,095	100.0

a. *Jurisdictional Distribution of America's Consumption Taxes.—*
Of the total of over $46 billion consumption taxes averaged for the five years 1958-62 for all tax jurisdictions of the country, over $32 billion, over 70 per cent, were collected by the State and local governments and less than 30 per cent by the Federal government. Over these five years the Federal government had an average of less than $14 billion of these taxes or less than 5 per cent of average consumption expenditures to manipulate as an anti-depression force. In the five recession quarters January 1960-January 1961, gross private domestic investment declined by nearly $16 billion and wages and salaries in the commodity producing industries fell by nearly $4½ billion. To offset the decline in the gross investment, these taxes would have had to be wholly extinguished (barring concurrent cuts in the rates of the lower-bracket income tax). They would have had to be cut by some 30 per cent to offset the fall of the wages and salaries, except for the counter-offset of the net unemployment benefit payments in those months.

Of course, this is crude reckoning. Maybe the fall of investment would not have gone so far, nor that of wages and salaries in the face of a timely downward tax adjustment. Maybe a cut in these taxes would have raised an offsetting consumer demand. On the other hand, it might have induced more saving—at a time when the gross investment was falling! We must bear in mind that the rich, who save, also pay consumption taxes, and a cut in the tax on mink coats may not necessarily induce them to buy another mink. They are more likely to buy a few more of the existing shares of stock of the mink farm. To make sure that a tax cut will increase *consumer spending*, the cut would have to be much larger than the desired increase in that spending.

Furthermore, the entire argument goes counter to the assumed relation between consumption and investment. With Hansen, we argued earlier (pp. 105-08, above) that a cyclical rise in investment is not uniquely geared to current consumption demand. There may be good reasons for eliminating consumption taxes altogether, and for lowering tax rates on the lower-bracket incomes. To the extent that tax cuts may help to sustain consumer demand, to that extent they will help maintain employment. But they cannot *lift* the economy out of a slump, unless they are projected on a much higher level of magnitudes than is currently politically feasible; unless they are projected as a long-range *continuing* program, *and* unless government spending is not correspondingly lessened; that is, unless deficit spending becomes the established government policy at least in capital outlays. (We come back to this subject again later. See Ch. 12, below.)

b. *The Personal Income Tax.*—We now turn to the personal income tax. To what extent may we expect cuts in this tax to raise consumer buying power? This tax, by definition, is a non-consumption tax.

In this case, State and local tax collections count for very little. In the five years 1958-1962, this tax collected by State and local governments averaged a little over $2.5 billion. Federal collections of this tax averaged $47.8 billion.

Here the question is, which portion of this tax most likely bears on consumer purchasing power? However, we can have no hard and fast rule to go by in this respect. We may merely assume that persons whose gross taxable income falls below a certain level are most likely to benefit, as consumers, from a cut in rates and from an increase in personal exemptions. Above that level, any reductions in the tax would go largely into personal savings.

For the present purpose we make the not wholly arbitrary assumption that for the lowest ⅔ of the individual income-tax payers the personal income tax represents a reduction of potential consumption expenditures. For the highest ⅓ per cent income-tax payers it represents a reduction of potential savings. This assumption is in consonance with all studies of the distribution of consumer income, consumer savings and consumer expenditures.[15] In 1961 the 66 per cent lower income-tax payers fell in the income bracket of under $6,000 and paid a little over 22 per cent of the total Federal income tax.

If, in view of the above figures, we may assume that the 66 per cent line of the returns for 1961 is applicable to the five recession quarters of 1960-61, then the accumulated personal income-tax liability at that line would amount to $9.4 billion (22.2 per cent of a $42.2

125

billion total).[16] Adding this amount to the $13.6 billion federal consumption taxes for that year, we get a total of $23.0 billion. To offset the concurrent effect of the $16 billion fall of the gross private domestic investment and the $4 billion loss in wages and salaries in the private sector of the economy, would have required a forgiveness of most all of these combined taxes. The government could not have been expected to do any such thing. In fact, despite every indication that the recession then in progress was likely to develop into a prolonged depression, the government decided to do precisely nothing in the matter of cutting taxes on consumers. Maybe it took that position because if these taxes were cut, taxes on the upper income brackets would have to be raised if expenditures for the military were not to drop. (But taxes on the upper incomes would, according to Keynes, cut into the marginal efficiency of capital, discouraging the very investment which increased consumer demand is presumed to encourage.)

Maybe the government took that position because consumption taxes are a powerful means of holding workers' real wages down. A recession is another such means. The unemployment it creates drives down workers' demands for increased wages. Reducing consumption taxes and tax rates on lower incomes would counteract these effects of a depression.

In the winter of 1962-63 unemployment was running close to the high recession rates of the preceding decade, and industrial production was barely maintaining the sluggish pace it had maintained since the Korean War. In his State of the Union message, delivered January 14, 1963, the late President Kennedy, therefore, proposed that Congress enact a tax cut of about $6 billion in individual and corporation taxes. That, he argued, would stimulate consumption, investment, employment *and* economic growth. He made no mention of consumer tax cuts. Said Dr. Robert Nathan, dissenting from a similar proposal urged by a C.E.D. panel at the time, "I know of no public finance economist who believes that a $6 billion tax reduction is adequate to achieve and maintain full employment and vigorous growth."[17] The G.N.P. at the time was running at about $550 billion a year; consumption expenditures at about $350 billion, and gross private domestic investment at over $75 billion.

As finally enacted in early 1964, the tax reductions, to run up close to $12.0 billion in two years, will add very little to consumer income. The reductions are in the personal and the corporation income taxes, with higher rates of reduction in the upper than in the lower personal income tax brackets. For the 66 per cent of the lowest bracket income-tax payers the deduction-withholdings will amount to $115 a year or a little over $2.00 a week in 1964 and to $135 a year or not quite $3.00 a week in 1965. For tax payers earning a salary of $25,000 a year the reductions will amount to $744.00 a year in 1964 and $893 in 1965. The millions of families whose annual income falls below taxable returns will not be reached at all. For the Federal government to raise consumer income through tax measures it should reduce or even abolish most of its excise taxes, which now run to near $15 billion a year. It might retain them on luxury goods, such as high-price jewelry, for example. The tax reduction law of 1964 can but tend to increase savings, as was very clearly demonstrated in the surge of individuals' savings to a postwar high in the second quarter 1964 when the law became effective.

The recovery from the 1960-61 recession has not been due to tax reductions, but was due in the main to increased government spending, Federal, State and local; in the case of the Federal government, chiefly in the national defense. In the years 1961-63 defense expenditures were increased by nearly $23 billion. In the same three years State and local governments raised their expenditures by nearly $24 billion.

From the second quarter of 1961 to the end of 1962 increased government expenditures accounted for more than 25 per cent of the rise in the GNP—"a proportion," we read in *S.C.B.* (January 1963; pp. 7-8) "that has been exceeded in postwar recoveries only in the Korean mobilization period." In this way both the Federal govermnent and the State and local governments continued to support the rise in private demand into 1964. In the course, they ran up a deficit of some $15.0 billion.

For the government to create new consumer demand, and new investment demand, as well, it must spend in excess of its tax receipts. It must engage in deficit spending. That alone, as we shall see, is sure to stimulate production, employment, consumer demand and economic growth. Deficit spending siphons off social surplus which may not otherwise be invested. To the extent that that may permit a reduction in consumer taxes it will tend also to raise real wages, assuming prices do not rise simultaneously. However, deficit spending raises new questions. Deficit spending as a condition for raising real wages may be good for the people, but it may not be good for the production of surplus-value. That is one reason why the capitalist class so vigorously opposes deficit spending except for armaments. But before we enter upon these subjects, we must examine still another of the Keynesian remedies for depressions, namely, monetary policies.

127

11.
MONETARY POLICIES

"Monetary and Fiscal" policy to combat depressions has come to be a twin shibboleth in the vocabulary of Keynesian economists. The two, "monetary" and "fiscal," are most always listed side by side and come right after the "built-in stabilizers" in their kit of anti-depression remedies. "Government spending" comes last on the list, as a last resort, so to speak. It comes last because it does not command the general acceptance by business leaders as do the others. If for the Keynesians, government spending can take us out of depressions, for the true defenders of the capitalist faith the government might spend us into a depression. For these, the "balanced budget" is the magic wand with which to scare away a depression.

Most literate Americans know about these anti-depression and anti-inflation (!) remedies. He reads of them in the daily press and in weekly journals. They are, perhaps, as familiar to him as radio and television commercials, but they are equally as vague and unsubstantial to his comprehension as the claims for preferring one brand of cigarettes or headache powder to another. In both instances, this is due to the utter chaos of claim and counterclaim concerning their merits. What *does* "monetary and fiscal policy" mean to most people as a remedy against unemployment, against inflation? What does "government spending" mean? What does a "balanced budget" mean? Do these economic measures possess, as is claimed, the power to sway the economy? We saw in the preceding chapter that the potency claimed for the built-in stabilizers was subject to considerable discount, even if we were to include taxation as an anti-depression fiscal policy. We wish to examine the validity of the claim for the power of monetary management to effect the swings of the economy. Government spending and the balanced budget are left for treatment in the next chapter.

A. The Quantity Theory of Money

1. *In the American Tradition*—Probably the most popular notion of how "the government" can hold down the violence of business

128

fluctuations is that it can do so by controlling the supply of money and credit. Americans have had this notion "in their blood" for generations. All of us who took a course in Public Speaking in high school or college before World War I imbibed this notion with Bryan's impassioned Cross of Gold oration: The argument of free coinage of silver *vs.* a rigid gold standard; of "soft" money *vs.* "hard" money. When "things are going bad," we want the government to "put more money into circulation." When business booms and the cost of living soars, we want the government to "put a stop to it." We do not quite know how the government should do it. But the monetary economists come to our aid.

All monetary theories, and there are many variations on the theme, stem from the initial assumption, arguable for the early stages of capitalist development, that the supply of money (and credit) uniquely affect business decisions to expand or contract investment and production. Some hold that the relation between the two is that of direct cause-and-effect. That the greater the supply of money the higher will the rate of business activity be, and the shorter the supply of money the lower will that rate be. Others hold that the relation comes from the effect of the money supply on the price level: That the greater the money supply the higher are prices, and the smaller the supply the lower are prices, and that business activity is stimulated by rising prices and depressed by falling prices.

Still others hold that the money effect operates *via* the interest rate. Interest rates are said to be lower when money is plentiful and higher when money is in short supply. The theory is that high interest rates discourage business enterprise, whereas lower interest rates encourage investment, production and employment.

In all these theories the one underlying assumption is that the money factor is the initiating cause and that the rate of business activity is the consequent effect. In the 1920's, in England as well as in America, these theories virtually became a credo. The business prosperity of that decade in America was attributed, in the main, to the stable prices of the period. And those were attributed to "wise" monetary policies.

In England, R. G. Hawtrey entertained the belief that "changes in 'the flow of money'," as another economist summed him up,[1] "are the sole and sufficient causes of changes in economic activity. . . ." Since, thought Hawtrey, we now knew how to regulate the money flow, we could therewith regulate also the business cycle, reducing it, as he put it, to "a thing of purely historical interest." This he wrote in 1926 and repeated in 1928,[2] just one year before the onset of the severest business depression in the history of capitalist crises.

Also in England, in his *Tract on Monetary Reform* (1923) and in his mature work *A Treatise on Money* (1930), Keynes looked to the central bank to control the fluctuations of the business cycle and stave off depressions by means of monetary and credit policies. As far back as 1924 he had written in the London *Nation* (May 24):

> I look, then, for the ultimate cure of unemployment and for the stimulus which shall initiate a cumulative prosperity to *monetary reform*—which will remove fear—and to the diversion of the National Savings from relatively barren foreign investment, into *State-encouraged* constructive enterprises at home, which will inspire confidence.[3]

And in his Treatise (Vol. II, p. 384) he wrote:

> I am bold to predict . . . that to the economic historians of the future the slump of 1930 may present itself as the death struggle of the [high] war-rates of interest and the re-emergence of the [lower] pre-war rates.

The abolition of the gold standard, which had required gold shipments to balance international payments, and the establishment in its place of a gold-exchange standard, which would permit such balancing in terms of gold through an international clearing house, or credit union; the creation of a supra-national central bank (which eventually took the milder form of the International Monetary Fund and of the International Bank of Reconstruction and Development); the control of the money supply and of the interest rate through central banking operations, and state direction of the flow of saving and investment—these were technical adjustments in an otherwise well-balanced social mechanism, required to cure unemployment and stimulate "cumulative prosperity"—to halt the secular decline of capitalism and to save the world from communism.[4]

In America, Professor Irving Fisher of Yale University was the chief protagonist of the monetary theory of business cycles. For him, in fact, the business cycle itself was but a price phenomenon. Price changes, he wrote, "can so nearly explain the behavior of business, that there is little room left for any cyclical, or regular factors" to explain it. It was, then, only a question of manipulating the money and credit supply, he argued, in order to set up the mechanism that would control the business cycle.[5]

So much did "money" pervade the thinking of business-cycle theorists of the time that, in the words of a later observer, they "developed an almost superstitious reverence for the supposed power of central banks [the Federal Reserve System in America] to stabilize business through rediscount rates and open-market operations."[6] Hansen has said that because of this preoccupation with the idea that money and prices were the primary factors in the formation of business cycles, "the coming of the Great Depression was not only not anticipated but appeared to be quite inexplicable."[7]

The "almost superstitious reverence" of economists of the 'twenties for the power of money to control business fluctuations was carried over into the early years of the New Deal. By going off the gold standard and by devaluing the dollar the American Government attempted to stimulate investment and employment by making money plentiful and cheap.

That these measures failed is one of the most conspicuous examples of how facts often belie a false theory.

Despite this experience, the notion has continued to persist that by altering the money supply, by regulating credit and by raising and lowering the interest rate one can control the major swings of the business cycle and even determine the rate of economic growth. So, for example, we have seen Seymour Harris advocate that, along with other measures, the government "pump money into the system" in a recession and "withdraw money" when a boom threatens to become inflationary.

In the same vein, the Economists' Committee *Report* (p. 515) reads:

> It follows . . . that one way to counter forces making for contraction is by monetary action designed to increase the amount of cash or other liquid resources held by individuals and firms and to reduce the cost [the interest rate] and increase the availability of loans [ease credit facilities]. Similarly, one way to offset any forces making for expansion is by monetary action designed to reduce the amount of cash or other liquid resources held by individuals and firms and to increase the cost and reduce the availability of loans.[8]

But money and credit and the rate of interest, we saw in Chapter 5, are not the forces which propel a capitalist economy to fluctuate between booms and depression. An expansion of money and credit and lowering the interest rate can do very little to stimulate new investment when business is in the doldrums. Business is in the doldrums when there is a lack of adequate new investment to keep it active. But that lack is not necessarily due to a lack of money and credit, or to high interest rates. It is due chiefly to a lack of profitable investment outlets. Why this lack in investment outlets develops is a question which has "stumped the experts" these past 150 years; since, indeed, the birth of the science of economics. We have seen Keynes try to explain it, without any success. We come back to it in the concluding chapters of this book. What we wish to emphasize here is that it is not a shortage of money or credit, or a rise in the interest rate that slows down the rate of investment. It is the crisis conditions which lead to a slowdown in the rate of investment that also cause a tightening of money and credit, and a rise of the interest rate. Normally, *prospective investment possibilities create their own money and credit supply*. Rarely will it happen that the banks will not underwrite a "sound" issue. And it is the prospective rate of profit from any new investment that determines the rate of interest businessmen will pay. Besides, nowadays, Big Business, whose investments chiefly determine whether we have prosperity or depression, command enough internal financial resources to go it alone for the most part, until a crisis puts a halter on investment and the money market.

The interest rate, we already know, counts for very little in most investment decisions. Once a slump is on, we saw Keynes himself argue, the interest rate cannot be made to fall fast enough nor low enough to reverse the trend. (Chapter 5, p. 55. above.) In Hansen's words, "The existing state of abstract theorizing about the rate of interest leaves us very uncertain about its possible effect on the volume of investment and consumption, while statistical and case studies enhance this skepticism."[9]

A striking example of the ineffectiveness of a rise of the interest rate in the matter of consumer demand was the failure of the Federal Reserve authorities in 1955 to slow down the growth of consumer credit by means of raising the rediscount rate. In the course of that year that rate was raised, in four $\frac{1}{4}$ per cent jumps, to $2\frac{1}{2}$ per cent from $1\frac{1}{2}$. In that same year total consumer credit rose by the unprecedented amount of nearly $6\frac{1}{2}$ billion. The few additional dollars a consumer had to pay in interest were apparently dwarfed in his mind in comparison with the vastly larger amount of the principal, or, if you please, with the emulative delight of becoming the owner of the latest model car.

Similarly, the reversal of these monetary measures in late 1957 and early 1958 proved equally ineffective. The lowering of interest rates and the reduction of reserve requirements failed to encourage borrowing or to stimulate new investment, or installment buying. Investment, it appeared, was to continue downward throughout the first half of 1958 and installment buying, for the first time since the end of the war, actually fell below repayments. The business recovery that came later that year, came in response largely to the spending by the Federal, State and local governments of upwards of a score of billions of dollars above tax receipts; that is, in response to government deficit spending. (See the concluding pages of the preceding chapter.) We return to this point at length in a later connection.

It is essential, if the American people are not again to develop a "superstitious reverence" for the supposed potency of the money supply as a measure to combat depressions (and inflation), that we take special pains to expose its shallow character. The persistence of the myth that the manipulation of the money supply can ensure full employment deceives the people and obscures the real issues that confront capitalism in its maturity—when the volume of investible funds tends to exceed investment possibilities. When the battery is dead, no amount of gas pumping will start the motor; it will only flood the carburetor.

As far back as 1940, the American economist Stuart Chase noted this untenable position of the monetary theorists. That year the money supply in America was $14 billion greater than in 1929, a lot of money those days, while unemployment was still at a depression level of over 8 million. "These figures," he commented, "reduce to nonsense all monetary schemes which depend for their action on increasing the amount of money in the system," as a means for stimulating production and employment.[10] In the midst of the depression, resources in the Federal Reserve Banks were 2 and 3 times greater than in 1929.

As Professor Edward S. Shaw of Stanford University put it recently:

> In the light of monetary experience, it appears that many
> of us have romanticized monetary control. The stop-and-
> go growth of money, dignified as "monetary management",
> is a nervous tic in the economic system that diverts to

finance attention and resources that should be spent on real aspects of development.

Even less credence, he said, should be given to the idea of credit control in relation to the money supply and economic growth: "The effect of linking the money supply to the cyclic yo-yo of credit demand is to intensify cycles.

"Real growth is measured in terms of goods. It is not measured in terms of credit," and he explained:

> In earlier phases of American economic growth, credit markets were embryonic. Then the banking system necessarily wore two hats, as supplier of money and as supplier of credit. Now the credit markets have matured, and there are efficient channels outside of the banking system for the flow of funds from savings to investment in real capital.[11]

Nor is the current slow motion of the American economy due to a shortage of money. The banks are loaded with money and so are many firms and individuals. "Our failure to achieve more rapid expansion and fuller utilization of resources [reads The First National City Bank of New York *Monthly Letter* of September 1962] does not stem from a scarcity of money. There is a plentiful supply of money today, the stock of other liquid assets has surged to unparalleled heights, and credit-worthy borrowers can obtain funds on favorable terms."

As regards the presumption that the credit and money supply affect business fluctuations *via* its effect on prices, it should be noted that America has experienced booms and busts in periods of long-term price inflation and long-term price deflation, as well as in periods of price stabilization, as was the case in the 1920's.

Unquestionably, in the early years of capitalist development in America, say, before the Civil War, the "money market" was a determining factor both in the rate of capital accumulation—economic growth—and in the contingencies of the business cycle. The main source of money capital then was the "thrifty citizen"—Keynes' "rentier"—who controlled the market through his high, often usurious interest charges. After the Civil War, the stringent gold reserve requirements and the inelastic credit base under the National Banking Act of 1863 were frequent causes of a tightened money market and "financial panics."

Today, money capital is accumulating at even a greater rate than the economy can profitably absorb. (I first pointed out this phenomenon in my *Falling Rate of Profit*.) Retained corporate profit, depreciation reserves, individual and business savings in savings banks, in savings and loan associations; mutual trusts, insurance company reserves, private pension funds; short-term government obligations—all combine to supply a stream of money capital that meets and more than meets all short-run as well as long-run capital requirements at the lowest interest rates in the capitalist world. One measure of this abundance is the fact, noted earlier, that in 1962 the interest paid by the 100 largest non-financial American corporations amounted to no more than 0.7 per cent of their total receipts and in 1963 to 0.5 per cent.

In a word, the causes of the current sluggishness of the American economy and of the repeated recessions since the end of the War have to be looked for elsewhere than in the money market. Except in times of domestic or international crisis, when a "flight of capital" becomes a visible symptom, enough monetary resources are generally available to the system to finance it out of a depression and to provide for continuous growth. As the book progresses we shall have reason to spell out further some of the causes which impede continuous capitalist production and retard the rate of economic growth. "Capital shortage" is not one of them, although it may have been in earlier days and may become one again under certain international tensions. Private money may run into hiding or seek safer havens when the domestic economy is threatened with an inflation or devaluation of the currency. As I first argued in *The Falling Rate of Profit*, the curse of present-day capitalism is not a shortage of money capital, but its relative overabundance.

12.
GOVERNMENT SPENDING

A. Objectives of Government Spending

With "government spending" we come to the ultimate of the Keynesian anti-depression weapons. The "built-in stabilizers" and monetary management, we have seen, are not the powerful anti-depression agents which Keynesians claim them to be. They do not possess the power to affect the basic issues making for depressions. They cannot affect seriously the imbalances developing between the social surplus potentially available for investment in an advanced capitalism and its investment potentials. Some mitigation might result if Social-Security benefits were paid out of excess savings, instead of from taxes on payrolls. The same would also be the case if the personal income tax were levied on actual or potential savings instead of on actual or potential consumption.

As regards monetary measures to combat depressions, even such a stanch Keynesian as Professor Hansen had his doubts as far back as 1947. The argument, he wrote, "vastly overemphasizes the efficiency of mere increases and decreases in the money supply."[1] Ten years later he perceived that, "In a rich country, there is no close relation between the quantity of money and aggregate spending."[2]

When treating of government spending as an anti-depression mechanism one must bear in mind these two questions: (1) Government spending *with* what? (2) Government spending *for* what? "The Government," Federal, State or local, has no money of its own to spend. In capitalist society it must get it from the private sector of the economy as taxes or as loans. If from taxes, and that is where most government spending money comes from, the net effect of that spending will depend upon whether the money comes from taxes on consumption or from taxes on potential savings. If it comes from taxes on consumption, the net effect on the economic drift may be neutral. The government spends what the consumers might have spent. What may affect this equivalence is the degree to which workers can compensate for the tax increases, through wage increases, and the degree

136

to which businessmen compensate the wage increases through price increases.

If the money which the government spends is derived from taxes on potential savings, such as the income of corporations, the net effect may again be largely neutral, depending on the extent to which the corporation income tax is passed on to consumers in increased prices.

Most effective, therefore, as a counter-cyclical measure is government spending income derived from loans. That would be deficit spending — spending in excess of tax receipts. Deficit spending has the special virtue in that it involves borrowing from the actual or potential pool of the community's savings which may not be planned to materialize as private investment. Deficit spending thereby becomes a withdrawal from the community of actual or potentially uninvestible social surplus. In other words, it is not government *spending* which counts. It is government spending which might not otherwise be spent at all that is of the essence, be it out of taxes or loans.

In the end, of course, government loans, principal and interest, are paid out of taxes, except in a few cases of self-liquidating investment, T.V.A., for example. Government spending, then, is for the most part a consumption item in the National Income Account, the same as private spending from wages and salaries. In fact, it shows up in the market mainly as consumers' expenditures of government, civilian and military personnel and of employees in industries producing goods and services for the government, as well as capitalist profit. It is not "investment" in any sense of the word, as it is often referred to, even though it may stimulate private investment as all consumer expenditures might do. The distinction would become clear if government kept a separate capital account.

Government spending *for* what? is the second question to be borne in mind in an evaluation of the probable effect of government spending on business fluctuations as well as on economic growth. Normally, State and local government expenditures go almost entirely to pay for the social services of the community: education, police and fire protection, the public health and sanitation, streets, highways, all of which create and protect social wealth. On the other hand, the Federal government spends but a fraction of its budget on the social services. As we will see shortly, it spends most of its income for the "National Defense," paying for past, current and future hot and cold wars. These expenditures, for the most part, consume social surplus without replacing it. They waste potential wealth. We have

137

Adam Smith's word for it, as we have seen.

To answer both these questions, Government spending *with* what? and Government spending *for* what?, we consult the figures.

B. Government Spending and the National Income

1. *Composition of the Gross National Product.* — In the productive efforts of a nation an income is generated which equals the money value of all the goods and services produced — the Gross National Product. GNP equals the income paid out in the course of its production.

After allowance is made for the depreciation of the capital used up in this production and for other capital consumption charges,[3] we get the Net National Product. Out of this Net figure come the wages and salaries of productive as well as unproductive workers, individual proprietors' income, corporate dividends and undivided profits, net interest payments and all direct and indirect taxes of the Federal, State and local governments. And out of all these payments, except the undivided profits come personal consumption expenditures and savings. Adding to these personal savings, corporate depreciation reserves and the undistributed corporate profits, we have, except for a few minor entries, the nation's "gross private saving." This is the source of the gross private productive investment; that is, investment for the replacement and renewal of capital in use, and for additions to it in the form of new net capital formation — for the expansion of the country's capital assets, for its economic growth. At the same time, the taxes in this Account serve as the source for government purchases of goods and services at all levels, Federal, State and local. Thus, personal consumption expenditures, plus the gross private domestic investment (plus or minus net exports of goods and services), plus government purchases of goods and services, add up to the Gross National Product.

In this way, the GNP Account serves a dual purpose. It measures the national income produced in any given time, say, a year, as well as all the income spent for consumption and investment in that time, and makes them equal to each other.[4] It is in this that we have the basis for the argument that for the economy to be in balance at a given level of employment, all income produced at that level must flow back into the production stream as individual and public consumer expenditures, and as private investment to maintain the current rate of production.

To advance to the next higher level of production, you must invest not only the current savings but also previously uninvested money capital, as well as newly created money capital in the form of credit which will be paid up from future "savings." It is in this way — if we disgregard for the moment the employment-depressing effects of the new automation investment — that investment exerts a multiplier effect on employment.

In the case of the government account, expenditures below revenue may signify a business boom, whereas expenditures above revenue may signify a business recession. When the latter is the case, we have, by definition, deficit spending. The government borrows to make its income and outgo equal to each other. Deficit spending, however, is not necessarily only a recession phenomenon. A country may resort to deficit spending in a business boom, as is notoriously the case in a war boom.

2. *Saving, Investment and Government Spending.*—Studying the data for the years 1929-1939 we find that gross private investment failed to absorb the gross private savings in every one of the years 1930-1939, with the one minor exception of 1937. For several of these depression years this investment failed to absorb even the depreciation allowance. Except 1937 and 1939, the index of industrial production never got back to where it had been in 1929. Private domestic investment was utterly insufficient to provide employment for millions of workers seeking jobs, and in 1939, unemployment still amounted to near 9½ million. Government expenditures did not rise appreciably until past the middle of the decade to offset this deficiency and then were not large enough nor of a character to get us out of the depression.

Until we reach the war years, State and local expenditures continuously exceeded Federal expenditures, and State and local taxes were then nearly 95 per cent consumption taxes. In those same years, between 40 and 60 per cent of the federal taxes also fell on consumption. To the extent that during the depression years government tax spending was aimed at raising mass consumption, the net effect was largely a case of robbing Peter to pay Paul — of sharing poverty, as the saying went.

In the years following the war, private domestic investment has, on the whole, tended to match total gross private savings, as recorded

139

in the National Income Account. The largest difference occurred in 1958, reflecting the 1957-58 recession. If in one year investment fell below savings, in the next it exceeded them by about the same amount. As a rule also, year-in and year-out, the gross private investment as a percentage of the GNP approximated the pre-depression full-employment level, that of 15.5 for 1929, for example, although with a declining trend since the Korean war. The percentage was abnormally low during the years 1942-45 because gross private savings were then abnormally high and a large portion of the new capital facilities was being financed by the Federal government. It remained lower than in 1929 during the immediate Reconversion years because of the large existing war-created capital facilities, both federally and privately financed. Something like 75 per cent of the wartime federally financed facilities were acquired by private industry when the War was over, at from 25 cents to 50 cents on the original dollar, which lessened the dollar total required for new private investment. Federally financed facilities, from machine tools, electronic equipment and typewriters to shipyards, steel mills and portable fire extinguishers were so acquired.

At any rate, after Reconversion private investment as a portion of the GNP came back to the pre-depression "normal" of, say, 12 to 15 per cent. The percentage rose to above 17 in the two war years (Korean) 1950 to 1951 and again in 1955. In all these cases the rise was due to an unusual rise in inventories, an upsurge in non-farm residential construction, or both. It was not due to an unusual rise of investment in plant and equipment. In fact, these expenditures as a per cent of the GNP remained relatively stationary with a tendency to fall. By 1962 this per cent had fallen to 9, compared to 11 in 1956 and 1957. ChartV, reproduced from the *S.C.B.* January 1964 (p. 8), illustrates this trend.

Chart V

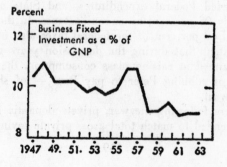

Even more striking has been the declining tendency in the expenditures for producer's durable equipment as a per cent of Gross Private Saving. Here we have the combined effect of the greater output of surplus value with equipment calling for lessened investment. The percentages for the same years as above follow:

1946	44.6	1950	46.9	1954	38.2	1958	33.2
1947	70.0	1951	43.3	1955	38.7	1959	35.0
1948	50.0	1952	40.8	1956	41.0	1960	38.0
1949	47.6	1953	41.0	1957	41.0	1961	32.5
						1962	33.2

Chart VI, next page, illustrates this tendency.

The average annual value, in constant dollars, of capital equipment per employed person rose 5.4 per cent in the years 1947-57 and by only 1.3 per cent in the years 1957-62. Capital-saving technologies had come to the fore. Between 1957 and 1962 the bulk of investment was devoted to "modernization" and "replacement." The proportion of manufacturers' capital spending allocated to automated machinery and equipment rose from roughly 11 and 12 per cent in 1955-1959 to around 18 per cent in 1962. (*Manpower Report of the President,* p. 51.)

All this time the economy was operating at relatively high employment levels, except for the four recessions — 1948-49, 1953-54, 1957-58, and 1960-61, although, again, with a declining trend.[5].

But now a new facet of the traditional saving-investment relationship appears. Since the end of the war ever-increasing amounts of government spending have been required to sustain the faltering employment levels, *in addition to private investment.* And the point should be made that a good portion of the private investment made during these years was conditioned by these large amounts of government spending. Undoubtedly, some of the income extracted in taxes might have been used for increased private investment, in the new automated equipment. But as we know, the United States is not suffering from an insufficiency of productive capacity. If not taxed, or taken up in government loans (deficit financing), that income would have gone to swell the reservoir of uninvested savings, and instead of the recurrent recessions we might have descended into a depression of the 1930-39 dimensions.

The figures for 1958 tell this story most vividly. Compared with 1956, gross private savings had risen by nearly 3½ billion dollars, but gross private domestic investment fell by nearly $10 billion. This was one measure of the extent of the recession of 1957-58. (Other

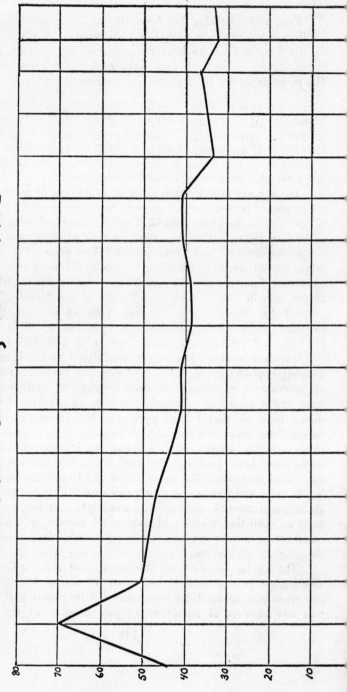

Percent Producers' Durable Equipment
Expenditures of Gross Private Saving
United States, 1946 - 1962

measures are the near-doubling of the number of unemployed and the fall in the index of industrial production.) What prevented that recession from deepening into a major depression was in the first place the increase of over $14 billion in government expenditures for goods and services, which was achieved through a combined deficit of Federal, State and local governments of nearly $11 billion.[6] The story repeats itself with the usual variations in the subsequent recessions. In 1963, a rise in government purchases of goods and services to the amount of $8 billion helped sustain the recovery from the 1960-61 recession. (*S.C.B.*, January 1964, p. 8.) In the years 1957-62 there was a net loss in employment in the private sector of the economy. What increase there was in total employment came from government operations, Federal, State and local.

> It is a fact [wrote Dr. Geoffrey H. Moore in 1959], that in four of the five contractions since 1929, (that of 1953-54 was the exception) the decline in output was predominantly a decline in output for the private sector. Government purchases of goods and services rose during the first year of each of the four contractions, thus off-setting part of the decline in the private component. *The offset, however, has been much larger in the postwar than in the prewar contractions.*[7]

One other item in our statistical findings deserves attention at this time. It is the rise of $25.0 billion of GNP in 1958 over 1956 in the face of the recession. This rise was a source of great jubilation among economic fiction writers, as also of many professional economists, as a signal sign of the recuperative powers of the economy and of the growth of the system. It was nothing of the sort. On a constant dollar (1954 = 100) — that is, allowing for the concurrent price inflation — the total for 1958 was practically the same as that for 1956. More important, the rise in current dollars was pure fiction for still another reason. In the National Income Account our economic statisticians include government wage and salary payments to the military personal as a *component* of the GNP, as if they were productive workers! Treating government spending of this sort as a component of the GNP imparts a spurious measure of economic growth. But it creates that illusion as well as of growing national wellbeing.

It is this spurious nature of the National Income Account which permits certain learned men to prattle about raising the rate of the economic growth of the country by increasing government spending (out of taxes!). As Dean Neil H. Jacoby of the Business School of the University of California at Los Angeles wisely reminds us, "We might hire a million men to dig holes and another million to fill them up and we are not going to get more growth just because we employ two million men."[8]

Economic growth is measurable by the physical output of goods and services or by the physical capacity to produce them, that is, by the new net capital formation. It is not measurable by the *sales* value of these goods and services which includes, among other unproductive expenditures, such "costs of sale" as advertising and sales promotion. These "costs" add no more to the real value of a nation's output than housewives would if they took in each others washing.

In the same way, government expenditures do not add to economic growth, unless it spends *social surplus* on productive social services. *In fact, as the rate of private real investment opportunities declines relative to the growth of the social surplus, economic growth must be looked to increasingly in the expansion of the productive social services of the community; and that sustained by taxes on the social surplus.* Military expenditures do not add to the economic growth of a nation, except as they substitute for private investment and consumption. Otherwise, they are a sheer social waste.

C. NEW SIGNIFICANCE OF GOVERNMENT SPENDING

We seem to have arrived at this fact:

At the beginning of the second half of the twentieth century we are apparently faced with a new relationship in the saving-investment potentials as these reflect the movement of business between prosperity and depression and the rate of economic growth. Before the War of 1940-45 it may have been true that, alone, the full private investment of a community's emerging savings was the sufficient (and necessary) means of assuring an economy of relatively full employment. Compensatory government spending, it could be argued, as the Keynesians did, would be necesary to maintain full employment only in the event private investment did not promise to absorb all the community's emerging savings on a cycle-to-cycle basis. Further, as the Keynesians correctly argue, this compensatory

144

spending by government must be in excess of current tax receipts. It has to be "deficit spending." Otherwise, government spending would only replace potential consumer spending to the extent of the taxes collected. Deficit spending means siphoning off accumulated and potential excess savings.

It now appears that private investment, even to the full extent of emerging private savings as reported in the National Income Account, can no longer alone guarantee an economy of full employment on a long-term basis. The gross private saving, against which we have matched gross private investment, does not measure *all* the savings (surplus-value) available for investment. Large and increasing amounts are wasted on unproductive expenditures (television advertising, for example) or are siphoned off by the government in taxes and in loans of even greater magnitude and spent on military projects. Such uses of savings do not add to the economic growth of the nation. They do not add to its productive capacity, but absorb increasing portions thereof, instead. *These expenditures thus conceal the conditions which constitute an economic crisis.* Henceforth, it appears, economic stability and the volume of production in America will depend less and less on the rate of new private domestic investment in productive assets and more and more on the magnitude of unproductive expenditures, be they socially useful or socially wasteful. This is the essence of the crisis of capitalism in its advanced stage of development.

13.
THE NEW CRISIS

Keynesian policies to ensure full employment, we may recollect from Chapter 9, stemmed from a theory which was aimed at explaining the length and depth of the depression of the 1930's. That theory held that capitalism had reached a stage in its development from which it was slowing down in the form of a long-run or "secular"' stagnation. "Maturity and Stagnation in American Capitalism," the title of Professor Steindl's book on the subject, succinctly describes that thinking.

Since the end of the war, however, America seems to have experienced a secular growth, rather than a secular decline. Except for the four recession years 1949, 1954, 1958 and 1960 gross private domestic investment in *current* dollars, that is, disregarding the rise in prices, advanced almost steadily over the years. It amounted to a little over $28 billion in 1946 and rose to nearly $73 billion for 1959. After the decline in the 1960-61 recession, the amount rose to $78.8 billion in 1962 and $82.3 in 1963.[1]

This, we all know, resulted initially from the rebuilding and expansion of the productive plant of the nation, first, to make good the deficiences of the long depression of the 1930's and then to meet the requirements of the hot and cold wars. After the wartime shortages were made up, the building of electronically controlled automation systems and the technically new productive equipment served as a new stimulus. Since the Korean War, especially large government spending for the cold war has been a major sustaining factor.

Yet with all this large private investment and with all the huge government expenditures for the military, the prosperous postwar American economy, up to the time of this writing, experienced four recessions — in terms of unemployment, each tending to become more insidious than the one preceding. In the years following the 1949 recession, unemployment was reduced to an average of no more than 3 per cent of the labor force; after the 1953-54 recession the unemployment residue amounted to over 4 per cent; since the 1958 recession unemployment has hovered between 5 and 6 per cent of the labor force. The number of those unemployed 27 weeks or more (26 weeks is the maximum statutory coverage in most States) has risen from .2 million for 1949, to .4 million for 1954; to .6 million for 1958, and to .9 million for 1961. (*S.C.B.*, June 1961 p. 3.) Early in 1962 the number reached 1.4 million and for the year averaged 20 per cent of the insured unemployed. In 1963 over 15,000,000 people were unemployed at one time or another. From peak to trough in the first three postwar cycles the drop in industrial production was 8 per cent in 1948-49, 10 per cent in 1953-54 and 14 per cent in 1957-58. It was little over 9 per cent in the 1960-61 recession. What these figures reflect is the fact that in *constant dollars*, that is allowing for the price inflation of the times, the gross private domestic investment reached peak for the period in 1955 and declined thereafter until 1962 when it barely surpassed it. When, further, allowance is made for the growth of population the G.N.P. has risen at the rate of no more than 1 per cent a year, as against the claimed 3.5% on the gross dollar basis (*Ibid*, Table 1-2.) Is America once more on the track of the secular stagnation observed by Hansen? If so, why?

A. The Theory of Secular Stagnation Reappraised

When Professor Hansen projected the theory of secular stagnation, he listed five "causes" for the phenomenon, we will recall. They were:

a. A declining rate of population growth.

b. Declining possibilities for new territorial expansion — the "closing of the frontier."

c. Declining possibilities for new great business-expanding and capital-absorbing innovations.

d. The growth of capital-saving innovations.

e. The retarding effects of the growth of monopoly on new investment ventures.[2]

These causes can hardly be the reasons for the *resumption* of a stagnation tendency in the 1950's. They were simply not operative then, except, as we will see, for item "d."

Take the case of population growth (item "a," above). For years before the Great Depression the rate of population growth had been declining in all advanced capitalist countries, including the United States. In the decade of depression the fall was especially sharp, and the outlook was very pessimistic. Before the war came to change it

147

all, forecasters for the United States saw its population reach about 140 million by 1960 and a peak of about 154 million by 1980. In May 1938, President James B. Conant of Harvard University wrote in *Harper's Magazine*: "By 1960 or thereabouts we shall have a stationary population. The expansive pressures on our schools will soon be gone." (!) By 1950 the projected peak was still estimated at no more than 165 million, with an indicated decline by the end of the century. Professor Hansen argued accordingly.

But the war and its aftermath changed all this. The war-induced and the immediate postwar demand for labor, and the consequent improvement in the general standard of living of American workers led to an upsurge in family formation and to the unprecedented crop of new babies. As a result, the formerly projected topmost peak of population was passed by mid-1950 and the new projections envisage a population for the United States running beyond 225 million before the end of the century.[3] Indeed, the great concern at the beginning of the 1960's was that at the present slow rate of economic growth millions of Americans reaching working age in the decade seemed doomed to joblessness. The population factor may, therefore, be counted out as a cause of the new stagnation trend of the American economy in the second half of the 20th century.

Nor can the "closing of the frontier" (item "b") explain it. The awakening of hitherto underprivileged, capital-hungry countries opens up untold potentials for capital exports. True, these countries are no longer available for "territorial expansion" in the old sense as areas for imperialist exploitation, but as outlets for capital investment on a non-imperialist basis they will for decades to come remain inexhaustible. That America is not availing herself of these new opportunities is another matter, of which we treat later.

Most damaging to the stagnationists' thesis, however, is their conception of monopoly as wholly a retarding factor in economic growth, and of the related significance of new innovational investments. (Items "c" and "e".) Since the end of World War II, Big Business has expanded investment and grown bigger; mergers increased concentration, and installation of new inventions accelerated.[4] The notion that monopolies, *because* they are monopolies, on balance exert a retarding influence on economic growth is clearly contrary to fact. Until we correct this erroneous notion we cannot have a correct conception of the place of monopoly in capitalist expansion and decline, the nature of twentieth century capitalist crises, nor for that matter, the Keynesian illusions regarding the means for containing them. True, monopoly *has the power* to retard innovation and on occasion has done so. But it also has the power to accelerate innovation and since World War I has done so increasingly.

B. The Role of Monopoly in Prosperity and Depression

As conceived by Keynesian and liberal economists generally, the power of monopoly is solely a power for evil. Monopoly, Seymour Harris has declared, is "the cancerous growth of large business units which consumes small unit cells." It is the power of one large business firm or a small group of large business firms ("oligopolies") to control output, prices and investment for their self-enrichment to the detriment of free competitive private enterprise. As such, monopolies tend to retard economic progress. This evil, it is argued, must be curbed and free competitive enterprise restored if capitalism is not to be driven down the path of secular stagnation.

The Congress, therefore, is asked to enact rigid anti-trust legislation and the Executive to enforce the law by vigorous court action. As one Keynesian has put it, "If private enterprise is to be preserved in this country, the process of economic concentration must be stopped . . . If it is not stopped, the time may come . . . when neither private enterprise nor political liberty any longer exist." And, again, "When competition is eliminated from a capitalist society, the system is in danger of breaking down."[5]

We have seen that, in the view of Steindl, the assumed retarding effect of monopoly on investment has been the principal, if not the sole cause of stagnation tendencies in American capitalism. In Kalecki's view, "the increasingly monopolistic character of capitalism" is one of the three broad reasons for "the decline in intensity of innovations" in the later stages of capitalist development.

Hansen brought out this notion most clearly when he wrote in 1938:[6]

> Under vigorous price competitions, new cost-reducing techniques were compulsorily introduced even though the scrapping of obsolete but undepreciated machinery entailed a capital loss. But under the monopoly principle of obsolscence new machines will not be introduced until the undepreciated value of the old machine will

at least be covered by the economies of the new technique. Thus progress is slowed down, and the outlets for new capital formation, available under a more ruthless competitive society, are cut off.

This is tantamount to saying that capitalism could and did make more technical progress in the era of small scale industry than in the era of monopoly and big business. But as we have elsewhere observed:[7]

> Little of the economic and cultural advances which American Capitalism made in the past half-century or so could have been achieved with the technologies commanded by the "hand and neighborhood" industries of the nineteenth century. Over a hundred years ago Marx could write of capitalism in its young years: "The bourgeoisie, during its rule of scarce one hundred years, has created more massive and more colossal productive forces than have all preceding generations together." Today it may as truthfully be said that in a scarce fifty years American Big Business of the twentieth century created "more massive and more colossal productive forces" than have all the generations preceding it.

Contrary to Hansen's view, whereas monopoly (or big business in general) may not, and as a rule does not, readily scrap the old plant, it continually raises productivity by introducing technological and managerial innovations in both the old and the new plants. The new technology and the scientific management which big business and monopoly make possible may minimize the rate of capital investment. They do not slow down economic "progress," if we define economic progress as a nation's potential for the expansion of the wellbeing of its people. On the contrary, as we have just noted, they advance that potential. That they do not utilize this potential is another matter, which resides in the very nature of capitalism as a scarcity economy and in the contradictions between full employment and the private accumulation of capital; of which more later.

Keynesian economics, like all the extant literature on the subject of monopoly, fails to advance its treatment beyond that which antedates the Sherman Act. Monopoly and big business in general, are treated as if they were forces extraneous to the capitalist system of production; as if they were imposed on that system by evildoers whose practices must and can be controlled away, curbed or even exorcised altogether by one "anti-trust" policy or another, and as if thereupon, the presumed blessings of pre-monopoly competition can be restored. Such a prevailing conception of the "monopoly problem" is a contortion of the thinking of economists of two centuries ago and a confusion of historical processes of capitalist development. It confuses the rise of monopoly out of free capitalist competition with the rise of free capitalist competition as a revolt against pre-capitalist monopoly. Besides, the economists who hold these views of monopoly never seem to face the question of how a capitalism which is dominated by big business will want to or can free itself of that domination.

Two hundred years ago the rise of the capitalist mode of production required the stimulus of free competitive business enterprise and, therefore, the elimination of existing, chiefly trading, monopolies.[8] Present-day monopolies came into being as a result of the intolerable consequences of that competition. The free unlimited competition of the 19th century tended to depress the rate of profit and jeopardize investment. Long ago the time came when such competition had ceased to be "the life of trade" and was getting to be the death of trade. It had become a fetter on the further growth and development of the capitalist mode of production. In particular, the new productive forces which were released by the invention of electric power, of new products and new processes could not find their full expression within the narrow confines of competing small business enterprise. They required large scale investment that had to be protected against the damaging vagaries of price wars. And they required integration into large scale enterprise which would command the large financial resources needed to promote the new technologies and to benefit from the economies of scale through mass production which the new technologies now made possible.

This interstimulation between the growth of the new technologies and large scale enterprise also sharpened the competitive struggle which is inherent in capitalism. That struggle took on new forms. It is carried on not as of old by means of price wars, depressing the rate of profit and jeopardizing investment, but as a struggle for markets, national and international, to improve profit potentials and safeguard investment; by means of mounting advertising and sales promotion expense; through product differentiation and brand monopolies and such inter-industry competition as that between steel, aluminum and plastics; between oil, gas and coal; between airlines, bus, truck and the railroad train. All this is done under a cover of price peace, the device of price maintenance and even price collusion.

To say that the struggle for markets by these means, which are not generally available to small business, spell "unfair competition," is merely to say that we are observing a law of capitalist production in its latest stage of development. It is the stage which was forced into being by the destructive effects of price competition, by intensified depressions since 1874-79, and by the rise of new technologies which require large scale business organization, large scale capital investment, assured markets for large output, stable costs, stable or even rising prices; surely, not falling prices. It is a historical fact that the early American trusts came into being as a defense against the destructiveness of the unbridled price competition of the 19th century.[9]

The "fight against monopoly," which the liberal and even the radical press is so full of, can only serve to befuddle the people. No amount of "antitrust" legislation can convert this new competition into the old. If the blacksmith shop has become a museum piece, that was not because of the growth of monopoly in automobiles. It was because, with the invention of the internal combustion engine, the horse-and-buggy and horseshoeing had become anachronisms, even as, with the advance in the science of aviation, long-distance railroad passenger service becomes an anachronism.

A still more cogent illustration may be drawn from the field of banking. With the gradual disappearance of "hand and neighborhood" industry, the small, independent local bank became a socially wasteful institution. Its continued existence for a quarter century beyond its historically allotted time of usefulness ended in the catastrophe of mass bankruptcy in 1930-33. That was not because of the "competition" of the Big Banks. It was because Big industry needed the services of the Big Bank. The small bank had no reason for its continued existence in large numbers.[10] Branch banking takes the place of the former small, independent bank.

What should be clear by now is that all the prosecutions under the Sherman Act and the Clayton Act and all the other acts "to enforce competition" have not "curbed" nor can they "curb monopoly"; they have not and cannot reverse historical processes. To "curb monopoly" would mean to curb capitalism as it has developed into the 20th century. It is naive to think otherwise. The "fight" against monopoly cannot be to *reform* it. It can only be transform it — to transform its private power into public power. That is, the fight has meaning only as a means of transforming capitalism into socialism.[11]

This does not mean that monopolies should not be fought, at least, for their grosser abuses — collusive price fixing which mulct the consumer, corruption of government agencies, wasting the natural resources of the nation. In fighting these and other abuses of monopoly power, the people will discover the intimate connection between Big Business and Big Government — executive, legislative, and judicial — in the interest of Big Business; will discover the baneful influences of what ex-President Eisenhower called the Military-Industrial Complex on both domestic and foreign policies of the American Government. To fight monopoly power, therefore, means fighting capitalism all along the line— its drift to war; its involvement in the suppression of the national liberation movement; its resistance to disarmament and to peaceful coexistence with the socialist nations.

For our present purpose we may focus on a facet of the monopoly problem of which our economists, Keynesians, anti-Keynesians and non-Keynesians alike, seem as yet to be wholly unaware. For this problem arises not, as our economists argue, because monopoly retards economic progress, but because monopoly accelerates economic progress in the sense of accelerating growth of productive capacity beyond the absorption power of a capitalist economy. The "excess capacity" that monopoly builds is not built in error, as Steindl would have us believe. Up to a point it is built by deliberate design. (It may result also from a relative shrinkage of markets.) Monopoly is ever alert to the new technologies: it builds the new machines *without* scrapping the old as long as they have any usable life. This old plant is stand-by or "excess" capacity which serves as a special source of monopoly profits. Always in normal times monopoly firms produce in their new plant, but set prices at or above the would-be cost of production at the old plant — their marginal, their low-efficiency "excess" capacity plant. They can do so because these represent the technological level at which their would-be competitors operate, either because they are too small and have not the financial means to keep abreast with the new inventions or because they lag behind the more venturesome innovators, as Schumpeter had it. Competition is thus carried on, on the innovational front as well as in the market.[12] In the process the weaker, generally the smaller, competitor is killed off and Big Business picks up the pieces.

But to establish this technological superiority over its rivals, a business firm must be in a position to control production, to control prices, to protect patents, to protect the benefits of its research. A business firm does not engage in innovational research for the benefit of its competitors, big or small. It will not invest in new ventures unless it can thereby improve its competitive advantages. Was not this also the motive of "free competitive enterprise?" If now extra benefits accrue to the monopolists, this is not due to a selfishness peculiar to them. It is capitalism in its more calculated exploitation of technological possibilities as well as the public.

With this new stage come also new, radically different economic problems. The command which monopoly and big business hold over financial, material and technological resources enables them to create ever-increasing productive capacity, ever-mounting masses of goods, at an ever-increasing mass of profits which the capitalistically-restricted consumers' markets and the new capital outlets cannot absorb on a continuing basis. This is one problem. Another is the fact that investment in the new technologies, including automation, cannot absorb all the investible profits they produce. This is so because present-day industrial technology is to an ever-increasing degree capital-saving as well as labor-saving. This means that under large-scale business organization and management, the economy's profit-producing potentials are greater than its profit-consuming potentials. Profits then fail to get invested and production and employment fall to lower investment levels. Why the ever-increasing profits do not get continually reinvested will be examined in the next several chapters.

14.
THE "SECOND INDUSTRIAL REVOLUTION"

A. AUTOMATION

Automation, the core of the "Second Industrial Revolution," may be defined as the use of instruments of production which by electronic impulses stimulate and activate manufacturing and data-recording processes so as to make them continuous and automatic. As one expert explained it, automation "embraces the automatic making, inspecting, assembling, testing, and packaging of parts and products in one continuous flow, without direct human intervention, except for the initial programming."[1] The process may involve the operation of a series of interconnected machines or no more than one self-integrating machine, such as the quarter-mile-long engine assembly installation at the Plymouth divisions of the Chrysler Corporation. The novel idea of it all is the automaticity of the sequence of machine operations, once the initial impulse is given.

In automation we have a qualitative change in the historical development of the mechanization of industry. As the American economist-engineer John Diebold has explained it, "Mechanization provided power-driven tools, eliminating many manual tasks and freeing labor from much of the physical work required in production. But no matter how small a portion of brute strength was involved in running a machine, a human worker was always needed to operate and control it. Now, through systematic application of the principle called feed-back, machines can be built which control their own operation . . . "[2] Automation replaces not only human muscle but, to an extent, the human brain as well. Automatic control of the movements of spaceships and data-gathering in orbit are spectacular examples.

As such, automation is potentially the most drastic capital-saving as well as labor-saving device yet invented by man.

This capital-saving aspect of automation has not been as adequately documented as the more immediately obvious labor-saving effect. This is so, in part, because capital-saving takes longer to materialize. In part, it is because, as a production process, it is essentially still largely in its innovational stages.

Yet, we have seen, Professor Hansen took the capital-saving effect of the new technologies for granted more than a dozen years ago. In *The Falling Rate of Profit* (published in 1957), I was able to cite several examples of the "cheapening of the constant capital" which resulted from instrumentation and automation. These were shown to have effected capital savings not only in the consumption of materials, fuel, electric power, etc., but also in the greater durability, productivity and efficiency of the new machine, even though the new installations may initially cost more than those they displace. It has been reported for the Soviet Union that the extra investment cost in the automation of electric power was recovered in from 8 months to 2 years. "By increasing production capacity and output," an article reads, "automation greatly reduces costs and thus ensures that the capital outlay involved can be recovered quickly." The initial cost of science and research is high, but this should be spread, the authors argued, over all subsequent installations where the capital invested is rapidly recovered in lowered operating costs. Output is increased and capital outlay is reduced. As an example, they cited the "multi-spindle automatic lathes." These, they reported, are "twenty-times more productive than ordinary universal lathes, and the extra cost of installing the automatic lathes can be recovered within two years from savings on wages alone."[3]

In the same publication, John Diebold makes the point that in our studies of the social effects of automation, "the possibility of capital savings so substantial as to dwarf any conceivable gains from labor savings is overlooked altogether." The increase in productivity and speed of equipment "results in a sizable decrease in the capital cost per unit of useful product in the manufacturing process." (p. 42) According to an official of the General Electric Company "complete automation" of a 500,000 Kw. H steam station "could realize capital savings of about $1¼ million to $2¾ million."[4] A certain tape-controlled machine tool introduced in 1958 is claimed to cut "direct labor time from about seven hours to two hours, saves 50% of the cost of jigs . . . and fixtures . . . saves 41% on time needed to set up production and replaces from 15 to 20 other machine tools."[5] In the continuous steel casting process, capital outlays are estimated at only 30 to 50 per cent of the cost of the blooming mill and its auxiliary equipment. (*Barron's Weekly*,

Examples can now be mutliplied to any extent desirable. John Diebold and others give a number in the Joint Committee Print cited earlier. (See, for instance, pp. 93 ff.)[6] When an automatic installation reduces labor requirements, it reduces *labor costs* not only in the production of final consumer goods, but also in the production of the new automated machines which produce these goods.

Automation unemployment is, therefore, not only *and not merely* a matter of displacement of man by machine—a decrease in *labor requirements*. The loss of employment through the relative decrease in *capital requirements* is the more insidious. A worker displaced by one labor-displacing machine might find work in building another— in the economic growth of the system—as was the case in the non-automated mechanization of industry over the two preceding centuries. But automation, to repeat, is capital-saving as well as labor-saving. Automation minimizes the rate of investment and hence retards the rate of economic growth in physical terms. Herein lies the core of "automation unemployment." If the system were growing and expanding, automation would prove a blessing. It would reduce drudgery, increase output and permit an increase in leisure to enjoy the increased output. It is when growth of the system slows down and ceases to expand, due in part to the effects of automation, that automation becomes a dread. Estimates have it that automation already costs us 2 million jobs a year. And this is only the beginning.

Automation, furthermore, makes possible the use of new mechanical and chemical *processes* that are capital-saving as well as labor-saving. The H-Iron Process of steel making is an example. (It was developed by Hydro-carbon Research, Inc., of New York, in collaboration with the Bethlehem Steel Co.) In this process, pulverized iron ore is "fluidized" with hydrogen and converted in an electric furnace to steel. The coke oven converter and the blast furnace are wholly by-passed, along with the labor attending them. An installation of a capacity of 2,000 to 3,000 tons of steel per day, would cost about half of a blast furnace and its coke ovens. The process is, of course, automated once started in operation. (Letter from the Corporation to the writer and an article in *Iron Age*, August 3, 1961.)

In short, most of our new technological advances, *using* automation, require less and less capital and less and less productive labor, relative to the growth of productive capacity. "From 1957 to 1962," we read in the *Manpower Report* (p. 5), "no major sector of the economy with a productivity gain averaging as much as 2.5

157

CHART VII

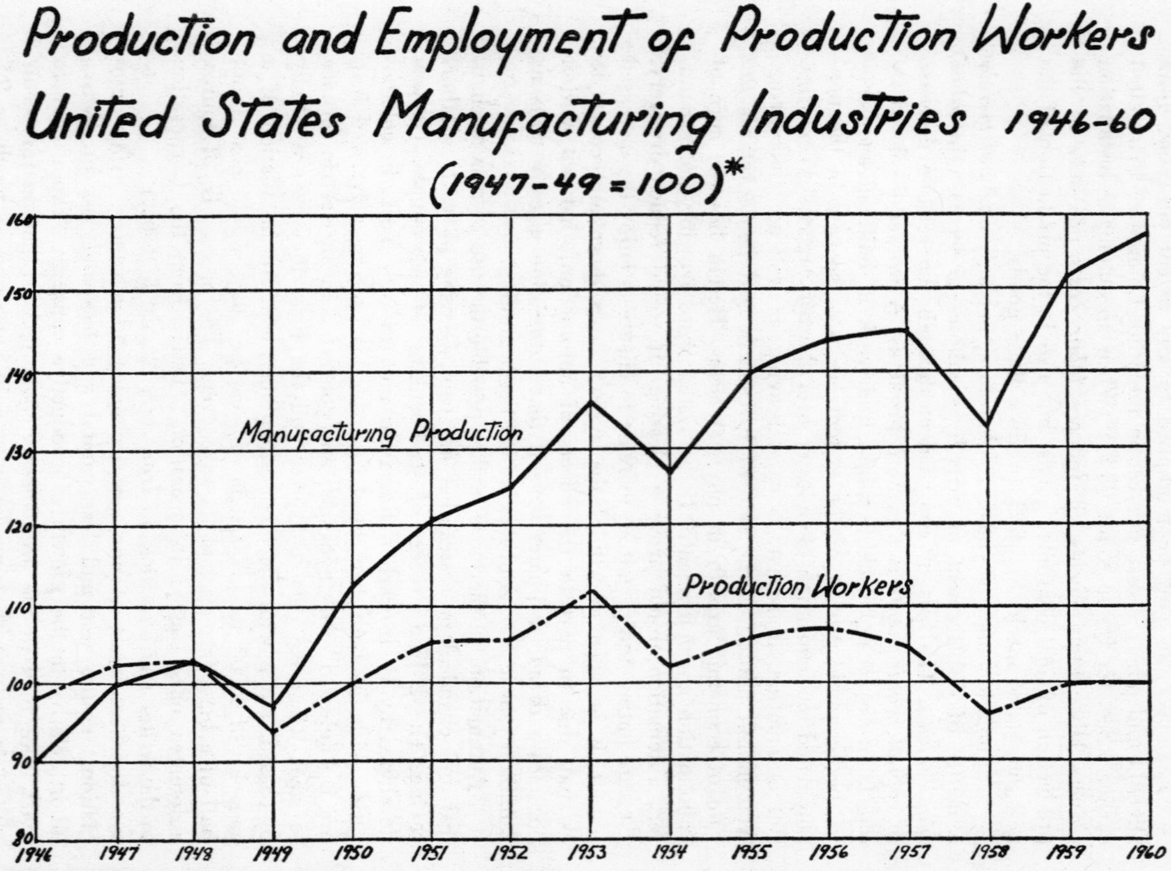
Production and Employment of Production Workers
United States Manufacturing Industries 1946-60
(1947-49 = 100)*
Manufacturing Production
Production Workers
160
150
140
130
120
110
100
90
80
1946
1947
1948
1949
1950
1951
1952
1953
1954
1955
1956
1957
1958
1959
1960

per cent a year achieved enough increase in demand for its products and services, and hence in its production, to prevent a reduction in its work force." The lag of employment of production workers in total employment is now notorious, as Charts VII and VIII testify. In an earlier page, we observed the persistent decline in the rate of investment in plant and equipment since the early 1950's.

In all the "recovery peaks" between 1957 and 1962, investment in plant and equipment never came back to the 1957 level. Excess social surplus tended to accumulate. While the need for investment capital has been diminished, the need for unproductive expenditures has been multiplied. This is the qualitative change which has taken place in the creation and absorption of investment funds in the monopoly period of capitalist production.

B. Historical Perspectives

For a hundred and more years before World War I the nation's social surplus was used to build its productive plant and pay up the capital borrowed abroad. These were the years when the capital ratio—the ratio of the value of the material capital in use to wages of production workers—was almost continuously rising.[7]

By the end of World War I, and in large measure as a consequence of that war, we had paid up our foreign debt.* In the decade following, the rate of capital formation was minimized by the growing elimination of waste in industry; by the standardization of parts, products and processes; by improving the efficiency of plant and labor, and the integration of production from raw materials to finished products.[8] Investment possibilities declined. The capital ratio ceased to rise.**

------

*This closed a "frontier" for British capital exports and may have accounted in no small way for the stagnation of the 1920's there.
Competition of other capital-export countries began to affect Britain's rate of economic growth even before that war and was the ultimate cause of it. When Keynes in 1924 (see p. 130 above) argued for a diversion of the nation's savings from "relatively barren foreign investments" to domestic investment, as a cure for the continuing unemployment, he was unconsciously recognizing the fact that British hegemony over the capital-export market had come to an end.
**Recent studies of the N.B.E.R. confirm these findings and bring them up to date. See, for example, S. Kuznets: *Capital in the American Economy, its Formation and Financing.* See also the able review by Charles L. Schultze in *A.E.R.*, Sept. 1962.

To be sure, we used much capital that decade in the electrification of factories, homes and household equipment; in a housing boom; in building the automobile and subsidiary industries. With all that, the social surplus grew faster than these and other likely private investment outlets would absorb. Large amounts of the surplus then found their way into luxury expenditures and worthless foreign investments, involving tortuous stock-market speculation and pyramiding holding companies.[9] When the speculative bubbles burst, the last outlets for the excess social surplus vanished, releasing the forces that make for capitalist crises. The Great Depression became inevitable.

During the Depression all net new investment virtually stopped. The new replacements from depreciation reserves were so productive that they sufficed to carry the economy through the 10 years of depression demand and into the first two years of war production. Beyond the use of depreciation allowances those 10 years, the potential social surplus had no place to go, and income, production and employment remained low. Replacements alone, we have learned, cannot advance employment; only net new investment can do that.

It was not until war production took over fully that the potential surplus found realization in the market, relieving its downward pressure on the economy. The war raised investment to the full level of the nation's social surplus potentials. The war "solved" the unemployment problem.

When the war was over, a number of temporary, war-induced stimuli at first kept the economy operating at relatively high production levels. Principal among these were financing reconversion and re-equipping industry; replacing plant and equipment worn out during the long depression and the war; the making up of shortages in housing, in household durables, in automobiles; equipping the large additions to the labor force; providing housing accommodations for the rapid rise in the rate of family formation and for the new high rate of population growth; and the migration of industry to new geographic areas South and West. When these stimuli waned, the oncoming war in Korea gave the economy a fillip.

Yet, despite all these large private investments, it was the increasing absorption of social surplus by expenditures on the military and foreign economic aid that, in the main, helped stave off a new round of major business depressions. When in the years immediately following the war domestic military expenditures were cut, foreign economic aid absorbed about $5½ billion of the social surplus a year. Together with military aid, some $84 billion were thus absorbed

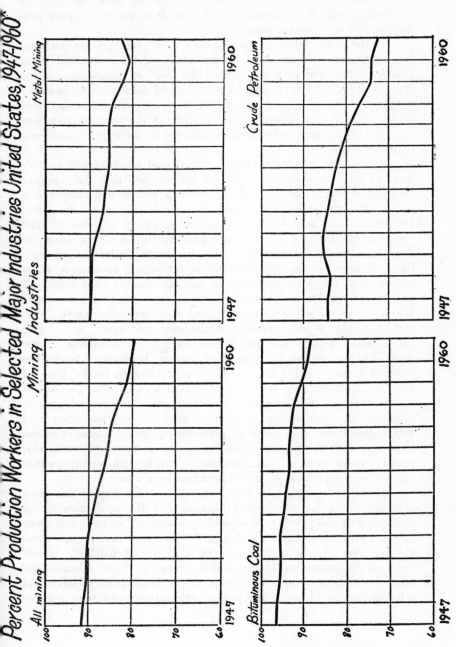

Percent Production Workers in Selected Major Industries United States, 1947-1960*

Mining Industries

All mining

Bituminous Coal

Metal Mining

Crude Petroleum

* Manufacturing Production, *F.R.B.* The production workers index computed from *Employment and Earning Statistics.*

in the years 1946-1960. Since most of this aid took the form of products produced in American factories, it served to support production and employment there.

In the years following the Korean war, gross private domestic investment, as we have seen, on the whole equalled recorded gross private saving, and as a per cent of the GNP at times exceeded the pre-war full-employment level. Yet large and increasing amounts of government spending were necessary to prop up production and employment. As we know, a good portion of the private investment since the end of the war has been conditioned by the large expenditures of government.

It is in this manner that the prosperity of mid-twentieth century America must be evaluated. First the hot war and then the cold war absorbed enormous amounts of accumulated and accumulating excess capital and excess output. These, first, took us out of the Great Depression, and then kept the economy operating at relatively full employment. Now we cannot relax these expenditures; we must, indeed, continually increase them, as the excess social surplus continues to grow, or find other substitutes for private investment, if we are to avoid another depression. In this lies the crisis of America's postwar prosperity. It is a new form of economic crisis. For it is also a new political crisis, superimposed upon and reflecting the long-run or secular world capitalist political-economic crisis, which fifty years earlier became manifest in the wars for a redivision of the world for exploitation by imperialist powers. In America today, the political-economic crisis is also of a cyclical nature in the form of armament expenditures as an absorbent of excess social surplus. It is the crisis of the increasing absorption of the social surplus in unproductive expenditures, in the first place military and other cold war expenditures, as a means of preventing prolonged massive unemployment. Indeed, the very viability of the system now seems suspended on the brink of war. Because we are so rich we must suffer poverty in a depression or risk destruction in a war.

At this point the reader may well ask, why not employ this great national wealth for the further expansion of the productive forces of the system and produce an expanding abundance of more consumer goods, such as housing, for instance, than we now do? To this there are two very closely related answers. One is that indefinite investment in the expansion of production sooner or later exhausts the unemployed labor supply. That causes a rise in the price of labor and a fall in the rate of profit. The private accumulation of capital *requires* a rate of employment below full employment, where wage rates can be held down to tolerable levels. We deal with this capitalist phenomenon at some length in later pages.

The other answer to our question is that capitalism is an economy which thrives on artificially-created scarcities. Recent discoveries of new iron ore reserves sent shivers down the steel market. Capitalist production is not production for use, but for profit, and only so much is produced as will yield a profit. To produce more than that would "flood the market." Prices would fall and profits and the rate of profit would fall. Capitalists, therefore, limit their outputs to what the market will take at prices that would yield the maximum possible total profit. When surpluses, nevertheless, threaten to accumulate, capitalists pull in their horns and precipitate the periodic crisis during which excesses are used up or dissipated. The government always stands by to help limit the "glut." In the past, tariffs were used to keep out imports. Today, the government stockpiles "strategic" goods. To keep up prices of raw mining products, it stockpiles 76 minerals and metals. Government stockpiles at the end of 1963 came to near-$14 billion. Storage costs alone ran to nearly $½ billion a year. To keep up farm prices the government takes cotton, wheat, corn and other crops off the market. In January 1964 the inventory dollar value of the Department of Defense was estimated at over $171 billion, $6.5 billion above the previous year. All such "government investment" serves to use up productive capacity, materials and labor which otherwise would be surplus.

The phenomenon of creating scarcities in a capitalist economy is practised all along the line. The medical profession limits the number of medical graduates. Workers organize in unions to control the labor supply and maintain occupational monopolies by limiting admission to apprenticeships. California peach growers destroy part of their annual crop to prevent a market glut and a fall in prices.

In mid-twentieth century the creation of artificial scarcities has become a compelling necessity. The social surplus which monopoly capitalism now produces is so great that if invested in the expansion of its productive capacity and in the production of civilian goods and services, it would exceed their market potentials. Over the years 1929-61 the rate of growth of the capital stock has been but half of the rate of growth of output. The economy now seems able to produce in two years what it can profitably consume in three. Hence the frequent "recessions," permitting the system to lie fallow a while. The capitalist division of the national income between capitalists

163

and workers makes this inevitable. To stave off a flooding of the market, billions are spent annually on advertising to induce socially-wasteful consumption—to "buy now and pay later," even though what you buy is tinsel and what you pay for is vanity status.* Artificially-induced super-consumption has become structured in the economy as firmly as has militarization. "Without the institution of consumer credit," declared Professor Arthur Smithies before the American Assembly (*loc. cit.*, p. 77) "it is doubtful whether the total rate of growth over the last generation would have been so rapid as it has been."

These supports to the "growth" of the American economy cannot go on forever. The militarization of the economy is contingent on the ability to maintain world tensions. But always there exists the "threat" of peace. Should peace become the choice of the peoples of the world, then military expenditures as a means of maintenance of capitalist viability would become increasingly difficult to support in sufficient magnitude to absorb the ever-increasing amounts of uninvestible social surplus which modern capitalism tends to create. Even today, the continued building up of arms is becoming absurd. The country already has enough atomic weapons to "kill and overkill" and contraction of their further production now seems probable. (See *N.Y.T.*, June 30, 1963, p. 1.)

Sooner or later, also, net increases in consumer financing must slow down as repayments are balanced off against new extensions. Sooner or later "depth consumer research" and sales promotion must cease to pay for themselves as the consumer dollar is stretched beyond the breaking point.[10]

These considerations point up the illusory character of the discussions, in and out of Congress, on the problem of raising the rate of the economic growth of America in the face of the "threat" of the rate of growth of the economy of the Soviet Union. After the "recovery" from the 1957-58 recession it became clear that the traditional 2.5 to 3.0 per cent annual growth rate in America is not only no match to the Soviet Union's 7 to 8 per cent growth rate, but can no longer suffice to absorb all the labor force seeking jobs here.

---

*It is very doubtful whether advertising, as such, much advances total consumer demand, except as it accelerates obsolescence. The real stimulus in the consumer market comes from the $15 billion annual income (in 1963) made available to "Madison Avenue" from otherwise uninvestible surplus-value.

As automation and other capital-saving technologies build up, less and less of the social surplus they will help to create will be required for investment and employment. More and more of unproductive expenditures will be required to maintain employment at even existing levels.[11] Since expenditures for the military may be tapering off as the horizon for world peace broadens and as the arms supply becomes absurdly over-extended, new and expanding outlets for the output of America's production potentials will need to be found if the rate of its economic growth is to come even within the shadow of the Soviet Union's. The Soviets gear their rate of growth to the unending rise of the material and cultural standard of living of its people. Can a capitalist America do that? You cannot, as we noted a few pages back, build factories just to build factories *ad infinitum*, in order to raise the rate of economic growth. But, if you supply the means, you can build factories up to the available labor supply to produce the goods and services that would supply the unending material and cultural wants of the people. The people's wants are insatiable, given the wherewithal to satisfy them. In a socialist country, like the Soviet Union, in fact, the satisfaction of the people's wants must always lag behind its output as the standard of living continually rises. In a capitalist country, like America, production must always tend to outrun consumption. This is the underlying condition for the periodic capitalist crises, recessions and depressions, except as unproductive expenditures, such as military expenditures, may dampen the rate of descent.

The question that arises, then, in the search for means of maintaining peacetime full employment in a capitalist country and of providing for its economic growth is: What outlets are available to such an economy, outlets of a more socially useful and socially productive nature than the military outlet, for absorbing the excess savings of the community?

And then will come the question of what the maintenance of full employment may signify to the viability of a capitalist economy.

We turn next to these questions.

PART IV

STEPS AND BARRIERS TO FULL EMPLOYMENT

15.
CAPITAL EXPORTS

In this and in the next three chapters we consider possible alternatives to military spending as means of absorbing social surplus which can find no outlets in the private sector of the economy. We consider also a new factor which has not hitherto been stressed in this book. This is the fact that all these alternatives, as is true also of military expenditures, carry with them built-in barriers to their effectiveness as absorbers of social surplus, and, as Keynes noted, in a capitalist economy, full employment itself creates conditions antagonistic to the maintenance of full employment.*

As alternatives to military expenditures, singly and in combination with one another, we consider:

    I. Capital Exports.
    II. Increased Social Consumption—building the Welfare State.
    III. Increased Mass Individual Consumption, Through
        a. Increased Real Wages;
        b. Reduction of Consumer Taxes .

A. CAPITAL EXPORTS AND COLONIAL EMANCIPATION

The traditional capitalist means of disposing of excess savings has been their export to less developed countries and building colonial empires. This was the case of Great Britain, France, Holland, Belgium, and later, Germany. For Great Britain, for example, it can be shown that in the last quarter of the 19th century, "in practically every year when the volume of domestic investment fell or remained the same, the volume of foreign investment rose," and "when a disparity developed between the growth of full-capacity output and actual output, the economy found profitable outlets for its excess saving overseas and, hence, was able to maintain a comparatively high volume of output and trade."[1]

Today, the export of capital to build colonial empires on a large

---

*But, as we will see, not for the reason he gave.

scale is no longer feasible. The revolt of the former colonies against foreign economic and political domination precludes that. Further, the major portion of the vast Eurasian continent, which before the Bolshevik Revolution in Russia was becoming the object of large amounts of foreign investment, is now socialist and not available for colonization. In these respects, "The frontier is closed." Advanced capitalisms can no longer look to this kind of "territorial expansion" as a major way for the export of capital.

This does not mean that the need for capital outside these capitalisms has been satisfied. On the contrary, the political emancipation of the former colonies has also meant their awakening to their economic needs. (The two, of course, are interrelated.) They want more of the material and cultural abundance which present-day technology makes possible. And so they want to put their hands on capital that would help them produce these worldly goods and services. Paul G. Hoffman, director of the United Nations Special Fund for Economic Development, has estimated these needs at $320,000,000,000 over a period of 10 years in trade and aid. One-half of the world's population is thus capital-hungry. The vast socialist camp, especially China, is eager for capital loans. In these respects the frontier is not closed; it is, indeed, wide open.

But the capitalist countries with excess capital, in particular their senior partner, the United States, will not enter. The United States will not lend to the socialist bloc of nations; it will not even carry on customary trade with them and seeks to prevent its allies from doing that,* in the naive and forlorn hope that thereby it will thwart their growth and, perhaps, even bring them to their knees in economic and political ruin. This was the official foreign policy of the United States in the reign of the late Secretary of State John Foster Dulles and still is as these lines are written. According to his surviving brother, Allen W. Dulles, then still Chief of Central Intelligence Agency, peaceful coexistence with the Soviet Union is a danger to the capitalist world since peace would make it possible for the Soviets to divert expenditures from the military to civilian consumption. (Speech before the National Association of Manufacturers in New York, December 4, 1959.) Instead, "Overload and Delay"

---

*The embargo on sale of big inch gas and oil pipe to the Soviet Union which the United States is imposing on its allies is a case in point.

has been the strategy for dealing with the Soviet Union.*

The advanced capitalist countries will not lend money to the sub-capitalist half of the world's population, except at high profit rates and on the forfeiture of their economic and political birthrights. These terms are no longer acceptable to these peoples. They are unwilling any longer to serve as the millennial source of material and human exploitation for the benefit of foreigners. As Professor Gunnar Myrdal once put it:

> The "world" of 1913 was, like Athens in the days of Pericles, in many respects a model civilization—if one forgets the fact that it excluded from its benefits the larger part of mankind. Any new international system ensuring stability, broadly shared progress, and a commonly felt confidence in the future must be attained on different terms, since the peoples who were then excluded are unwilling to resume their earlier passive role.[2]

Robert L. Garner, until lately President of the International Finance Corporation, private investment-stimulation arm of the World Bank, was clearly out of tune with the times, then, when in his address to the First Annual Meeting of its Board of Governors, he declared:

> I conceive that a goal of the IFC is to demonstrate in concrete form that soundly conducted investment in the less developed areas *can be highly profitable,* and by that demonstration to stimulate the flow of private management and capital into such investment.
> Such a concept requires, first, that we select projects which are well-conceived, well-executed, well-managed—with proper financial set-up and prospects of attractive profits related to the risk; and, second, *that our investment be made on terms which promise returns greater*

---

*In 1951 or 1952, we are told, "The Government called to Washington some of the best brains in the universities to help work out a 'cold war' strategy. The planners came up with a powerful idea condensed in the capsule that bore the label 'Overload and Delay'." This was to pressure the top Soviet leadership with overpowering problems for decision, delaying responses to any rapprochments, thus wearing them out and leading to a political breakdown. Wallace Carroll, in the *New York Times,* June 9, 1959.

*than those available from more familiar, and generally
safer, opportunities in the more developed countries.*[(3)]

There can be no socialist nonsense, either, in these strictly private
profit business transactions. The IFC will not lend where the state
in any way interferes with free enterprise, as he made explicit in
his address to the Third Annual Meeting of the IFC. If an economy,
he said then, "is to benefit from the vigor of individual effort and
from the imagination and courage of the able man, government must
not put him in shackles of bureaucratic regulation, nor attempt to
substitute the judgment of officials for his business judgment." To
be sure, he regretted, there are "more than a few sincere and responsible people who still retain doubt as to the effectiveness and suit-
ability of private enterprise for their countries. . . . One also frequently detects a distrust of private business in the minds of some
well-meaning people because it enables certain individuals to make
large profits."[4] Well, these benighted heathen will have to change
their thinking, or they won't get our money. In the words of columnist
C. L. Sulzberger (*New York Times*, January 25, 1958): "We are
openly wary of helping regimes we regard as 'socialistic'." So the
American Congress rejects India's request for a loan of $1.5 billion
to build a steel plant because it is to be government owned and government operated. The Soviet Union will build it. Our aid aims at
containing this socialist nonsense. As the late President Kennedy
declared before the Economic Club of New York, December 14, 1962,

> I would like to cut out foreign aid; it is unpopular.
> But this is a method by which the United States main-
> tains a position of influence and control around the
> world, and sustains a good many countries which would
> definitely collapse or pass into the Communist bloc.[(5)]

The historical fact is that the people who but yesterday shook
off the yoke of the old imperialisms will not consciously reach their
necks out into a new one, no matter how beguiling the inscription
on it. And they are impatient to the point of revolt. They are impatient to free themselves from the social and economic stagnation
so long perpetuated for them by imperialist exploitation. The per
capita income of most Latin American countries is less than $300
a year. In almost all African countries it is less than $100 a year.
It is less than $100 a year also in Pakistan, India, Burma, Laos,
Thailand, Indonesia, Cambodia, New Guinea—colonies or former col-

170

onies all.[6] When we hear of the much higher standard of living in the "civilized" portion of the "free" world, we should bear in mind the fact that to a considerable extent this has come about *because* these other countries have been kept so poor. It is on the wealth extracted from these lands that the "mother" countries have fattened. So, for example, Mr. Goodhue Livingston, former special assistant to the United States Ambassador to the Union of South Africa, wrote in a letter to *The New York Times* (August 7, 1960), relative to the exploitation of the Katanga mines by a Belgian corporation: "Most of the profits from these operations during the past seventy years have been funneled back to the stockholders in Belgium. Only a very small percentage has been used toward the development and welfare of the Congo."

The per capita United States annual income in 1963 was over $2,100. It was about half of that in Great Britain. In the judgment of Professor R. B. Williams of University College of North Stafford-shire, England (*Economic Journal*, Sept. 1959) : "Even if real income per head in [the] poor countries were raised 10 per cent per annum, Egypt would take twenty-five years to reach the present British level; Burma, Ethiopia, Ecuador, Korea, Phillipines, Saudi Arabia, thirty-five years, and Indonesia, forty-five."

The affluence of capitalist society, which is the envy and goal of these countries, took several hundred years to develop through the slow process of private capital accumulation and mass exploitation, including the exploitation of hundreds of millions of colonial peoples. The socialist countries, they know, take decades, instead of centuries, to achieve potentially broader and more certain affluence through public ownership and government organization of material and human resources. These socialist countries have extended loans to under-developed countries at minimal interest rates. No individuals in the socialist countries can make "large profits" from such loans. Besides, to many of the emancipating countries the capitalist path towards economic development appears an anachronism. Capitalism, as they see it, is an economic system of the past, not the future.

Whether the President of the IFC likes it or not, government direction in the accumulation of the capital required to lift these economically backward peoples out of their primitive poverty has become a categorical imperative for them. "I am convinced," wrote Professor Benjamin Higgins, discussing a paper at a session of the American Economic Association on "Economic Progress in Under-developed Countries," in December 1958, that the economic progress of these countries must be predicated on a "drastic structural change,

171

involving wholesale transfers of population from peasant agriculture to industry, which market forces alone [as was the case of the development of existing capitalisms] and unaided will not produce. Such transfers," he held, "require simultaneous industrialization and agricultural revolution and so necessitate substantially increased capital accumulation and government intervention in the allocation of resources."[7]

This, substantially, is the view also of the British economist Ursula K. Hicks. "The low rate of saving and entrepreneurial ability," prevailing in the underdeveloped countries, she wrote in 1957,[8]

> implies that in practically all backward countries there
> is need for the state to undertake a good deal of invest-
> ment, not only in social and economic overheads, but
> also, directly or indirectly, in manufacturing industry.
> . . . The basic obstacle . . . is the small size of the
> public sector . . .

Morocco, formerly a French colony, was perhaps the first to point in this direction. Under a five-year plan that went into effect in 1960, the Moroccan government has assumed "effective control" of all transport, communication and energy, and will participate in setting up basic industries. The going will be slow, its leaders are aware, because of "the need to change the economic, social and administrative structures," the need "to mobilize national savings to avoid dependence on foreign sources," and because of a lack in qualified personnel in "every branch of the economy." (*The New York Times*, Nov. 25, 1959.)

The question of capital exports to underdeveloped countries, thus, is seen to be of a political as well as of an economic nature. A large measure of public ownership and control; anti-imperialist ideologies; the urge to national liberation; the ever-present threat of confiscation by nationalization—all these make investment in the emancipating countries a risky venture, unless the government guarantees its safety. This means an agreement on a government-to-government basis, and in the case of the small, weaker countries may mean jeopardizing the sovereignty of the borrowing country.

B. AMERICAN CAPITAL EXPORTS COME HOME TO ROOST

What has been said thus far does not mean that the United States is not engaging in capital exports. On the contrary, these have risen considerably since the end of the last war. But, balanced by capital imports and particularly by repatriated earnings, they have not been large enough to make any serious dent in our excess savings. By the end of 1963 long-term foreign investments and assets in this country amounted to some 40 per cent of the long-term American private investment and assets abroad. European long-term investments in the United States were actually greater than American long-term private investments in Europe, $16 billion and $15 billion, respectively. Total foreign assets and investments in the United States equalled nearly 59 per cent of total United States assets and investments abroad. (*S.C.B.*, August 1964, p. 24.) Capital exports from the United States as a means of reducing the domestic surplus are thereby being offset by this counter-movement of foreign capital to the United States.

Repatriated earnings over the decade ended in 1961 have exceeded the long-term direct overseas investment by an average of nearly $1 billion a year, increasing the domestic social surplus. In 1963, income from overseas direct investment exceeded $3 billion, but new direct investment amounted to $1.9 billion. In general, in recent years income received from direct investments of United States corporations abroad has been about twice as large as our new direct investment outlays in foreign countries. In the years 1950-61 new private investment in the major Latin American countries amounted to not quite $3.0 billion. Remittances amounted to $2\frac{1}{3}$ times that amount.

American private investment in foreign countries has not been directed at building up the economies of underdeveloped nations. "Capital Avoiding Poorest Nations," reads the caption over an article by Brendan N. Jones in the *New York Times* of December 7, 1958. And a sub-caption explains: "Extreme Nationalism and Fear of Expropriation Called Difficulties." When American capital does enter these "poorest nations" it is, first of all, to build "bastions of freedom" and money gets dammed up at the top layers of the political and business hierarchy. Little gets trickled down to the people. For example, since the liberation of Korea from the Japanese, America has poured in over $3.5 billion in economic aid and $2 billion in military assistance. Yet, after 15 years of this aid Korea [and by this is meant South Korea] "still lacks: A major manufacturing for exports; a sufficient water supply; enough power; a reliable sanitary system; highways other than a string of bumpy gravel tracks; any kind of employment at all for 3,000,000 persons, and anything more

173

than part-time work for another 4,000,000." That, in a total population of about 23,000,000. One of every three male adults is in the Korean Army, maintained by American dollars. (Richard J. M. Johnson, *N.Y.T.*, September 1960.)

The United States' aim in the underdeveloped areas, as that of all affluent capitalist countries, has been the exploitation of human and natural resources and the establishment of economic domination. With respect to America's effort to counter the influence of the Cuban Revolution on the other Latin American countries, a *New York Times* editorial of September 6, 1960 ("The Bogota Conference") reads: "There can be few North Americans who do not realize that Latin America is vital to our *economic supremacy* and that this is a crucial period in the history of the region." (italics supplied) Everywhere military and economic aid is aimed at propping up kinglings, princelings and petty dictators against the wrath of the people. "The new stress," of a special military aid program for Latin America asked of Congress, reads an item by correspondent Tad Szulc in the *New York Times*, July 4, 1961, "is on internal defense against subversion." The United States has "military commitments" of this nature in 44 countries. (*N.Y.T.*, May 7, 1961, maps on p. E3). The size of our "counter-insurgency" forces was increased several hundred per cent in recent years.

An AP dispatch from Durham, N. C., dated April 29, 1961, reported Associate Justice William O. Douglas as declaring at a "Law Day 1961" banquet that the underdeveloped nations that have received billions of dollars in American aid in the past 15 years "are mostly worse off for it." The funds have gone not to build schools and hospitals, but military bases, army barracks and a few factories. "Instead," he is quoted as saying:

> the aid launched the countries on military projects that gave them such an amount of armament that they crushed all dissident elements. The result was the liquidation of democratic influences and the entrenchment of feudal overlords.

In some countries, he went on to say, "The overlords became rich on the American aid while the people at the bottom starved. Consequently, American aid accentuated the gulf between the rich and the poor. . . ."

To soothe Latin American discontent in view of the Cuban Revolution, the United States offered to extend them $500,000,000 in new aid. A "political rescue operation," United States Senator J. W. Fulbright called it. (*New York Times*, September 26, 1960.) The United States has actually resorted to the secondary boycott to put an economic squeeze on Cuba. Countries that receive economic aid from America are forbidden to buy Cuban sugar! The first country so warned was Morocco. (*New York Times*, August 20, 1960.) * Early in 1964 we cut off economic and military aid (piddling amounts) to Britain, France and Yugoslavia for trading with Cuba and halted new aid commitments to Spain and Morocco until they explained what steps they are taking to stop their trading in line with American policy to isolate Cuba.

Permanent industrial investment of American capital is placed in safe, capitalistically developed countries, as the figures in Tables 2 and 3 testify.

TABLE 2

American Private Foreign Investment by Major Areas, and Foreign Assets and Investment in the U.S.A., in million dollars. At the end of 1956, 1958, 1960 and 1962[9]

Area	1956	1958	1960	1962
Western Europe	6,137	7,768	11,234	14,460
Canada	12,029	14,249	17,235	19,746
Latin American Republics(a) .	9,355	11,133	11,473	12,190
All Other and Unallocated....	5,479	7,674	10,343	13,414
Total U.S. Private Foreign Investment	33,000	40,824	50,285	59,810
Foreign Assets and Investments in U.S.	31,607	34,816	44,682	47,368

(a) Including Western European Dependencies.

Table 2 shows that the largest private American investment abroad has been made, first, in Canada, next in Latin America, and next in Western Europe. All the rest of the world, including Asia and Africa, where lie most of the economically backward nations, and the socialist bloc of nations have received about 20 per cent of the total. Partly this is so because the Asian and African markets have long been

---

*Since this was written, the United States became involved, in mid-April 1961, in the intrigue of a counter-revolutionary invasion of the island. That ended in a disastrous fiasco. But it did not end the intrigue.

preempted by the European imperialist powers and American penetration is a slow process involving "free world" rivalries. Partly it is because American money has hastened to get in on the ground floor in the rapidly developing European markets. In the main, however, this is so because the European markets *are* safe and offer immediate high-rate returns, whereas the Asian and African markets are still only a distant promise, are of doubtful safety and hold forth no immediate prospects of high rates of profit.

In Table 3 we find that the greatest concentration of the *direct* private American investment in Latin America and the Middle East has been in the extractive industries—in mining and petroleum. Direct investment in manufacturing has been concentrated in Canada and in Western Europe, with the United Kingdom the major base. In Canada, it is reported, direct American private investment accounts for roughly half of all of that country's mining and manufacturing capital expenditures. American companies are "taking over," either by investing in the expansion of existing native businesses or by building branches of their own home establishments. Competitive international capitalism is becoming integrated transnational capitalism. For the investment capitalist, it seems, it is not the color or shape of the national flag that counts, but the profit made under it.

TABLE 3

Value of Direct American Private Investment Abroad, by
Major Areas and Major Industries in 1963
(In millions of dollars)

	Mining Smelting	Petroleum	Manu- facturing	All Other
All areas, total	3,350	13,698	14,890	8,707(a)
Canada	1,540	3,133	5,746	2,137
Latin American Republics (Total)	1,093	3,094	2,103	1,667
Dependencies in Western Hemisphere	(b)	533	108	320
Western Europe	55	2,828	5,610	1,235
(United Kingdom)	(2)	(939)	(2,735)	(13)
Africa (Total)	351	701	176	186
Middle East	(b)	1,207	33	—
Far East (Total) (c)	31	718	387	31
"International"	—	988	—	—

(a) Includes investment in public utilities not distributed by area here.
(b) Included in total.
(c) Includes Australia, India, Japan, Philippines, etc.

176

This form of American investment in industrially advanced capitalisms is not conducive to the maintenance of full employment
at home, and explains in no small way why these countries have out-
stripped America in the rate of economic growth in the recent past.
It explains also why Western Europe already by 1960 was suffering
from a "dollar glut" and was trying desperately to get rid of its
excess investible surplus through exports. The excess social surplus
is becoming a universal capitalist phenomenon.

It would be different if these excess capitals were used in the
industrialization of undeveloped countries. There capital would give
employment to the millions of underemployed peasants, raise their
per capita income and their standard of living, and create a market
for exports of goods and services from the investing country. Capital
exports under these conditions would reduce the excess social surplus
at home.

In their present form, most American capital exports set up opposite conditions. They not only set up competition with homemade
goods, they tend also to enhance America's social surplus which
capital exports are presumed to reduce. In 1957, United States exports
of goods and services amounted to $27 billion. At the same time the
sales of the 2,500 or so American companies that had branches or
subsidiaries abroad ran up to an estimated $32 billion, *including
exports back to the United States*. The sales originating in American
overseas establishments thus ran to nearly 18 per cent above the
total "American" export trade.

American firms operating branches and subsidiaries abroad benefit from the lower wage rates prevailing there, as well as from the
up-to-date machinery they install. The profit rate on American foreign investment is probably twice as high as on domestic investment.
(See, for example, *U.S. News and World Report*, December 17, 1962,
p. 84.) They reap the same kind of advantage that they do when they
move their factories, say, from New England to the low-wage South.
In 87 per cent of American firms manufacturing in the United Kingdom, labor costs are lower than in the United States, and in 74 per
cent of the firms, total unit costs are lower. Initially, when capital
is exported to build abroad, these foreign investments reduce the
domestic excess social surplus. But in the end, when their foreign
output begins to cut down American export potentials at the same
time that the larger earnings from the foreign investment enrich the
home corporations, the domestic excess social surplus is increased
while domestic employment potentials have been decreased to the
extent that American capital employs labor abroad.

It would be different, we have noted, if this capital were exported, in the main, to underdeveloped countries. There industrialization would raise the income and the standard of living and the demand for American goods and services. But the dilemma for the capitalist class is real. Whether to waste uninvestible social surplus on military expenditures and "contain Communism," or invest it in underdeveloped countries with potentially "socialistic" tendencies. Socialism is a living reality in ⅓ of the world and the former colonies cannot lift themselves out of grinding poverty without substantial doses of this "poison," as Walter Lippmann has called it. But official America does not seem to know it yet.

The irony of it all is that *some* Americans do know that, and so also do America's Allies as well as her former enemies whom our economic and military aid has made prosperous.* West Germany is selling goods to the Chinese-Russian bloc to the value of over $900 million a year *and is extending credit to East Germany* (!) which, like China, does not exist in the eyes of the State Department. And a considerable portion of the output of American branches and subsidiaries in Western Europe and Japan is similarly exported. But "their less-favored domestic rivals," as the *Nation* (Nov. 28, 1959, p. 391) has phrased it "—those without subsidiaries—are handcuffed by the pretense that a boycott on East-West trade is still in effect." Further, quoting Harvey Williams, President of Philco International Corporation, Moscow seems to be getting all the credit it wants in Western Europe and "its credit standing with European insurance companies is particularly high." *(ibid.)* During the past decade Western Europe tripled its commerce with the Communist countries which now runs at about $5 billion a year. As these lines are written, Britain is reported to have agreed to build a synthetic fiber plant for the Russians in the amount of $84 million, 80 per cent, on the basis of a 15-year credit. This extended credit is especially irksome to the State Department. It goes counter to its policy of denying the Soviet Union long-term credit, a policy which was in the making already when we were still its allies in fighting the war against Hitler.

This failure to develop capital exports to the underdeveloped regions and the communist bloc of nations aggravates America's problem of disposal of its uninvestible social surplus. It will become aggravated still further with the likelihood that American foreign,

---

*American defense expenditures abroad have been largest in Germany and Japan, over 1/3 of the 1960 total of $3,048 million going to these erstwhile enemy countries. See *S.C.B.*, Jaunary 1962, p. 15, Table 2,

military and economic aid may be tapering off in the near future. This, curiously, is likely to happen precisely because of the competition in foreign trade which American investors have stimulated abroad, narrowing domestic foreign trade balances. What is involved here is that the traditional American favorable balance of trade is not high enough to offset the new American overseas dollar payments in "foreign aid." Since the United States has undertaken to bolster the economic and military potentials of the "free world," its dollar outflow has outrun its dollar inflow. The deficit since 1950 has amounted to about $2 billion a year. In 1963 it ran up to $2½ billion. At first these went to build up the very weak foreign dollar reserves— to close the "dollar gap ." By now this gap has been closed, and the incoming dollars are no longer needed as reserves. Instead, they are being converted into gold. This has led to a drain on the American gold stock amounting to over $10 billion in the three years 1958-60. By contrast, by the end of 1960 West Germany alone had accumulated a gold and dollar reserve of more than $7 billion.

This drain on American gold stocks has reduced them from the near-$23 billion at the end of 1957 to less than $16 billion by the end of 1962. This is still a tidy sum. But foreign investments in this country, in large part short-term holdings, amount to much more than that. Short-term liabilities alone came to nearly $20 billion in the Summer of 1962. This combined "threat" against America's gold reserves may lead to a weakening of the value of the dollar reserves in the United States and so of the whole international trade structure of the "free world" countries which mainly rests on dollar balances. The condition may deteriorate further when the "inner 6," the "Common Market," and the "outer 7" blocs of European nations, which are now forming and which America has encouraged to come into being, create tariff walls to impede imports from America.

It is significant that of the three interacting causes adversely affecting American dollar balances—capital exports, the export-import balance, and cold war expenditures abroad—the First National City Bank of New York points the accusing finger at the last. In its December 1960 *Monthly Letter*, it declared:

> The chief weakness in the U.S. balance of payments is neither in our trade nor in our private capital account: it stems from the vast overseas expenditures of the U.S. Government.
> These expenditures — military outlays abroad, military and economic grants, and loans by the U.S. Treasury, the

179

Export-Import Bank, etc. — have reached the staggering total of close to $110 billion over the past fifteen years.[10]

This view expressed by the Bank constitutes a new orientation, an "agonizing reappraisal" of the Dulles policy of containment from a "position of strength." It must lead to a reduction of international tensions, to a reduction of arms expenditures and to a reduction in taxes. It should also lead to the cooperation of the U.S.A. with the U.S.S.R. and other "have" countries, under U.N. auspices, in the export of the large amounts of capital required to build up the economies of the unindustrialized nations—some $32 billion a year for the next ten years, to follow Paul Hoffman's estimates. Yet, even if the United States participated in proportionate measure, the need for new outlets at home, outside private investment to absorb a rising volume of social surplus would still be great. And this leads us to the consideration in the next chapter of one of the other alternatives to military expenditures listed at the opening of this chapter, namely, building the Welfare State.

16.
INCREASING SOCIAL CONSUMPTION

"Building the Welfare State" as a means of assuring full employment in an advanced capitalist economy is now as common a cliché of economists and publicists as are "monetary and fiscal policy" and "built-in stabilizers." As is becoming in a "democracy," some hold that building the Welfare State is *the* solution to the problem of full employment, while others believe that Welfare Statism endangers the very life blood of a free enterprise system.

What is commonly thought of as the Welfare State is that the people living under one are adequately provided by the government with decent, low-cost housing; with free and high standard education from the nursery through the university; free or low-cost medical care; free recreational and cultural facilities and, of course, old age economic security and economic protection in the case of loss of job. Some will go as far as to include a fair minimum wage, and other economic and social service benefits for wage earners. The underlying thought is that government provision for these needs would help maintain full employment. In the present context, government spending for the social welfare would absorb much of the social surplus which world peace and universal disarmament would release for productive social consumption.*

It should be noted at once, however, that the absorption of excess social surplus is not the ultimate justification for increasing the expenditures for the social welfare. Expenditures for the better health, the better housing, the better education, as for all the other social services, are their own justification. These are related to the excess social surplus only insofar as that is now so largely absorbed by the military. So long as this holds true, the social services will be espe-

---

*We define as productive social consumption all government expenditures which enhance the physical, cultural and mental health of the community, in short, investment in social capital. This precludes the military expenditures of a nation, which we designate as unproductive and wasteful social consumption. The military consumes income which might otherwise go to the enrichment of the individual and communal life of the people.

181

cially skimped. The "tax dollar" which now goes to pay for intercontinental ballistic missiles and hydrogen bomb warheads is not available for the public schools. In all the areas of social welfare the United States is at present incredibly deficient, considering its wealth-producing capacity. This condition would be largely corrected if what the country now spends on the military were to be diverted to the social services—to increased social consumption of a productive nature.

Furthermore, in the face of the burgeoning population of the United States since the end of World War II, it must become increasingly impossible to maintain the social services even at their present inadequate levels unless more of the tax dollar is so diverted. There are increasingly more families requiring decent housing, more children in the schools, more in need of medical care. Besides, if our theory of the impact of a potentially uninvestible social surplus on employment is correct, then, if we are to have full employment, productive social consumption must be increased in the coming years even if expenditures for the military are maintained at their present high levels. The rising productivity of labor and the prospective large annual additions to the labor force will lead to increasing unemployment unless new ways of consuming the nation's potential output at full employment are developed. In large measure these could be found in increased expenditures for the social welfare. Increasing production alone—increasing "the size of the national pie" for personal consumption—will not supply jobs for the increasing labor force. Increasing labor productivity makes possible increased production of consumer goods without a corresponding increase of employment of production workers, as the recovery from the 1957-58 recession and the "bottoming up" of the recession of 1960-61 have amply demonstrated. Further, there is a limit to "increasing" current production, insofar as a large share of present-day production is geared to wasteful consumption. Gadgetry and "conspicuously wasteful consumption," as Veblen phrased it, have their satiation points, as has the vogue of "buy now and pay later."

To meet the "prodigious increase" of population alone "will require," in the words of Professor Henry Steele Commager of Amherst,

> a bold program of repair, renewal, and expansion of our
> physical plant on a scale comparable to that by which we
> are developing our national defense at the present time
> [1957]. It will require a rebuilding of cities, now rotting
> away at the core: vast slum clearance and housing projects; the construction of innumerable playgrounds and

recreational centers; an immense increase in provision
for health — in preventive medical centers and in hospitals; a reconstruction of city traffic. . . It will require
the replacement of obsolete and the construction of new
educational plants on a vast scale, from the nursery
school to the university and research institutes. . .

These [he added] are elementary and obvious necessities.
*We cannot provide for them — we can scarcely initiate
them if we are required, at the same time, to provide for
the defense of the free world at current costs.* . . [1]

I select for the present discussion three of these "elementary and
obvious necessities": Housing, Education and the Public Health.

A. HOUSING

1. *Shortages and Inadequacies: The Slums.*—It has been estimated that at the close of the 1950's, 17 million American lived "in
dwellings that are beyond rehabilitation—decayed, dirty, rat infested,
without decent heat or light or plumbing."[2] The rate of slum clearance has not kept up with the rate of slum formation. In the 10 years
after slum clearance financing was authorized by the Federal Housing
Act of 1949 (Title I), only 36 projects were completed, in the
sense that land had been acquired, cleared, sold to private builders
for development, and capital grants approved by the authorities, even
though "planning had been initiated on 647 projects in 385 communities."[3] And "projects completed" does not mean houses or apartments
erected. If present trends are allowed to continue, reads an article
by Edward L. Logue in the New York Times *Magazine*, November 9,
1958, "30,000,000 Americans will be living in slums by 1975." In
Westchester County, New York, one of the richest counties in the
country, 70,000 persons were living in 20,000 slum dwellings in 1959.
Three times as many substandard houses needed to be replaced each
year until 1970 than were then being planned if the accumulating
blight was to be overtaken. (See item in *New York Times*, January
28, 1960, p. L33.)

One reason for the snail's pace in slum clearance is the problem
of relocating slum families. The majority of slum dwellers in America
are non-whites of middle and lower-middle incomes. (In preceding
generations they were the newly arriving immigrants.) Decent, rea-
sonably-priced private housing for non-whites in these income ranges

183

is virtually non-existent, and to open up white neighborhoods for them meets with the baneful race prejudice of the American white population. The direct answer to this problem would seem to be the construction of interracial low-rent public housing, but America is a white man's country and Congress acts accordingly. Congressional appropriations for such housing have been forthcoming in driblets. Besides, low-cost, low-rent housing in any meaningful quantities meets with the powerful opposition of private real estate interests.

The country has needed some 2.5 million new dwelling units each year for the 15 years beginning in 1955, to provide for an expanding population; to replace annual losses and dwellings becoming obsolete and substandard, and to eliminate the accumulated deficiencies. Any lesser volume of new housing construction, it has been calculated, will never reduce or eliminate existing and newly forming slums. Here are the estimates, in million dwelling units, of one authority on housing, those of Professor William L. Wheaton of the University of Pennsylvania:[4]

Assumed new construction per year	Number of substandard units remaining			
	1955	1960	1965	1970
1.2 to 1.4................	15	14	15	17
1.4 to 1.6................	15	13	13	14
1.6 to 1.8................	15	12	10	9
2.0 to 2.4................	15	10	7	5

Even at the construction rate of 2 to 2.4 million housing units a year beginning with 1955, the number of substandard housing units remaining in 1970 would still amount to 5 million.

In the years 1955-59 average annual starts of private non-farm dwellings have amounted to scarcely 1.2 million. Since 1959 they have averaged 1.4 million. Low-rent, low-cost public housing units built those same years have averaged no more than about 40,000—just a little over 3 per cent of total private housing starts.[5] These rates of housing construction will clearly not eliminate the slums or provide for the relocation of the non-white slum dwellers.

2. *A Private Business.*—The reason private real estate builds only about half of the number of dwelling units needed for the decent housing of the American people is not far to seek. In accordance with the principles of an artificially-created scarcity economy, only so much new housing is built each year as will sell at the highest possible profit to the builders. Any measurable increase in total con-

184

struction would reduce the scarcity value of the houses. Private real estate, thus, has a vested interest in housing shortages. And this, also, is one of the reasons why private real estate interests obstruct any moves to increase the construction of low-cost, low-rent public housing. Private housing is geared to the purchasing power of the 30 per cent top-income families of the community. The "median minimum" cost of private houses built in 1959 in 25 sample cities was priced at near $11,000. To purchase a house at that price that year a family would need to have had an annual income of over $6,600.00, figuring the family income at five times the annual mortgage payments, taxes, heat and light, insurance and maintenance costs. Yet only about 29 per cent of American families had that much income (or more) in 1959.[6]

The need, then, is for government-financed housing construction to accommodate the 70 per cent low and lower-middle income families of the nation. Something like 1.5 million units a year each for the next 15 years of that price housing seems to be required to meet that need. By eliminating profit and other "overhead" costs, the government might be able to build such housing at $5,000 to $6,000 per dwelling unit, in 1959 prices. This would run up to about 7½ to 9 billion dollars a year, or to about 15 to 20 per cent of the present military outlays. It would run in rental or purchase price at about one-half of the "median minimum" cost of private housing.*

But any suggestion that the government provide low-cost housing in any meaningful numbers is decried as rank socialism and any legislation proposed in that direction as "communist inspired." When the Taft-Ellender-Wagner low-cost housing bill was before the Congress in 1948, the President of the National Home and Property Owners' Foundation (a Mr. Arthur Binns) declared it to be "the last beach-head" in the struggle "between public enterprise and private enterprise." If, he said, "the government now takes over the housing of the nation under a bill which provides at the beginning twice as much public housing as we had prior to Pearl Harbor, we have started down the path which can only lead to the nationalization of all property."[7]

When after World War II Senator Taft proposed in the Housing Act of 1949 that 10 per cent of all new housing starts be low-rent

---

*For 1961-62 the median annual income of white families is estimated at $5,800; of non-white, at $3,200, and the median price for a new one-family home, at about $14,900. Statistics of the Federal Housing Home Finance Agency. For 1962 the corresponding family incomes were $6,237 and $3,330.

public housing, private real estate forces closed ranks and fought his program to a standstill. Opposing that provision of the Act, President Thomas S. Holden of the F. W. Dodge Corporation, which collects and disseminates real estate statistics, published a pamphlet entitled "Housing Dictatorship and Soft Socialism" which the Corporation broadcast among real estate and related business interests of the country. A *Los Angeles Times* editorial (March 1, 1949) announced that occupants of government housing were on strike demanding a "24-inch screen television in each housing unit and a two-car garage for every family." Representative Jesse P. Wolcott (R., Michigan) opposed the Act in the House, declaring, "My objective is to make sure that my boy does not have to say that his dad contributed to the deterioration of the American government."[8]

As finally passed, that Housing Act provided that a total of 1,050,000 low-rent dwelling units be built in six years, a rate of 135,000 a year. In the next 10 years 232,000 dwelling units, an average of 23,200 a year, were built under that Act. At that, the major portion consisted of housing on military installations and temporary war housing for military personnel. (*N.H.C.* Yearbook for 1959, table on p. 54.)

It should be added that "public" housing as it is supplied today, is not wholly a government expense. It is *government financed*. Once construction is completed and occupied, 60 per cent of the cost is paid for by tenants as rent. Twenty-five per cent of the cost is borne by the federal government and 15 per cent by the local community. (Yearbook for 1954, p. 47.) Built by private contractors, they are also profit-producing.

This is where public housing in America stands in 1964.* In opposing a provision in the Emergency Housing Act of 1957 authorizing $1 billion for secondary financing of moderate-cost housing—to combat the then developing recession—President Eisenhower warned in his budget message in January, 1958, that the pending legislation was wholly inconsistent with his Administration's policy "to encourage private capital and private investors to finance in competitive markets the myriad activities in our economy, including housing construction,"

---

*In the Nov. 1964 general elections, California real estate interests induced citizens to nullify, 2 to 1, an existing anti-discrimination law in housing. The action was justified by the National Association of Real Estate Boards, which claimed that private property rights — to sell or not to sell real estate — were more basic to human liberty than the civil rights of minority groups. (Glenn Fowler, *N.Y.T.*, Nov. 11, 1964.)

and that it was inconsistent with "the philosophy of a free enterprise system. . . ." In his January 1960 Budget Message he saw no additional obligational authority necessary for the existing, meager housing programs.

At a Hearing before the Senate Subcommittee on Housing, May 9, 1960, Mr. Norman P. Mason, Administrator of the Housing and Home Finance Agency, declared that the liberal housing philosophy of the Subcommittee would lead to a "completely managed economy. These things start small," he warned, and added: "There should be a greater dependence on the private economy."

It was in line with this reasoning that the Federal Housing Administration in April 1960, lowered minimum down payments on houses costing more than $15,000 (!), the reduction running from $300 on a $17,000 house and $500 on a $20,000 home and over. The move was made in order to bolster a sagging housing construction trend (Edwin L. Dale, Jr., *New York Times*, April 30, 1960.), but that obviously would not help build low-cost housing.

3. *The Need for Public Housing.*—That "free enterprise" has not given us the housing the country needs has been made abundantly clear in the preceding paragraphs. That it will not do so in the future is also clear, so long as the consideration of private profit rules the rate of housing construction. *Within* the industry there undoubtedly is keen competition—for choice building sites and for construction contracts. But in one thing the industry is wholly united—in opposition to low-cost housing and especially low-cost public housing. Emphasis must, therefore, be placed on the construction of public housing if the 70 per cent lower income families are to be placed in decent homes and the slum blight of the cities eliminated and housing construction become an outlet for the country's social surplus. Public housing costs less than private housing because the housing authorities can finance their projects at low interest rates; because they can save money through large scale planning, construction and maintenance; they can whittle down costs by eliminating "frills"; they sustain virtually no vacancy or rent collection losses. One leak in this process is the variety of "overhead" costs charged by private contractors and sub-contractors.[9] Further, government housing construction is beset with parasites, "fixers" and various types of leeches which drain the public purse. The experience with slum clearance skulduggery in New York is revealing in this respect.[10]

What will induce the public authorities to change the slow pace of slum clearance and undertake the construction of low-cost housing in America? One thing, if one wished to indulge in fancy, would be for the slum-dwellers *en masse* to leave their filthy habitations and go squat in near-by parks, playgrounds, parking lots—any open spaces —until the "government" bestirs itself and builds them decent homes within reach of their family income.* More immediately likely, under present circumstances, public housing may conceivably come as a "crash program" to meet the Soviet "Housing Challenge." The Soviet Union has been suffering from a housing shortage incomparably greater than our own. The Soviets inherited several centuries of mud huts. In World War II, the Fascist invaders destroyed some 20 million homes in the heartland of the country. Only now are the Russians beginning to make up for these shortages. In the first year of their Seven-Year Plan ending in 1965, the Soviet Union constructed more than 2,200,000 modern apartments in towns and 850,000 dwelling units in villages.[11] The program is to build 15 million dwelling units for workers in towns and 7 million in the countryside as the Seven-Year Plan progresses. These may not be split-level ranch houses as are built in American Suburbia, but they will house the Russians decently and comfortably at low rentals. This will be the Soviet Housing Challenge that may call forth a housing "crash program" here. Americans love crash programs, but all this is still reckoning without the assent of "free enterprise" real estate. This is the big barrier to housing the people in a capitalist society. It constricts one of the means of substituting productive social consumption for wasteful social consumption, and it denies millions of new jobs in the housing construction industries and their suppliers.

B. EDUCATION

1. *Low Esteem.*—On October 4, 1957, the Russians put an artificial satellite in orbit around the Earth. At once America became aware that it had fallen behind the U.S.S.R. in education, particularly in the new, revolutionary physical sciences. It had fallen behind in curricular content of its public schools and colleges; in teaching standards; in teacher qualifications; in school and college plant equipment. Despite a certain amount of ado in the two years following, in the fall of 1959 the American public elementary and high schools were operating with nearly 100,000 teachers of substandard credentials and were short over 132,000 classrooms—66,400 to accommodate excess enrollment and 66,000 to replace obsolete facilities. An Office

---

*The American Negro is winning civil rights by just such mass movement!

188

of Education study published in spring 1962 (Circular #21026) reported nearly 168,000 classrooms in combustible permanent school buildings and additions. Besides, approximately 202,000 classrooms have been in use over 40 years.* Between 1957-58 and 1959-60 classroom construction had actually declined by some 9,000, increasing overcrowding, the number of split sessions and the use of makeshift facilities.[12] At the opening of the school year 1962-63 the shortage was estimated at over 120,000. The enrollment had meanwhile increased by 4 million. Some 82,000 full-time classroom teachers, or 5.5 per cent of all teachers did not meet regular State certification requirements for the positions which they occupied. Thirty-seven States and the District of Columbia reported 418,000 pupils attending less than full or normal school day—almost ⅔ in elementary schools. Over 1½ million pupils were in excess of the normal capacity of the accessible publicly owned school plants in use. (O.E. Circular #703: *Enrollment, Teachers and Schoolhousing.*)

In the colleges and universities, towards the end of the decade, ¼ of the students were attending classes or living in temporary buildings that were fire and health hazards.[13] At the same time, some 200,000 "gifted students" each year withdrew from high school before graduation or failed to go to college because they could not pay the cost.[14] The situation remains essentially the same at this writing (summer 1964).

That the government must do something about it is now almost universally admitted. By "government" is meant the Federal Government. The tax base of the State and local governments, which carry the entire burden of the public schools and over half of the burden of higher education in America, is neither broad enough nor flexible enough to meet this challenge. In fiscal 1962 the publicly controlled institutions of higher learning spent 56 per cent of the total for the country. (O.E. Circular #52008)

American education suffers from two kinds of deficiencies—deficiencies in quality and in quantity. The deficiencies in quality arise from the fact that, for decades now, "learning" in the United States has generally been held in low esteem. The injunction that gave content to that condition has been the Shavian aphorism that "He

---

*In New York, on February 12, 1960, a school wall collapsed throwing tons of brick and mortar into two empty classrooms—the school was closed on Lincoln's Birthday. According to an account in the *New York Times* (February 14, 1960), "the building was erected in 1876 on foundations from previous school structures that go back to 1835."

who can does; he who cannot teaches." At the time Sputnik soared
into space the belief was common in high places in Washington that
basic research except for military purposes was something "you can't
make a living by." A man of intellect was an "egghead." Educational
standards were held down in conformity with these beliefs. The cost
of construction of new facilities for *teachers colleges,* as per cent
of new construction for all institutions of higher learning, fell from
16.2 in 1951 to 6.5 in 1955.[15]

It was this denigrating attitude toward scholarship that in large
measure contributed to the financial niggardliness in regard to school-
ing. In turn, the niggardly financing of schools froze educational
standards at low levels. One conditioned and reinforced the other.

2. *A Consumer Tax Burden.*—The quantitative deficiencies in
American education below college level arise, in the main, from the
dependence of the public school system on a narrow tax base, namely,
the real estate tax of the local governments. The responsibility for the
maintenance of public schools, the standards of instruction as well
as the physical facilities, is lodged with the more than two scores
of thousands of independent "local School Boards." It was so in the
horse and buggy days of over a hundred years ago, when the free
public schools were first established, and it is still so today in the
jet age. In 1957, some 30,000 school districts had less than 50 students
each, when a complete modern school program can hardly be conducted with fewer than 2,000 students, according to the judgment
of the Committee for Economic Development cited on p. 250, n. 25.
And the source of financing has equally remained the same as at
the beginning of the system, that is, the general property tax, increasingly the real estate tax.

Revenue receipts for public school purposes in 1962 amounted
to $17.5 billion. Of these the share of the local governments was
nearly $10.0 billion or 57 per cent of the total. State contributions
ran up to $6.8 billion, or to not quite 39 per cent. The Federal
Government's contribution was less than $1 billion or 4.5 per cent,
and that went largely to federally impacted school areas and for such
non-school purposes as school luncheons for children of poor families.
Most of the local revenue is obtained from the real estate tax; most
of the State revenue is derived from sales and business taxes—all
consumption taxes.

The real estate tax is a highly inelastic tax. It is not expandable
in the degree of the growing needs of the local communities, and,
as a consumption tax, it is regressive. It weighs most heavily on the
lower incomes. The lower the income the greater relatively is the

bite a consumption tax takes out of it. Raising the real estate tax to expand or improve the school system is, therefore, fiercely resisted, whether that rise takes the form of an increase in rent or as an addition to the home owner's mortgage costs. Hence the phenomenon of the repeated defeats of school bond issue in recent years. The real estate tax and the quality of the public school stand in opposition to each other.

On the college level, as regards State institutions, the same type of restriction exists as in the case of the public schools on the local level. Nearly 60 per cent of the States' tax revenues are derived from sales taxes of various kinds. Some 25 per cent come from various licenses, charges (highway tolls, for example) and fees, and only about 15 per cent from individual and corporation income taxes. The income taxes cannot be raised much by the States, since that tax is preempted by the Federal government, in the first place. In the second place, many wealthy people escape that tax by establishing legal domicile in States with no income tax laws. There are many of these States, among which are some of the richest—for example, Connecticut, Florida, Illinois, Michigan, New Jersey, Ohio, Pennsylvania, Rhode Island, Texas.[16] State legislatures can raise the appropriations for the State-supported educational institutions, including contributions to local School revenue, only by raising the rates of existing sales taxes or by devising new sales taxes. But that would penalize the very people who most depend on the low-cost college education which the State institutions are designed to afford—the low-income 70 per cent of American families. The 200,000 gifted youths who now fail to get to college because they lack the finances would double and redouble in number as the higher and new sales taxes raised family living costs.

Private institutions of higher learning are limited in their operating and expansion possibilities by their dependence on endowment income and by the limits to which tuition fees might be raised. Endowment fund income has declined from providing 14 per cent of college income in 1930 to 5 per cent in 1956. This affects especially the smaller colleges. These have little endowment and draw their student body from the less affluent portions of the local populations that cannot afford to pay high tuition fees. The more affluent parents send their children to the large "Ivy League" colleges which also have the largest endowments. For the year 1956, for which the latest information is available at this writing, 22 per cent of the total college endowment fund of $3.7 billion (book value) was concentrated in 5 institutions and 50 per cent in 24 institutions, out of a total of nearly 1,100 that reported as having endowments. "In order to finance new educational programs as well as to meet increased operating costs of established programs," reads a report of the Department of Health, Education and Welfare, "a much broader base of support of higher education is needed."[17]

Education, then, is a potentially large and expanding outlet for federal expenditures, and, in addition to public housing, another potential absorber of otherwise uninvestible social surplus. The new educational requirements of the nation could absorb a large portion of what now goes to the military. Dr. Louis H. Conger of the above Department has estimated that capital outlay requirements for the public schools in the 10 years ending 1968-69 would amount to $24.4 billion, even if no change in *present standards* of equipment were made.[18] His projection took into account merely the anticipated increase in enrollment, the elimination of classroom shortages existing in 1959, and prospective replacements and abandonments. On the basis of the prospective increase in enrollment it may be similarly estimated that the current operating costs of the public schools of about $17 billion a year will rise to about $25 billion by the end of the decade, again, without allowing for improved standards of instruction, higher teachers' salaries, or for the inflationary rise in general costs.

Similar reckoning applies to colleges and universities. On the basis of the projected increase in college enrollment of about 70 per cent in the next 10 years, the present operating costs of about $4½ billion a year, including about $1 billion in capital expenditures, will rise to about $10 billion by 1970.[19] The investment needs in higher education facilities "to clear up the present backlog and to provide for increases in enrollment and for new programs expected periodically to 1970" run up to $18 billion for the decade.[20] If no new drastic provision for expansion of college facilities is made now, a shortage of a million seats is foreseen for 1970. (Education Facilities Laboratories.)

3. *Need for Federal Financing.*—Where shall the money to meet these requirements come from? It cannot come from increased real estate taxes, even if many new taxable structures are erected in the next 10 years. Nor can it come from sales taxes, existing or newly devised. It can come only from the general funds of the United States Treasury, the major portion of which is derived from taxes on income, the same as the costs of foreign military bases and hydrogen bombs. Only thus financed can American educational standards and facilities be brought up to the requirements of the times, and only thus

financed can expenditures for education serve to absorb social surplus which in an advanced capitalism tends to become excessive relative to private investment outlets.

Here there would seem to be no direct private profit interests to obstruct progress, as is the case in public housing, but here too a barrier is interposed which appears to be as insurmountable. It is the political barrier which private wealth erects against any sharp advance in expenditures for the social welfare, whether it is public housing, education or, as we will see, free or low-cost medical care for the common people. Whereas capital will permit itself to be taxed for the purpose of the military, it will not tolerate taxation of the same magnitude for the social welfare. In the first it sees compensating benefits: Expenditures for the military help expand and safeguard foreign markets; they cause the "enemy" to forego butter to build guns, which is expected to create public discontent and possibly lead to the overthrow of his government. At home the propaganda required to win the people's support for the large military expenditures and the business booms they generate from time to time help create the atmosphere of conformity and unquestioned acceptance of "our way of life."*

Expenditures for the social welfare, on the other hand, appear to be sheer extravagance—as an unrewarding consumption of private profits. Public housing for the ill-housed millions is deemed a threat to private real estate interests. Free or low-cost medical care is resisted as "socialized medicine." A higher order of mass education than now prevails may teach people to "think." When people think, they may ask questions, and questions are dangerous in a democracy which demands conformity and which punishes nonconformity.

Further, expenses for the military can be revoked when the expected rewards begin to diminish. Expenses for the public welfare,

---

*The cruelty and tragedy of it all is the fact that most countries whose people live in abject poverty, in Latin America and in Asia, spend inordinate proportions of their national incomes, from 15 to 30 per cent, for the "national defense" — for the protection of *their* "way of life." In many cases these run 2 or 3 times the amounts spent for education and the public health, in the national budgets. Thus, of Iran's 1960 budget of 60 billion rials, 17 billion went for the national defense. Little Jordan spent over 21 billion dinars on defense and only 2.6 billion on education, health and the social services. Indonesia in 1959 spent over 7 billion rupiahs on defense and only a little over 2 billion for health and education. And so on and on — for Brazil, Haiti, Colombia. See the *Statistical Yearbook* of the United Nations.

once embarked upon, cannot so readily be revoked. The people will not easily relinquish prerogatives which at once, through the absorption of excess social surplus, give them protection against unemployment, at the same time that they advance their physical and cultural well-being.

The big excitement which Sputnik caused among the American people, leading to an awareness of the educational deficiencies of the country has resulted in no more than what may be called token aid from the federal government. Indeed, by January 1960, President Eisenhower felt free to declare at a Republican fund raising campaign dinner in Los Angeles that all this talk about deficiencies in the American educational system was largely "spurious." "Time and again," he told his audience, "we hear spurious assertions that America's . . . educaional . . . efforts are deficient."[21]

The token aid of the federal government to education came in the form of "The National Defense Education Act of 1958." With this Act Congress appropriated a niggardly $250 million a year to aid education in the ensuing four years.* The amount just about equalled 1 per cent of the nation's current expenditures for education on all levels. Further, about ¾ of this amount was to be apportioned among the States, mostly on a dollar for dollar matching basis, to set up counseling and pupil testing services; for vocational training; for improving statistical reporting, and, to use Secretary Flemming's words, "to institutes to train counselors, and foreign language centers, and to agencies, organizations, and individuals for research in educational uses of television, radio, motion pictures, and related means of communication." None was assigned to help build new classrooms or to raise teachers' salaries. And these niggardly provisions would probably not have passed the Congress if not cloaked in the mantle of "national security."

The remaining ¼ of the annual appropriation, about $61½ million, in all, was to go to college students as scholarship *loans*, and as fellowships to graduate students preparing to teach. The fellowships, if the graduate took up teaching as a profession, would not be repaid. The student loans, which may total $5,000 over a five-year period, must be repaid, principal and interest (of 3%), over a span of 10 years beginning one year after graduation. Assume an average of $1,000 per loan or fellowship, the number that would benefit by this largesse equals exactly 61,500. There are some 200,000 "gifted" youth, we will remember, who are annually kept out of college because of lack of funds.

---

*The Act was extended in December 1963 to run another 3 years.

The loan provision was in line with recommendations of a Presidential Citizens' Committee on Education Beyond High School. The rationale behind this recommendation was the calculation that a college education enhanced the earning power of the graduates and they should pay for it out of these future greater earnings. In other words, they should buy their education on the installment plan, just as they will, upon graduation, buy cars and, upon marriage, furniture and furnishings. To obtain a loan, furthermore, the student was required to sign a loyalty oath.

Aside from the fact that scholarships granted as loans degrade scholarship,[22] a college education may not be avilable to millions of American homes even on the installment plan. In 1957-8, when the Act was passed, 50 per cent of America's families had annual incomes of less than $5,000 a year: 35 per cent between $2,000 and $5,000, and 15 per cent less than $2,000. The 50 per cent lower-income families cannot pay their children's other college expenses, which run about ⅔ above the tuition fees which a scholarship would cover. "In an Eastern factory city, with a population of 180,000," we are told, "the local high schools this year [1959] sent only 15 to 20 per cent of their graduates to college. A residential suburb, only ten miles away, sent more than 80 per cent."[23]

In the land of sputniks all students go to college tuition-free and those of special talent are *paid* to do so.[24] Even in England, hoary with the commercial spirit and financially much less able than the United States, "All students deemed of superior ability are put through the university at government expense."[25] Both in England and the Soviet Union scholarship is an honor, not a commercial investment. In the Soviet Union over 750,000,000 library books are available to its people, compared with 200,000,000 books available in the United States. This may explain in no small way why in the Soviet Union children in the 4th grade use books with a vocabulary of about 10,000 words, while American children of the same grade use books with a vocabulary of less than 1,800 words.[26]

A way out in the present circumstances might lie in Federal construction of the capital plants of the schools and colleges.* Re-

---

*The College Construction bill enacted by Congress in early December 1963 is a token in this direction. It provides $400 million for each of three years to construct classrooms designed for instruction in the sciences, mathematics and modern languages. The States are required to meet this aid on a 2-1 matching basis.

lieved of that cost, the public schools could afford to raise educational standards, recruit a better paid staff, improve operating facilities.* The colleges and universities would be enabled to raise teaching standards and extend fellowships and scholarships to promising students. Deduction of educational expense from the family income tax has also been proposed as relieving the private cost of education.

C. THE PUBLIC HEALTH

1. *A Private Burden.*—Free and low-cost medical care is the last of the four principal components of a Welfare State as here conceived. The other three, we will remember, are low-cost public housing; free public education, from the nursery school through the university and research institutes; and a social security system financed from the general funds of the Federal Treasury, rather than, as at present, from taxes on payrolls; that is, rather than from taxes on personal consumption.

Medicine in America, like housing, is in the main a free enterprise business and is deemed a social service only by "eggheads"— by certain college professors and long-haired intellectuals. Physicians and dentists are individual entrepreneurs and the fees they charge are the purchase price for individual, personal services. Medicines and drugs are priced to yield the maximum possible profit to private manufacturers, irrespective of the ability of the sick to pay. Profit mark-ups on certain essential drugs, it has been revealed, range from 1,100 to 7,500 per cent of cost.[27] Care in non-profit private hospitals—60 per cent of all non-Federal hospitals—is today posible for millions of Americans largely through hospitalization insurance, borne by the insured at a profit to the insuring companies. Private spending for health and medical care in 1958 amounted to near 79 per cent of the country's total; the other 21 per cent were public spending. (Eighteen per cent of the private spending was covered by insurance benefits.) Health is a business commodity, bought and paid for like any other commodity or service, and based on what the traffic will bear, and medicine is a free private enterprise operating under one of the strictest of American monopolies, the American Medical Association.

---

*The average salary of the instructional staff in the public schools in 1961-62 was less than 10 per cent above the average for factory workers — $5,700 against $5,200.

The cost of care in municipal hospitals is met from the same regressive taxes as meet the cost of most other social services, such as education. The cost of care in non-profit private hospitals is met from personal donations and philanthropic contributions, and from patients' fees. These municipal and private hospitals supply the short-term medical care required by the general public. Long-term medical care, chiefly for mental patients, but also for tubercular and other degenerative diseases, is provided by Federal and State hospitals. The health services of the Federal government are directed largely to military personnel and war veterans, and to medical research.[28]

Placing the principal burden of dispensing medical care to the general public on municipal governments and on private philanthropies has meant a growing shortage of hospital and medical facilities in recent years, in the face of a growing population, especially of its aged portion; in the face of an increased health consciousness of the American people, and in the face of the growing demand for expensive hospital equipment called for by new medical discoveries. The archaic tax system of the local governments, and the private philanthropies, are too limited in scope and too inelastic in form to permit the expansion and improvement of these facilities to meet the new needs. Shortages have developed in the supply of doctors, dentists, hospital nurses, new entrants to the medical schools, and in the number of hospital beds and in nursing homes, and sanitariums.

2. *Shortages and Inadequacies.*—In 1949 there were 135 physicians for every 100,000 Americans; today there are only about 133.* To maintain even the present ratio until 1970, some 10,000 new doctors will have to be graduated each year until then. At the 1963 rate of less than 7,300 graduates from the existing 85 four-year medical schools, from 14 to 20 new medical schools will have to be built in that period, at a cost of $½ billion to $1 billion. In his State of the Union Message in January 1963, the late President Kennedy estimated the need as a 50 per cent increase in capacity for medical schools and 100 per cent increase for dental schools. Where is the money to come from?

A new inadequacy in this connection, and not unrelated to the money question, is the falling off in recent years of new entrants

---

*There are country-wide ratios. They are higher in the North than in the South, and in urban than in rural areas. Thus, in the Northeastern States, the ratio, in mid-1959, was 160; in the South 102. In Mississippi, it was 75.

into medical schools. The number of applicants to medical schools in recent years has been as follows: 1957—15,917; 1958—15,791; 1959—15,165, and 14,951 in 1960. What is more, there has occurred a serious decline in the scholastic quality of the applicants. In the academic year 1950-51, about 40 per cent of the students entering medical schools had a college average grade of A; by 1957-58, the last tabulated record, the number of A students had fallen to 18 per cent.[29]

The falling off in the *number* of medical school applicants is probably due mainly to the high costs of a medical education. "Studying medicine" is a costly business, both in time and money. To "become a doctor" means spending one's way through 4 years of college, 4 years of medical school, 1 to 2 years as intern, and, depending on the specialty one wishes to pursue, 3 to 5 years as resident physician. The median cost of the four years in a medical school runs up to near $12,000, of which, a recent Johns Hopkins University study reports, 80 per cent is paid by the student or his family. No more than 10 years ago, a medical intern would get room, board and laundry, and just about enough "wages" to keep him in cigarettes. In 1960, the average stipend was still only $166 a month in hospitals affiliated with medical schools and $207 in non-affiliated hospitals—that, after 4 years in college and 4 in a medical school. As a resident physician, the doctor gets annual earnings about ½ the average American factory worker's. As Dr. Geiger has put it: "Even for the 40 per cent of our current medical graduates who come from families with incomes over $10,000 (the top 8 per cent in the nation), it usually means being supported by one's wife and isolated from one's children. . . . And it means going into debt; of the 1959 graduates, 52 per cent were in debt and 6 per cent owed more than $10,000." For the very top income families, one may suppose, it would make no sense to send their sons to a medical school, then to work an additional 2 to 5 years before he can begin "producing." They can begin producing in their father's business in a high post immediately on graduating from one or another of the expensive colleges.

It should be added that while a considerable number of fellowships are now becoming available for graduate study and research in the physical sciences, (chiefly serving the military), students in medicine have not been so favored.

The average Ph.D. candidate gets approximately $2,000 a year from stipends, fellowships and similar sources; the average medical student gets only about $500 a year.[30] *The medical profession is a private preserve, no matter how intimately it relates to the well-being of the people. Any outside interference financially, especially if it originates from the Federal government, is opposed by official medical organizations as an "entering wedge for socialized medicine," the anathema of all bourgeois anathemas.

Incidentally, the low financial rewards of medical graduates explain in no small way the increasing dependence in America on foreign graduates to fill internships and residencies. Most American hospitals, private and municipal, increasingly employ South Koreans. Formosans, Filipinos, and anti-communist European refugees in these capacities. Dr. Geiger recites these facts: in 1949 there were 2,000 physicians in United States hospitals trained in foreign medical schools. In 1958 there were 7,622, and in 1959 more than 8,300, that is, more than are graduated annually from American medical schools. In 1960 the total was 9,457, according to H.E.W.'s *Health Manpower Source Book*, Section 13, filling equally 25 per cent of the internships and 25 per cent of the residencies. In New York City more than half of the interns and residents are foreign-trained. In the municipal non-teaching hospitals the figure was 285 out of 293. This is high exploitation on high professional levels. There are over 12,000 internships open each year in American hospitals. In 1963 American medical schools graduated 7,270 doctors.

The falling off in the *quality* of medical school entrants is no doubt due to what the United States Surgeon General has called "unreasonably restrictive medical school admissions policies," affecting, as we know, Jews, Negroes, and women.[31] For decades American medical schools maintained an unofficial *numerus clausus* against Jewish applicants. These had to come truly with an "A average" and with considerable "pull" to get admitted. The potential Sabins and Salks and Waksmans usually had to wait for a "vacancy" to occur just before school opened to pass through the Pearly Gates of the medical Heavens. Now, these "A" students study mathematics and theoretical physics, perhaps even on science scholarships and without suffering the trauma of rejection.

In dentistry, two new schools, each with a graduating class of 50, are required to be added each year to the existing dental schools, merely to retain the present ratio of practicing dentists per 100,000

---

*Loans of about $1,000 a year at 3 per cent interest to students in medicine, dentistry and osteopathy are provided for in the medical aid bill passed by Congress in September 1963.

199

population. (Study Paper, pp. 67-70.)

To supply the hospitals with a full complement of nurses, their salary scales will have to be raised and their labors eased through the employment of non-professional hospital aides at decent wages, but in all cases hospital help is paid very poorly. This is due, in the first place, to the fact that nine out of ten of these employees are women and most of them, especially nurses, do not consider employment in hospitals as their life career. Many of them quit to get married or take jobs in industrial medicine where they find work more congenial and better paid than in hospitals. In the New York City hospitals, in early 1960, only 42 per cent of nurses' jobs were filled. (*New York Times*, March 2, 1960.)

In the second place, in the case of both the nurses and the non-professional hospital employees, lack of trade union organization helps perpetuate their lowly status. In the spring of 1959 a strike of non-professional workers in New York's private hospitals, demanding union recognition and wage increases, revealed that most of them, chiefly Negroes and Puerto Ricans, were being paid less than $40 for a 40-hour week. City "welfare" had been supplying the additional funds that enabled them to subsist, for the most part in the city's slum areas. The municipality had been subsidizing these hospitals in the employment of their non-professional help.*

The number of hospital beds in this country, counting public and private hospitals together, is no higher today than it was a half-dozen years ago, despite the rapid rise of the total population and despite the increasing demand for hospital services. The number of government hospital beds has been decreasing as fewer mental patients are institutionalized and the tuberculosis rate has been diminishing. Yet, it has been estimated, only 55 per cent of the total needs are met by existing acceptable mental beds. It has also been estimated by the same authorities that acceptable skilled nursing home beds, which would ease the pressure on hospital facilities, are meeting only $\frac{1}{4}$ of the needs. (Study Paper, p. 75.)

---

*The economic deprivations of the Negro, his low educational opportunities and his wretched housing accommodations, all in their interrelated hopelessness, point up the general inadequacies of these social services in affluent America. It may yet turn out that the rising revolt of the American Negro against these injustices, at the moment in the form of his demands for civil rights, will serve as the battering ram that will break down the walls of complacency of the white power elite and compel them to yield to the needs of all Americans for the social welfare which their labor can create.

Private non-profit hospitals have maintained a steady growth in the number of hospitals, due in part to Federal contribution to hospital construction of about 25 per cent of all non-Federal health facilities. (Study Paper, p. 78.) Further, the decline in the average length of patient stay in these hospitals has reduced the pressure on existing facilities. This average has fallen from 15.4 days in 1932 to 11.1 days in 1948 and 9.6 days in 1957. At the same time, hospital costs have continually risen. They amounted to $10.04 per day in 1946, but rose to about $40.0 by 1963.

For low-income families, and especially for the aged, the rising costs of hospitalization spell severe hardships. A study for 1956 showed that medical costs ranged from 3.0 per cent of family incomes of $7,500 and over to 11.8 per cent of family incomes falling below $2,000. For families with incomes under $2,000 and without health insurance, medical costs claimed an average of 13.4 per cent of family income. Most of the aging population fall in the "under $2,000" income bracket, and the largest uninsured percentage outlay for medical care also falls in this bracket. Sixty per cent of the men and women past 65 received less than $1,000 in cash income in 1958, and only about 40 per cent of them had some kind of health insurance. (Study Paper, pp. 55-60.) About one-half of the near-18 million Americans of this age group are now wholly dependent on old-age and survivors' insurance and/or old-age assistance; about $\frac{2}{3}$ are OASDI beneficiaries. In the spring of 1959, old-age retirement benefits averaged $72.50 a month and old-age assistance less than $65.00 a month. By early 1964 average old-age benefit was still only $77.20 a month and old-age assistance $78.83.

3. *Need for Federal Financing.*—Here, then, is a gaping lack in the public welfare requiring large financial outlays to fill. New funds are needed to build new medical schools, new hospitals, new nursing homes; new funds are needed to raise the wages of hospital employees, *including interns and resident physicians;* new funds are needed for scholarships to induce more students and more quality students to enter medical schools, and for fellowships to enable them to pursue post-graduate work. New funds are needed to provide free health insurance for low-income families and especially for the aged. The *present* total public and private annual outlay for health and medical care, $22¾ billion, is twice what it was 10 years earlier. It will evidently need to be doubled again in the next 10 years, even if only to maintain present standards. Where might all the new money come from? There is not enough "give" in State and local taxes, nor in the philanthropies to finance the indicated expansion

and improvement requirements. Only the Federal government commands the necessary resources to finance them. This seems to be the consensus of most agencies concerned with the problem; all, except the American Medical Association (A.M.A.), which speaks for the free enterprise of the American medical profession.

> "Several times in recent years, for example," writes Dr. Geiger, "there have been proposals in Congress for direct federal aid to medical schools to help them meet their teaching and operating costs. The medical colleges have fought for this valiantly. . . The A.M.A. has been opposed on the grounds that this is . . . an 'entering wedge for socialized medicine'. . .
>
> "There have been similar proposals for federal scholarships or other subsidies for needy medical school applicants. Again, the A.M.A. and its sister professional organizations have been opposed, and the measures have gone down the drain. There have been plans . . . for limited federal aid in the medical care of the elderly. . . "

Again, the "entering wedge to socialism" argument won out against them.

This was the position of the Republican Administration under President Eisenhower: medical care, like all the social services, is the responsibility of the State and local governments and of the generously inclined wealthy citizens. Not only federal expenditures for medical care, but all federal expenditures for the public welfare smacked of socialism. In his first post-Sputnik budget (January 1958) President Eisenhower proposed to reduce the Federal government's share in the cost of State old-age assistance programs, hospital construction projects and schools affected by federal activities, a sharp decrease in public housing and in federal aid to house construction financing, and to shift more of the cost of slum clearance to local communities and the States. In a speech in Oklahoma City, some two months earlier, he recommended curtailments, revisions or eliminations of a host of the Government's "Welfare" programs.

The above is a summary of President Eisenhower's views as related in the *Monthly Letter* of the First National City Bank of New York, February 1958. In June 1959, the *Monthly Letter* gives its own summary views of the Welfare State:

> Modern-day Welfare economics [it reads] contains the most essential elements of socialism which is, in the name of social justice, to weaken self-reliance. . .
>
> There is a good tendency to forget how we got ahead in the past and to seek progress on a foundation of government-administered welfare, replacing *charitable instincts* of the individual and making the government a philanthropic institution. [italics supplied]

President Eisenhower's successor, the late John F. Kennedy, at first put these questions up for a rehearing. But in the three years in office he got nowhere with Congress. Even his proposal for medical care for the aged, "Medicare," self-financed from a payroll tax as part of the Social Security System, was "stalled in the lobby"—the private insurance companies would lose 10,000,000 health insurance customers.* By the beginning of his third year in office, he too veered away from new social legislation, as he more than implied in a speech before the Economic Club of New York, December 14, 1962. He spelled this out in his 1963 State of the Union Message. To keep a planned budget deficit for fiscal 1964 to a stated minimum, while raising expenditures for the military, he would, he said, hold back on increases for all other Federal outlays, including the social services, some even at below 1963 levels. The "Welfare State" thus remains a mirage for Keynesians and an idea with which to frighten capitalists.**

---

*The Medicare bill passed the Senate in early September 1964, but is stalled in the House as these lines are written.
**Since this was written, Congress passed the "medical aid" bill of 1963 which provides a piddling $230 million for the construction of new and the rehabilitation of old medical facilities. That is the bill that passed also the $31 million for student loans cited earlier.

17.
INCREASING PERSONAL CONSUMPTION

A. WAGES, PROFITS AND INFLATION

1. *The Cost of Full Employment.*—If capital exports and Federal expenditures for the social services cannot be relied on to absorb the excess social surplus and thereby guarantee full employment, might it not be possible to devise means to prevent the excess from emerging at all? This might be done, for instance, by increasing workers' real wages. Raising workers' real wages would, in fact, have a double effect, the effect as a cost and the effect as income. It would limit the magnitude of the potential surplus excess and would increase consumer purchasing power and consumer demand. Lowering the work week without lowering weekly wages would lead to similar results, while it would also directly increase employment, at least temporarily. Similarly, though indirectly, the same ends might be gained, in part, through a reduction of taxes on consumption and an increase of taxes on the social surplus, or "savings." Together, increased capital exports to undeveloped nations, increased expenditures for the public welfare, increased consumer demand and higher taxes on savings, plus a feasible rate of private domestic investment, might be so contrived as to match all the potential national income at full employment, with no surplus remaining to exert a depressing effect on the economy. All this, of course, would be on the assumption that the nations of the world had learned to live at peace with one another and expenditures for the military had ceased to be the major absorbent of the excess social surplus. Depressions would then become a thing of purely historical interest, as Hawtrey had it away back in the late 1920's.

All such steps toward a solution of the problem of maintaining peacetime full employment in a capitalist society meet with what seem to be impenetrable barriers. As we saw in the preceding chapters, mid-twentieth century capitalist political, economic and social philosophy puts rather severe limits on net capital exports. The largest potential outlets for foreign capital are the socialist countries and the erstwhile colonial peoples. Monopoly capitalism will not extend its wealth to bolster the already rapidly developing socialisms, and it will not finance the emerging anti-imperialist state capitalisms of the under-developed nations, except under great new political pressures, such as might be generated by the competition of Soviet investment there. The rate of economic progress these nations impatiently demand requires the active participation of the state in organizing the economy, beyond the extent acceptable in opulent systems of "free private enterprise." Besides, as we have seen, monopoly capital insists on the traditionally high profit returns on foreign investments which these newly awakened peoples will no longer pay. Such high returns to foreign capital would greatly slow down their desired rate of capital formation. For the most part, these high profits would be expatriated, rather than reinvested where derived.

Similarly, private profit and political considerations will not permit the expansion and improvement of the social services to the extent of absorbing a major portion of the excess social surplus. Capitalists are unwilling to bear the cost, in the first place. They are even more unwilling to permit the emergence of a social policy which, once embarked upon, may imbue the underlying population with "unhealthy ideas" to want more of the same. If improvement of the social services might help secure the loyalty of the workers to the system that feeds them, it might also lead to the demand that capitalists pay for them directly out of profits, instead of pushing the costs onto consumers.

This leaves us the problem of increasing workers' wages and salaries, reducing consumer taxes and raising taxes on savings income as the major means of limiting the potential excess social surplus of modern capitalism. We deal with the tax question in the next chapter. In the present chapter we raise this question: Why not increase wages and reduce work hours so as to reduce the social surplus to magnitudes compatible with domestic and foreign investment potentials at full employment? Here we come to the dilemma which a capitalist economy faces in the choice between maintaining viability as a system of the private accumulation of capital and full employment.

Full employment achieved and sustained by way of increasing wages and salaries, as by way of expanding the social services—in short, by way of increasing individual and social consumption—tends to raise the value of labor power and to cut the capitalists' surplus-value at the source of its creation. The historical tendency of the rate of profit to fall is accentuated. The potential for the private accumulation of capital is permanently diminished. Further, the rate of profit becomes a mere residual in the full employment formula. Full employment becomes the negation of the essence of the capitalist mode of production; it negates its essence as a system of the private accumulation of capital. This is the major reason why capitalists as a class stand in opposition to a policy of full employment on a continuing basis, even though individual capitalists there be who would support such a program.

To make workers' consumption and social well-being primary and capital accumulation secondary as a condition of full employment, requires *socially* planned allocation of resources and, hence, the gradual atrophy of the power of private investment decision. It means *social planning* and the beginnings of the transition from capitalism to socialism. But capitalists, to survive *as* capitalists, must be free and able to make quick upward changes in policy with respect to production and investment as new markets, new sources of raw materials, new inventions, new technologies open up new business opportunities at home and abroad. They must, likewise, be free and able to make downward changes in policy as these are dictated by adverse conditions. Capitalists will not consciously and willingly acquiesce in a social policy which threatens to deny them these freedoms. This is what capitalist publicists and capitalist politicians mean when they declaim on the blessings of "free private enterprise" and on the need to "protect our freedoms against the menace of Communism."

Manifestly, capitalists will resist a policy of full employment if that means a falling rate of profit, a gradual decline in their power to control the rate of investment, and a gradual conversion of capitalism into a consumption economy—its gradual transformation into socialism. A growing subordination of investment to consumption requirements can lead to no other end. All this they will resist with all the political and economic power available to them. They will try to prevent the enactment of social welfare legislation, as the preceding chapters showed. They will promote the enactment of legislation, such as "right-to-work" laws, that weaken the trade unions and their power of collective bargaining, as for generations they held back their very emergence. (The right-to-work laws prohibit the requirement of union membership as a condition of employment.) They will hasten the introduction of labor-saving innovations that increase labor-productivity beyond wage increases, that create technological disemployment and increase competition for jobs. They will resist demands for wage increases. They will resist the demands for a shorter workday and a shorter workweek that would counter the negative effects of automation on employment opportunities.* Where this resistance proves ineffective, they will, where they can, raise prices to offset and, often, more than offset the wage increases. Inflation becomes an escape valve, even if only a temporary one, for staving off a falling rate of profit and in the rate of capital accumulation potentials.

This does not mean that raising wage rates is the cause of rising prices and of inflation. The causal sequence for the most part runs the other way around. Nor does it mean that employers do not raise prices except as wages rise. They raise prices for any number of reasons, as we will presently see, not related to wages of production workers. They will raise prices because they can do so without running the risk of competition, often in collaboration with ostensible competitors. This is where the power of oligopoly comes in—where a handful of "competing" firms dominate an industry.[1] Employers will nearly always use a wage increase as justification for a price increase, until, at full employment, inflation itself may impose a barrier to further price increases.

What is involved here is the continuing conflict between the capitalists' necessity to maintain a viable rate of profit and the market necessity to advance individual and social living standards of the workers. The workers' living standards must be continually raised to enable them to absorb the ever-increasing output of consumer goods by an expanding economy. And they must be raised to meet the demands of labor for a growing share in this abundance. So far, this conflict has led to a relatively steady increase in real wages and to a still greater increase in the capitalists' surplus-value as labor productivity increases and the "production pie" is enlarged. Thus, between 1939-40 and 1955-59, net spendable real weekly earnings of production workers in American manufacturing industries rose at an average of about 2 to 2½ per cent a year.[2] In the period 1947-49 to 1958 labor productivity was raised at the rate of between 3 and 3.5 per cent, as variously computed.[3] It is this excess of productivity above the net spendable real wages that is the source of a nation's social surplus.

---

*The last nation-wide reduction in standard work hours was that effected by the New Deal legislation in the late 1930's, when the workday was cut to 8 hours from the prevailing 10-12 hour day, and the workweek was cut to 40 hours from the prevailing 50+ hours.
In this speech before the Economic Club of New York, Dec. 14, 1962, the late President Kennedy virtually foreclosed any consideration of a new reduction in the workweek at this time.

B. INFLATION, MONOPOLY AND FULL EMPLOYMENT

1. *Conventional Notions.*—Anyone bred on the economics of the daily press, or even of professional journals and official government reports, has learned that inflation comes about in either one or both of two ways. One, as is popularly put, is that we get inflation when "too many dollars chase too few goods." The other is that we get inflation as the result of a "wage-price spiral"; that prices rise because wages rise.

The argument that we get inflation because too many dollars chase too few goods generally runs in terms of the effect of the money supply on the rates of production and employment. As profit expectations rise with the recovery phase of a business cycle, the explanation is, the money supply is increased by the release of hoarded cash, by an expansion of bank credit and by the increase in the velocity of circulation. (How the recovery started is not our concern here. Say, a war scare prompted it, or the discovery of interplanetary market potentials.) The increased money and credit supply, functioning as new money capital, stimulates the speed in the rising rate of investment and production and increases the demand for raw materials and services beyond available supplies. A consequent rise of prices raises further profit expectations, stimulates a further increase in the money and credit supply, which makes possible further expansion of investment and production and further demand for the still lagging supplies of materials and services. Prices rise again, and so on and so on, in cumulative inflation as too many dollars chase the relatively fewer capital goods.

In the same manner, it is argued, wage payments rise with the recovery as employment and wage rates rise and move ahead of the supply of consumer goods. The price of consumer goods then rises, stimulating a further rise in the supply of investment money and credit, for the further rise of production and employment, for the further advance of wage payments ahead of the output of wage goods, again cumulating the inflation. Too many wage dollars, it is now said, chase too few wage goods.

The other explanation of how inflation comes about is that as recovery advances and the labor market "grows tight," the trade unions' bargaining power rises and they demand and get wage increases for their members. Management is then compelled to raise prices to protect profit margins. As prices are raised, workers demand and get new raises to meet the rising cost of living, further causing management to advance prices. Now, as prices try to keep ahead of wages an inflationary "wage-price spiral" is created. In this explanation, inflation comes about initially and cumulatively because of the insatiable demands of organized labor.

Although both these explanations appear to equate with everyday, common-sense observation, just as our senses tell us the earth is flat, they both fail in one vital respect. Neither of them can explain why prices rise when investment, production and employment are no longer advancing and even when they are falling, as was the case, for example, in the business boom of 1956-57 and in the recession that followed. Evidently, we should probe a little deeper into the matter.

2. *In the Period of Monoply Capitalism.*—Given a plentiful supply of money and credit, largely left over from the preceding boom, recovery from a depression typically develops on the basis of new investment in the production of capital goods (pp. 102-05, above). As production and employment in the capital goods industries rise, the demand for raw materials, components and semi-manufactures rises faster than the immediately available supply. (There are no hoards of these goods left over from the previous boom as is the case with the money supply or labor.) Producers then raise prices as entrepreneurs compete for the limited supplies. Wages also rise in this period, but not so fast as commodity prices. The reason wages lag behind these other prices is that a recovery starts from conditions of a large supply of unemployed workers and the competition that then exists in the labor market is not so much for workers as for jobs (the opposite of the case of raw materials, components and semi-manufactures). As prices move ahead of wages, workers demand and get a raise of wages to meet the rising cost of living.[4] Employers then raise prices to offset, and often more than offset, the wage raise, and cause it to be known that it is wage demands that are responsible for the developing inflation.[5] Economists oblige by discovering the "wage-price spiral."

As the recovery develops boom proportions, still other factors (the rising cost of capital goods, among them) come forth to cause prices to rise. One of the most important of these is the increased use of the less efficient, standby capacity of which we have spoken earlier. Under normal conditions of demand, we will recall, the existence of this less efficient, "excess" capacity serves big business as the norm from which to *figure* costs and to set prices, but the output to satisfy the existing demand is produced at the more efficient, up-to-date plant where costs are lower. This, we argued, (pp. 149-54) is one of the sources of the above-average rate of profit which accrues to monopolies and big business in general. (We shall speak later of other means by which monopoly contrives to command above-average prices.)

Under conditions of full-employment demand, the less economical equipment and the least efficient workers are brought into operation. This lowers average productivity and raises the average unit cost of production. Big business in the face of expanding markets thereupon exercises its monopoly power to raise prices to cover these increased costs.[6]

At the same time there occurs a rise in the *cost of sales*. At *full employment* or near full employment the size of the employed labor force ceases to grow. Everybody who is able and willing to work has a job and draws wages or a salary. When not much more labor is available for employment, the total wage bill ceases to expand significantly. Even if wage and salary rates are still rising, the mass of effective consumer purchasing power, which wages and salaries represent, levels off. The rising wage and salary rates are not adequate to compensate for the lack of a further significant rise in employment. Furthermore, conscious of the likelihood that the good time may sooner or later turn into a depression, workers at this point start saving for the rainy day and pay off debts. All along the upgrade of the business cycle their consumer demand equalled wages + increases in installment credit. As employment levels off, consumer demand tends to equal wages minus some cash savings for the rainy day. When employment begins to decline, consumer demand begins to equal the diminishing payrolls, minus a certain amount of cash savings and a decline of consumer credit.

To offset these rising costs, entrepreneurs seek to increase labor productivity by installing new labor-saving machinery, and capital goods industries continue to boom. The result is that at the peak of the boom consumer market potentials decline relatively to output and relatively to productive capacity which is still rising. Now it is a case of too many consumer goods chasing too few dollars. In the past when too many goods chased too few dollars, businessmen cut prices. Now they cut production and increase sales and promotion expense to "overcome sales resistance." This expense, we know, is not profit-creating, but profit-consuming. It eats into the surplus-value which the productive workers produce. Entrepreneurs, thereupon, raise prices to protect the falling profit rate.

Put this in the form a "law," namely: to the extent that industry raises the proportion of service employment it must resort to a rise in prices, that is, to inflation, unless the rate of productivity of productive labor is raised in the form of an increase in the rate of surplus-value. Otherwise, an increase in the proportion of service employment would mean a decline in the rate of profit. (See *The Falling Rate of Profit*, p. 81, ff.) This is how it comes about that prices may be raised when production and productive capacity are at their highest. They are raised because at the peak of the boom, production and sales costs are rising when the consumer market is no longer expanding! Thus we get the "inflation" which was so "baffling" to "economic observers" when the great prosperity of the 1950's had turned the corner downward in 1957.[7] The classical law of inflation— that prices rise when demand exceeds supply, and fall when supply exceeds demand—became inexplicable. Since 1957, with production at below full capacity—"excess" capacity standing idle—the rate of profit has been high and prices stable.

The classical law becomes explicable when it is recalled that it was formulated for the pre-monopoly period, when competitive pricing ruled the market place. It does not apply in the monopoly period, when prices are increasingly determined—"administered"—largely independently of the rate of production. Up to a certain point monopolies can and do maintain or even raise prices in the face of excess supply, excess capacity and falling demand. So, for example, between January 1956, approximately the peak of the preceding cycle, and September 1958, when a new recession was in full swing, production of motor vehicles declined 34½ per cent, but prices advanced over 9 per cent; production of steel fell 28 per cent, while prices were raised 15 per cent; for electrical machinery the corresponding figures were 7.4 per cent and 15+ per cent, respectively. With a fall in total receipts the rate of return on the existing capital plant tends to fall. Big Business then raises prices *because* of a falling market, to protect profit margins.

But the power even of monopoly to raise prices has limits, which a prolonged period of full employment generates. As full employment continues on a rising price level, the cost of production of capital goods rises. Prices cannot then be raised high enough to offset the profit-depressing effects of the decline in consumer market potentials relative to production potentials, the rising cost of sales, and the pressure of high wage rates. Further price raising, also, weakens the competitive position in foreign markets; leads to speculative excesses in the construction industry, in the stock market and in inventory accumulation; leads to a credit stringency, rising interest rates and falling bond prices, signaling a crisis and the beginning of a downturn in production and employment. Rising prices had reached their culmination in near full employment and a crisis.

In a recession conditions are gradually recreated for a renewal of investment and capital accumulation. The money supply is replenished and credit made easier. Prices recede, especially prices of raw materials imported from subservient colonies and ex-colonies. Production is carried on with equipment of the newest design and of highest efficiency. Above all, the industrial reserve army, the pool of unemployed workers, is being refilled, and labor, once more, can be "put in its place."[8] The problem that now confronts the system is how to contain the recession so that it does not spill over into an all-out depression. As an economist for a national association of American industrialists once put it to the present writer,[9] like the farmer who prays for a "sizzle," but not a "sizzle-sozzle" rain to help ripen his grain for harvest, so the capitalist asks for a "sizzle" depression to help put a collar on labor's growing pretensions. A "sizzle-sozzle" rain would ruin the ripening crop. A "sizzle-sozzle" depression, with its attendant mass unemployment, is now no longer politically feasible. For this and for the reasons mentioned above, capitalists as a class oppose inflation because it leads to and tends to prolong full employment, and seek to stabilize the economy at less than full employment. Hence, the seemingly paradoxical phenomenon of the attempt on the part of the Federal Reserve Board to "stop the inflation" in late 1958 by raising the discount rate when unemployment still stood at around 5,000,000.

At the peak of the boom both the creation of surplus value and its realization are seriously impaired. Its creation is impaired by the high cost of labor and by the high unit cost of production and sale. Its realization is impaired in two ways. It is impaired in its initial form, in its conversion into money capital through sale of product, as market potentials decline and the costs of sales rise. It is impaired in its final form, in the conversion of money capital into real capital, into capital formation, as net new investment must be slowed down. Both are the negation of capitalist viability as a system of the endless accumulation of private capital.

The recession which develops in an advanced capitalism differs in many essentials from the historical pattern. In earlier days, a downturn from a boom meant declining production and employment, and a price deflation until a bottom was reached in a depression of mass unemployment and wide-spread financial bankruptcy, in a "slaughtering of the values of capitals," as Marx had it. In extreme form this was the case of the depression of the 1930's. A generation of unbridled rule of monopoly capitalism brought the economy to the brink. In an advanced capitalism the state links its political power

212

with the power of big business and by its own spending seeks to arrest the rate of these declines. This is what the New Deal attempted to do and failed because, as we noted earlier, its expenditures were too small and were not of the kind to fill the gaping holes in the economy. In the period of large scale creation of social surplus these government expenditures must be large enough to absorb the uninvestible portions and of a nature that does not glut the consumer market—they must be largely unproductive expenditures. With the rise of unproductive expenditures, government and private, unproductive employment becomes a substitute for the unemployment of productive workers and places a bottom to the decline of total employment.[10] If now inflationary tendencies could be curbed, it is argued, the economy could be stabilized at this recession level of unemployment.[11] The problem is, how control inflation?

C. Controlling Inflation

1. *The "Uneasy Triangle."*—In a series of three articles published by the London *Economist* some years ago, under the title "The Uneasy Triangle,"[12] the thesis was presented that "It is impossible for any [capitalist] community to have very full employment *and* completely free collective bargaining *and* stable prices. Either one of the three will be completely sacrificed, or else all three will be modified." Full employment *and* collective bargaining must mean rising prices: "Full employment means high bargaining power for the workers, high bargaining power means wage increases which, in greater or less degree, outrun the growth of productivity." The result is inflation.

Inflation, as is well known, works severe hardship on large segments of the population. It hits hard the large and growing white collar class of workers who, generally, are not organized in trade unions and so lack their protection against it. It takes it out on the large and growing class of pensioners and annuitants, as of all other citizens who live on fixed incomes. It cuts the buying value of your life insurance. It adversely affects the bondholders, especially small bondholders, of the trillion dollars public and private debt. The savings bonds which wage earners bought during the War have long since lost half of their face value in terms of current purchasing power. (The big bondholders have more than balanced off their losses on bonds with the doubling and more than doubling of the value of stocks.) Rising prices cause a rise in the cost of government and a deterioration of its social services. Inflation causes a rise in interest rates the government has to pay. Already in mid-1957 the United States Treasury had to offer 4 per cent interest on a conversion loan of $24 billion, a rate which was twice the average of but two years earlier and the highest since the distressful 1933. The Treasury has since been asking permission of Congress to raise the rate to 5 per cent. Higher costs of government mean higher taxes and further hardship on the people already hard pressed by the inflation.

Yet all this touches the problem of inflation on the surface only. It misses the essence of inflation as a means of capital accumulation. The "severe hardships" which inflation inflicts on pensioners, white collar workers, etc., is a form of forced savings which are siphoned off by the industrial capitalists. These benefit by inflation so long as they can keep ahead of the rising prices by still further raising prices. This is the way the rising bourgeoisie in the 18th and early part of the 19th century expropriated the savings of the land-owning gentry. For the industrial capitalists, and they are the controlling power of the system, rising prices mean increased values of property assets, both financial (shares of stock) and material (plant and equipment, inventories, real estate). Until full employment is reached, they thrive on inflation and stimulate it by increasing investment, made in anticipation of further price rises. They will raise wages so long as they can recoup the raise by further price rise.

In the latter, an element of collusion may even enter. Big Industry grants a wage increase to Big Labor with the tacit understanding of a greater price increase to follow. The consideration is the benefit of the workers immediately concerned. The inflationary effect on the economy as a whole is something to make speeches and write articles about. In the end, of course, the workers pay all this back in the higher prices of the goods and services they buy, especially the unorganized and weakly organized, and all of them through the loss of the dollar value of their savings. To the employers it is pure gain until full employment is reached and profit expectations begin to grow dim. Until then they gain not only the greater profit through the raised prices, but also in public relations: The blame is not theirs if they raise prices; it is labor's! At the same time, they gain labor peace, as well as the workers' loyalties to the business economy which gives them higher money wages and a trade union contract.

Once full employment begins to dominate the economy and capital accumulation potentials become impaired, the cry is raised to stop the inflationary spiral which brings on full employment and the untoward profit expectations. The drive is on to stop the inflation and, in fact, to reverse the trend. The problem is, how? In the *Economist's* view, we must either abandon full employment or lessen the wage demands of labor. In a word, labor must pay the cost of full employment. Its choice lies between stationary wage rates and full employment, even if the latter means paying higher prices.

There is, of course, a third alternative to controlling inflation. That is that capitalists take a cut in profits. Profits, in the last analysis, are an element in the "costs" which entrepreneurs would control by way of raising prices. What this alternative is saying is: Put a limit, by a reduction in profits, to rising prices by which management escapes the inflationary effects of full employment and, on our reckoning, benefits by them. The *Economist* did not discuss this alternative.

Still another alternative is that taken by the late Professor Sumner Slichter of Harvard University. Rather than choose between wages and profits to *combat* inflation, he would choose inflation. He would have what has become known as "creeping inflation" — small increases in prices of, say, 2 or 3 per cent a year. (That would just about put a clamp on the trend of real wages which, we saw above [p. 207] has been rising at about this rate.) In a speech before the New York Society of Security Analysts on November 8, 1956, he declared, as quoted in the *Monthly Letter* of the First National City Bank of New York for July 1957:

> In this imperfect world we are often compelled to choose between evils, and if the choice is between enough unemployment to halt the rise of labor costs, direct control of wages and profits, and creeping inflation, let us by all means have creeping inflation. It is the least of the three evils.

Aside from the fact that there can be no such thing as a little inflation, any more than there can be such a thing as being just a little bit pregnant, Professor Slichter's choice stemmed from the erroneous premise that "inflation is initiated by a rise in labor costs to which commodity prices more or less sluggishly adjust themselves," (*ibid.*), instead of the other way around.

In his very able review article on the Economists' *Report on Economic Stabilization*, to which we referred in an earlier chapter, Professor Arthur Smithies, also of Harvard University, wrote:

> Whenever one encounters a proposal for [economic] stabilization through fiscal and monetary methods, wheth-

> er it be by Keynes, Beveridge, Hansen, the U.N. Report,
> one can be quite sure that the inflationary dilemma would
> be recognized but left unresolved. The present report is
> no exception. The consensus evaporates when it comes
> to questions of how full employment and price stability
> are to be achieved at the same time.[13]

As would be expected, the *Report* proceded from the premise that inflation is labor-made. "The power of organized labor today," it stated, "suggests that we may be faced with the danger of chronic inflation resulting from general wage increases which recurrently out-run the growth of productivity of the economy as a whole."[14] "Thus," the *Report* continued, "inflation induced by rising costs rather than excess demand [meaning, by wages rising faster than productivity, rather than by too many dollars chasing too few goods] offers a very grave dilemma for fiscal and monetary policy." A money policy tight enough and an increase in taxes above expenditures high enough to halt the inflation will as surely reduce output and employment. On the other hand, "Direct government control of wages is incompatible with a free-enterprise economy. . . Limited statutory restrictions upon the right to strike are unlikely to curtail seriously the bargaining strength of labor organizations. . . For the present," therefore, the Report concluded, "reconciling full employment with price level stability within a free-enterprise framework must be regarded as a major unsolved problem."[15]

As one way out of this dilemma, the Economists would call upon Big Business and Big Labor to moderate their demands on each other and on the economy as a whole. How illusory! So long as raising prices means enhancing, or even only safeguarding profits, capitalists will not voluntarily give up inflation until compelled to do so by the contingencies of full employment. Nor will workers give up their demands for full employment *and* higher wages to protect their living standards. Full employment, *as a national policy* is not a gift of the capitalists to the working class. The idea did not originate with some "radical," crackpot college professor, nor did it come from an awakened "social conscience," as Sir William Beveridge, the British Keynesian, would have us believe. The nation's employment policy — the Employment Act of 1946 — came in response to the insistence of the workers that they will tolerate no more depressions, no more devastating unemployment, no more subsisting on a dole. They demand, and will continue to demand as their right as productive workers, jobs at full employment, at rising real wages. *If*, they would

216

say, *these demands threaten an inflation, it is because capitalists insist on a rate of profit which a full employment economy does not permit and which, in any case, current capital-saving investment no longer requires.* Progressively, the people will learn that twentieth-century capital-saving technology, and integrated business organization and management minimize the amount of profits required for the growth of the system. Indeed, the larger profits which these new productive forces make possible, when not invested, become an impediment to its growth. *In this view, increasing portions of the national output can and should be diverted to mass personal consumption by way of increased payments to workers and to productive social consumption by way of building a Welfare State.* A decreasing portion need now go to payment to property by way of profits. In this view a basis might be established for the maintenance of full employment without an accompanying inflation. Whether these objectives are realizable without a prior radical transformation in the relative class powers of workers and capitalists is another matter, which is left for consideration elsewhere.* From what we have learned so far, it does not seem that they are.

A further note is pertinent to the question of inflation, for the whole argument which we have followed in the preceding pages is an artificial construction conceived to support the theory of the wage-price spiral, distorting the meaning of the concept. In a strict sense and historically speaking, inflation occurs when a government engages in deliberate creation of money and credit without the backing of gold or other convertible assets. Such inflation does not stimulate production or even, in the end, prices. The contingencies, such as war or revolution, which lead a government to issue printing press money, makes it possible for entrepreneurs to raise prices and it is this that calls forth the increase in the circulating medium beyond the normal money supply. The price inflation *anticipates and conditions* the credit inflation, unless, indeed, it is dampened by price controls as was the case in the United States during World War II.

The inflation or "threat" of inflation publicists write about today is a fiction, indeed a shibboleth. The economy has a surfeit of monetary and credit facilities. The widening gap between existing productive capacity and output is a measure of that surfeit. So long as that gap exists, prices need not rise, as in fact they have not since the mid-1950's when this gap became chronic. When produc-

---

*In a work projected under the title, *Capitalist Crises and Capitalist Destiny.*

tion rises the credit supply rises with it; when production falls the credit supply contracts or finds an outlet in the speculative markets. The "inflation" of today is nothing more than rising prices maneuvered by entrepreneurs to cover a wage rise, increased costs of profit realization, a fall in productive efficiency or for no visible reasons except that they will it so. In a word, inflation is not an automatic monetary phenomenon; it is not God-given. It is manmade — made deliberately and with a purpose — to protect or enhance profit margins.

D. CONCLUSIONS

The way capitalist economists and business leaders would curb inflation has now been told: They would enact laws to curb the power of labor to act collectively (e.g., C.E.D. *Defense Against Inflation*, p. 63). They would contrive to reduce the rate of production to less than full employment levels. "It may be," Professor Galbraith wrote in his *Affluent Society* (p. 339), "that we need not use all the labor force all the time." (See again, notes 8 and 11 above.) As for the unemployed, C.G.C., like the gods of old, will provide.*

In no case, even implicitly, would they take action to reduce the share of the national income that now goes to property ownership. To do that, they say, would reduce the incentive to invest. As for improving the social services, let everybody share the cost, rich and poor alike, by way of an expanded sales tax, says Professor Galbraith. (*Ibid.*, p. 305.) Which brings us to the next chapter and the question of taxation.

---

*C.G.C.—Cyclically Graduated Compensation. Employment benefits would be raised with the rise of the rate of unemployment. C.G.C. would supply "a reasonably satisfactory substitute for production as a source of income." It would also calm down the rising clamor for the 4-day week (p. 305). Which millions of workers Professor Galbraith would consign to C.G.C., he did not say.

18.
TAXES

A. TAXES AND CONSUMER DEMAND

1. *Steps.*—Besides raising personal consumption, by way of increasing real wages, as a means of retarding the growth of uninvestible social surplus in an advanced capitalism, argued in the
preceding chapter, personal consumption could also be raised by
reducing or even altogether abolishing consumer taxes. The government would derive its tax revenue mostly or wholly from a universal progressive income tax, graduated in accordance with tax-
payers' ability to pay. In the five years 1958-62, consumption taxes,
including social security payroll taxes, averaged $46 billion. This sum
absorbed 19 per cent of the personal consumption expenditures those
years of all American consumers, the rich and the poor. The percentage for the poor, that is, for the mass of consumers, was of
course much higher than that. The mass of consumers spend a larger
portion of their income on consumption than do the rich of theirs and,
therefore, a greater proportionate share in consumption taxes. This
is what is meant when it is said that consumption taxes are regressive.
The poorer you are the harder they hit you. Property and sales taxes,
for example, consume from 5 to 6 per cent of the lower incomes,
but only a little over 2 per cent of incomes of $15,000 and above.[1]

When to the $46 billion direct consumption taxes about one-half
of the personal income taxes is added—they averaged some $26 bil-
lion for those same five years—the amount rises to near 23 per cent
of the personal consumption expenditures. (In this $26 billion we
include all of the personal income taxes of the 75 per cent lower-
bracket incomes and half of the taxes of the highest 25 per cent
bracket incomes.) This is still exclusive of the corporation income
tax, a large part of which finds its way into consumer prices.

It is with considerations such as these in mind that Keynesians
and liberal economists in general propose that government use its
tax arm as a weapon to fight depressions and to hold down inflation.
In general, the argument has run in terms of easing up on consumer
taxes in a business recession and tightening up on them when infla-

tion threatened. Reduction of these taxes, it is asserted, would release consumer purchasing power and increase consumer demand, which would stimulate production and employment. An increase in consumer taxes, the argument runs on, would reduce consumer demand and ease its inflationary pressures.

An increase in consumer buying power through a lowering of consumer taxes would, however, raise the *total* consumer demand in the economy, only if at the same time the government replaced the consumer taxes with borrowed money or with taxes on savings, in order to maintain its own rate of spending. Otherwise, the tax forgiveness would merely serve to shift demand from the government to individual consumers. The government raises taxes not to hoard the money, but to spend it. If it were to raise less taxes in order that consumers have more of their own income to spend, it would of necessity have to contract its own spending. Unless the government replaced its reduced tax revenue with borrowed money or with new taxes on savings and maintained its rate of spending, the total market demand would remain the same or even fall, insofar as consumers may not spend all the retrieved tax money.

In fact, under the circumstances, the government may have to increase its spending, if the total consumer demand is not to fall. It would have to spend more money than it gave up in taxes. In view of a threatening depression, most consumers may choose to save some of this money for the rainy day (or pay up consumer debts), rather than spend it all. The more well-to-do consumers, in particular, are not likely to spend this tax money on increased consumption. Their rate of consumption is not held down by taxes; rather it is their rate of saving that may so be held down. They are most likely, therefore, to save the bulk, if not all of the forgiven taxes. The tax-forgiving policy, in short, may call for government deficit spending as a counter-cyclical measure. We covered that subject earlier (pp. 118-27 and chapter 12 above).

Furthermore, the American tax structure and the separation of functions between Federal, State and local tax jurisdictions, which goes with that structure, preclude any significant shifts in consumer taxes, unless the structure and the functions were radically realigned at the same time. By far the major portion of consumer taxes lies within the State and local tax jurisdictions, where the Federal government may not enter. Some of the principal functions of these tax jurisdictions, such as education, are imbedded in these taxes. The powers that be will not surrender to the Federal government either these tax sources or these functions so long as the politico-economic structure of the country remains as it is. Yet, it is to Washington that Keynesians look for the manipulation of consumer taxes as a contra-cyclical device and, to an extent, as a means of stimulating the rate of economic growth.

If, then, taxation is to be used as a means of aiding in the maintenance of full employment, the tax structure of the country must first be changed and the functions of the Federal, State and local governments reallocated. Taxes would be shifted from their regressive form of the State and local governments, where they are imposed mainly on consumption, to the progressive form of the Federal government, where they are imposed mainly on income. The Federal government would then take over, wholly or in part, the financing of the social services as well as other State and local functions which are national, rather than local in character, such, for instance, as education, highways, soil conservation, water pollution control.

A regressive system, as that of the United States, is one in which the major portion of the country's taxes falls on the workers as consumers. This tends to enlarge the gross surplus-value of the economy, in that it tends to hold down the workers' living standards. Holding down the workers' living standards lowers the value of labor-power. Low cost of labor-power, together with a continuing increase in labor productivity, spells the creation of an ever-increasing total surplus-value. This may not always mean an increase in the *share* of surplus-value accruing to the capitalists. That would depend on the share absorbed by the state. But it always must mean an increase in the *total* surplus-value capitalists would get, as the share the workers get is lessened by regressive taxation.

A progressive tax system would be one in which an increasing proportion of the nation's taxes is raised from taxes on savings and a decreasing proportion from taxes on consumption. That would tend to raise the workers' standard of living, to raise the value of labor-power, and reduce the total surplus-value created. It may even reduce the capitalists' profit. That would depend on the concurrent rate of increase of labor productivity. In any case, a reduction in the total surplus value created would hit the capitalists' profit harder than it would the workers' standard of living.

This is why only a progressive tax system might serve to mitigate the violence of the movement of the business cycle and the slow rate of economic growth. It would help to reduce the gap between the amount of surplus value which the system tends to create and the amount that can be invested in private capital formation. It would reduce the social surplus which tends to exceed investment potentials.

In the period of monopoly capitalism and capital-saving technology, a progressive tax system would serve as a corrective to this tendency.

2. *Barriers.*—To propose to substitute a progressive tax system as just defined for the existing regressive tax system in America is to reckon without the interests of its ruling class. The tax structure of a capitalist society is not detachable from its economic structure. It is, in fact, one of its main pillars. It is a means of enhancement, distribution and control of the social surplus. *It has been a major source of capital accumulation:* It provides the mechanism, in short, for holding down workers' pretensions for an advancing standard of living. If, for example, they would have more of social welfare, let *them* pay for it, for example, by an "expanded sales tax," such as we just saw Professor Galbraith advocate.

The capitalist class will oppose with all the political power at its command any serious impairment of its hold over the existing tax structure. If defeated, as they were in the one case of the enactment of the corporation and personal income tax laws a half century ago, they contrive legal, and illegal, loopholes of escape from untoward effects on themselves. They may not always succeed entirely, but to a major extent they do, as any elementary study of the history of American taxation will reveal.*

B. The Dynamics of Capitalist Taxation

1. *Taxes and Capital Accumulation.*—A full appreciation of the place of taxation in a capitalist economy cannot stop with an evaluation merely of the *form* of the tax structure. One must know also the relation of that structure to the dynamics of capitalism as a system of the private accumulation of capital. Here we come to a phase of capitalist taxation which is conceptually elusive and apparently self-contradictory. It is that in a capitalist society taxes are both a deduction from surplus-value *and* a source of private capital accumulation. We have been saying all along, and our daily experience bears us out, that the common people, the consumers of the country pay the major portion of its taxes. They pay them as direct consumption taxes, as direct personal income taxes, and as the taxes which businessmen pass on in the prices of goods and servics they sell. To the extent that all these taxes press down on the workers' standard

---

*See, for example, *The Great Treasury Raid*, by Philip M. Stern, Random House, 1964.

of living they reduce the value of labor-power and raise the rate of surplus-value, the source of private capital accumulation. *Yet, from the long-run point of view and the economy as a whole, all taxes ultimately derive from the gross surplus value of the capitalists—are a deduction from potential profits.*

Recall the premise laid down in our first chapter. In a capitalist society, we said, wages must be set at levels which at least permit the productive workers of the system to recreate their own labor-power and to provide for the procreation of the new and additional labor force required for the growth of the system. All income from production above these wages is the surplus-value of the economy which the capitalists appropriate. This they share with the unproductive workers of the system and with the state. The unproductive workers get their share by way of salaries and wages; the state, by way of taxes. *Taxes are the portion of the capitalists' gross surplus-value consumed by the government.* Thus all taxes which go to maintain the state apparatus, as all other unproductive expenditures, emanate from the capitalists' income as a class; that is, from surplus-value. Yet, it is also true that the workers, as consumers, pay the greater portion of the country's taxes. They pay them with the income they get above the rock-bottom wage required to recreate their own labor-power and to provide a decent living for their families. What these standards are depends in large part on the workers' ability to set through their power of collective bargaining.

The capitalist tax structure is an arena in which capitalists and workers struggle for shares of the surplus-value which the workers create. The capitalists strive to procure the greatest possible share *for their own use* by placing the greatest possible portion of the nation's taxes on the workers as consumers. The workers try to retain as much of the surplus-value as possible for *their* own use in higher wages and by increased services of the state paid for by taxes on the income of the capitalists. This tug-of-war is possible because neither the rate of surplus-value created nor the reproduction value of labor-power is a fixed, or rigid quantum. The rate of surplus-value created fluctuates in accordance with the technological and managerial competence of the system and with the effective demands of labor for increased wages. The reproduction value of labor-power is affected by the productivity of labor, by the collective bargaining power of organized labor, and by what Marx called the "historical and moral element" which enters into the determination of the workers' differing standards of living in time and place—say, a public school education for their children in 1910; a college education in 1960.

Taxes, thus, constitute a dividing line, albeit shifting line, between the workers' standard of living and the net surplus-value accruing to the capitalists and the state. The higher the proportion of consumer taxes and the lower the workers' standard of living, the higher is the share of the surplus-value accruing to the capitalists. To the extent that the workers can be denied the "historical and moral element" in the determination of wage rates, to that extent are real wages depressed and the value of labor-power lowered. And to that extent are the rates of surplus-value and the potentials for the accumulation of capital enhanced.

What we observe in real life is that *within* the capitalist tax structure a constant maneuvering goes on among business firms and between capitalist and workers to shift their taxes from one to the other. Business firms seek to shift their taxes *to* one another in the prices of goods and services they sell to or buy *from* one another. Capitalists seek to pass on their taxes to the workers through lowered wages and higher consumer prices, while the workers seek to cover their taxes and higher consumer prices through increased wages. Producers of raw materials seek to pass on their taxes in the prices they charge to producers of finished products. Producers of finished products seek to pass their taxes backwards in lower prices they would pay their suppliers of raw materials, to a large extent colonial and other underdeveloped countries, and forward in higher prices to their own customers. The latter in their turn seek to pass some of their taxes backwards in lower prices they would pay the producers and forward in higher prices to the ultimate consumer.

In these maneuverings some business firms succeed, for shorter or longer times, to shift a portion of their taxes backwards and forward at the expense of the surplus-value of other firms. The thousands of firms that go bankrupt each year, mostly small businesses, are probably to a large extent victims of these maneuverings. In the long run, however, and for the solvent business firms as a whole, gains balance losses, averaging out their taxes as portions of their shares of the nation' surplus-value, where they are not passed on to the ultimate consumers. Marx's "average rate of profit" shows its face here.

It is different with the tax shifts to the workers as consumers. Here not only the purpose but the end result must be a lessened rate of advance of real wages. And insofar as this is so, taxes in a capitalist economy become a source of capital accumulation. This was almost unqualifiedly the case in America throughout the 125 years from the birth of the Republic to the First World War, when a radical shift began in the composition of the wage earning class away from its unskilled, immigrant component to semi-skilled immigrant and native Americans. Until then the unskilled predominated and their wage was just about enough to keep them and their families above the poverty line, *when there was work.* This applied especially to woman and child labor. Their wages did not need to be high enough to cover the cost of their labor-power, and less so to provide for the reproduction of their kind. That was presumably covered in the wages of the family head breadwinners. Woman and child labor was thus a most fruitful source of surplus-value.

When breadwinners those years were unemployed or otherwise unable to work, their own physical survival as that of their families depended on the mercy of organized charity. Organized charity subsidized poverty, and the capitalists preferred to have it so. They would give to charity out of their surplus-value rather than pay a minimum living wage to their workers. Charity giving assuaged the workers' inarticulate discontent as well as the capitalists' conscience before their God. Besides, charity could be given or withheld. The newly arived immigrants, who made up the bulk of these workers, were expendable. A wage raise once granted cannot so easily be withdrawn. It was not, indeed, until the Great Depression placed the whole capitalist wage system in question, when millions of the expendables were thrown on the scrap heap, that a semblance of a floor was placed under wage rates through the Congressional enactment of a minimum wage law and the 8-hour day. It was also only then that the spurt in trade union organization compelled the capitalist class to advance wages in at least rough conformity with basic living standards, including coverage for the increased taxes. Social Security benefits and unemployment insurance were in large part substituted for the dole of organized charity.

As may be seen from Table 4, before the income tax became effective with America's involvement in World War I, almost all taxes of the country were consumption taxes. An unending stream of unskilled immigrant labor kept the rate of growth of the labor force high and its wage-bargaining power low. The capitalist class was under no compulsion then to cushion the workers' standard of living against tax pressures. The value of labor-power was low and the cost of government low. Practically all the surplus-value created accrued to the capitalist as capital accumulation. Only in the case of the skilled and the relatively few organized workers was it necessary for the capitalists to pay wages high enough to cover taxes. There were, in addition, the taxes which they themselves and their retainers paid as consumers, and of course, the taxes paid by the farmers.

The crucial factor all those years was the high rate of growth of the labor force: it was the continuous growth of the labor force that, despite the low wages, provided a consumer market for the outpourings of the factories and a demand for capital goods to equip it as industrial workers. When the rate of growth of the labor force began to decline, in large part because of the cessation of immigration with the onset of the war in 1914, the maintenance of prewar wage rates became unfeasible.[2] This was so, first, because the new technologies of the time effected a shift in the labor market from unskilled to semiskilled and skilled workers. The rising demands of these workers necessitated an increase in wages to cover taxes—to meet their higher living standards. Now when tax exactions would reduce basic wage standards, consumer demand would be so low (the mass of surplus-value accruing to the capitalists would be so high) that the economy, in the absence of demand of an expanding labor force, would soon fall into a deep depression. The consumer market would shrivel, while the social surplus would rapidly draw away from the economy's investment potentials.

Table 4

CONSUMPTION TAXES IN THE UNITED STATES, 1789-1917

Percent of Total

Period	Federal	State and Local	Combined
1789-1913	97.6	100.0	99.0
1914-1917	78.1*	97.5	92.4

SOURCES: *Federal Taxes*
For 1789-1913, computed from the *Statistical Abstract of the United States*; For 1914-1917, computed from data in *Double Taxation* — House Committee Print, 72nd Congress, 2nd Session, Government Printing Office, 1933.
State and Local Taxes
1789-1849, estimated on the basis of the per capita tax in 1850; 1850-1913, based on the decennial census figures as given in *Wealth, Debt, and Taxation* and interpolations for the intercensal years in arithmetic progression.
*Decline reflects the application, beginning in 1910, of the corporation and in 1914 of the personal income tax. 1914-1917 are estimates.

Still, this does not mean that all workers are always covered for taxes. In a large number of cases, the millions of pensioners and the unemployed, for instance, taxes do bring down consumer income below the poverty line. (Yes! pensioners and the unemployed also pay taxes: in the rent they pay, in the cigarettes they smoke, in the clothes they wear—all taxes except the personal income tax, for which their income falls below the taxable base.) Several million American workers keep above the poverty line and so are able to pay their taxes through holding more than one job and through multiple family jobs. For consumers as a whole, taxes must be covered by income above the minimal living standards. In the long run, wages to maintain these living standards are raised by the amount of the taxes consumers have to pay. *In the long run and for all consumers taken together, income must be high enough to support a "reasonable" standard of living, including the ability to pay taxes,* even though for millions of American families this is not so. Put it this way: if your annual salary is $5,000 and you pay $1,000 in taxes, your spendable income is $4,000. By paying the $1,000 in taxes you serve, so to say, as transmission agent between the capitalists and the state.

An example of a conscious policy to cover taxes, although only personal income taxes, in the wage bill is that established at the United Nations. There, salaries for the employes of the Secretariat are set on an after-tax basis. A $10,000-a-year statistician, say, is paid $12,000 to cover the $2,000 income tax he may have to pay to his native country. The equivalence may not always be exact, but the idea is there.

The after-tax basis of compensation for major executives is frequently found in American corporations, where it takes many different forms. Expense account allowances, pension benefits, deferred compensation schemes are some of the devices used. Here "devices" are necessary in order to escape the eye of the Office of the Internal Revenue Service of the United States Treasury Department.

All taxes, thus, ultimately derive from gross surplus-value and the capitalists' gross profits, either as paid by business firms as buyers or sellers, or as paid by consumers from income above their basic living requirements. Hence, the perennial demand of the capitalist class for less and less taxes—for less and less government "extravagance," meaning for restricted social services—even though these are ostensibly paid for by the consumers.[3] Capitalists would not complain about taxes if they did not really ultimately pay them out of their surplus-value, any more than they are concerned about the loss of purchasing power by pensioners and by holders of government savings bonds because of inflation. Hence, also their perpetual policy to maintain a tax structure which presses down upon the standard of living of the people to the margin of labor-force viability and consumer market potentials. It is one of their means of "keeping the working class in its place." It is the historical fact which explains the regressive nature of capitalist tax structures everywhere. In sum, a regressive tax structure serves to enhance the rate of capital accumulation; a progressive tax structure, to retard it. Progressive taxation spells a decline in savings potentials, and so a decline in the rate of capital accumulation.

Put it this way. Since real wages in the United States are adequate to support a growing population under improving health standards (as evidenced by mortality and morbidity statistics), it cannot be said that wages are below the value of labor-power. Hence, by definition, all taxes are paid out of surplus-value. Nevertheless, if sales and other consumption taxes were reduced, or eliminated altogether, real wages, the standard of living and the value of labor-power would all rise. Surplus-value would fall and the capitalists would have to make good the tax deficiencies by way of increased taxes on income from profits.

Some economists, among them disillusioned radicals, wish us to believe that a progressive tax system as here defined is not only feasible in a capitalist society, but that the capitalists themselves will ultimately call for it as a means of saving the system from the effects of the increasing violence of the business cycle. Capitalists are expected voluntarily to give up a principal means of the private accumulation of capital. Maybe so. Maybe the world is again entering an age of miracles, but history does not record the phenomenon of a ruling class ever voluntarily surrendering to history.

Suppose that, contrary to history, all-embracing and exclusively progressive taxation becomes a capitalist fact? Would that arrest the capitalist tendency to move in cycles of prosperity and depression? Taxation, in the last analysis, is not a propelling force of capitalism, but one of the means through which capitalist propelling forces operate. It is these that must be controlled if depressions are to be abolished.

PART V

SUMMARY AND CONCLUSIONS

19.
THE CONTINUING CRISIS

A. Capitalist Incompatibilities

1. *Social Surplus and Social Welfare.*—The task of this book has been to discover the means that may be available in an advanced capitalist economy for absorbing all the investible funds, or social surplus, which it can create. Lacking such means, we argued, an advanced capitalism cannot sustain full employment on a continuing basis.

We have defined the social surplus as the amount left of the national income of a capitalist economy after deduction of payment to the productive workers of the system and for the personal consumption of the capitalists. Label this portion of the national income the community's saving potential. The social surplus, then, is the amount potentially available for the capital expansion of the economy, for the maintenance of the state and of the social services of the community. The discussion has proceeded from the theory that in a highly developed economy, in the period of large-scale concentrated business organization and capital-saving technology, the portion of the social surplus that can be profitably invested in the expansion of the economy tends to decline.

At the same time, the total social surplus *created* tends to rise with the rising productivity of labor. The portion of the social surplus available for investment then tends to exceed real investment potentials; the community's saving potentials tend to exceed its investment potentials, as the Keynesians would put it. Unless the uninvested social surplus is elsewhere absorbed in the system, this tendency must eventually lead to a fall in the rates of production and employment. This is so, because the total income which a nation produces at a given level of production and employment must *all* flow back into the stream of production if that level of production and employment is to be maintained, let alone prevented from falling.

In America, this tendency of saving potentials to exceed investment potentials has grown with the growing monopolization of industry since about the turn of the century and, particularly, since the

230

end of World War I. It has become especially manifest since the end of World War II as the newer technologies of electronics and automation have been generating still greater disparities between potential savings and potential investments. What, in the main, has so far prevented these disparities from precipitating a major crisis, such as happened in 1929, has been the increasing absorption of the excess savings in expenditures for the military, among other forms of unproductive and wasteful consumption.

The question, therefore, was raised: suppose peace comes, as sooner or later it must if the human race is not to be exterminated in a nuclear war, and the huge military expenditures are eliminated as an absorbent of the otherwise uninvestible social surplus? What civilian-type expenditures might there be to replace them, if we are to avoid falling into a condition of mass unemployment?

Keynesians treat this capitalist tendency to underemployment largely in mechanical terms. They would mitigate it by "stabilizing" the economy. Some of the measures they rely on, like Social Security and unemployment benefits and taxes, they call "built-in stabilizers." Others like monetary and fiscal policies, are controlling "mechanisms." Aside from the fact that an economy might be "stabilizing" at any level below full employment, none of these Keynesian measures relate or can relate to the new fact of capitalism: that in its monopoly stage, capitalism tends to produce ever-more social surplus than can be profitably invested in the growth of the economy on a continuing basis. Not even "government spending" is so related in their minds. They do not see that new investment can now proceed only in fits and starts with a tendency to decline, unless a good portion of the excess was siphoned off in unproductive expenditures, as in recent years for military purposes. The question that really matters now is, suppose peace comes, what civilian-type outlets, to replace the military, are available to the community that are compatible with capitalist viability in the long run?

In preceding chapters it was suggested that the excess social surplus might be absorbed by increased expenditures for the social services: Expand and improve the school, health, low-cost housing and cultural facilities with these excess funds. Build and expand the social security system in the same way. In short, build the Welfare State as an absorbent of otherwise uninvestible social surplus. There are no other visible means for absorbing the excessive riches of a modern capitalism, except by these and similar outlets for productive social consumption.*

What we have found, however, was that the capitalist class opposes the building of a welfare state. Whether paid for by direct or indirect taxes the cost becomes a charge on surplus-value, on capitalist profit. All taxes, all costs of government, as noted in the preceding chapter, are ultimately a charge on surplus-value.

So also are the costs of the military paid out of taxes—a charge on the surplus-value of the capitalists. But whereas capitalists permit themselves to be taxed to build up the military, they are not willing to be taxed for the building up of the Welfare State—for improving and expanding the social services. If, they say, the people want more and better social services, let them pay for them, by way of a sales tax, say, as Galbraith advocates. Thus financed, of course, real wages are reduced and the "Welfare State" becomes a hollow pretense—the bread and circuses of decadent ancient Rome. Professors who talk of the Welfare State as a realizable ideal in a capitalist society are guilty of deluding the people.

None of this, of course, means that the people should give up the fight for improved and expanded social services, to be met out of taxes on the social surplus, but they must not be led to believe that building the Welfare State is a ready possibility of replacing the military as the major absorbent of the social surplus that tends to become excess, and as an immediate measure for achieving full employment. If our theory is correct that the present-day capitalist tendency to create ever-mounting excess social surplus becomes the condition for recessions and increasing unemployment, the people must move on still another front to hold back that tendency. Simultaneously with struggles for improving the social services as a means of reducing the uninvestible surplus, they must take action to reduce it at the source of its creation. Such action would aim at reducing the profit take through increased real wages, shortened workweek without reduction in pay, and a shifting of taxation from consumption to savings.

So long as private enterprise predominates in an economy, so long will the drive toward the private accumulation of capital remain the controlling factor of the rates of investment and employment. As long as this holds true, the system will continue to create uninvestible social surpluses, and as long as this potentiality exists, the condi-

---

*Capital exports in the manner of 19th century empire building are no longer available as a relief from excess investment funds. See Chapter 15, above.

tions for growing unemployment and the precipitation of economic crises continue to be operative. The severity of the crises, the depth and duration of depressions, and the rate of economic growth may differ from country to country in any given time and over the years in any given country. They are partly a reflection of the different stages of their capitalist development and of the difference in their rates of creation and absorption of the capital surplus in private investment and government spending. But the underlying menace of the periodic inability to realize in investment and social consumption all of the potential surplus remains essentially the same for all of them, at all stages of their development.

Indeed, it may be laid down as a law of capitalist economic crises that their degree of severity varies in time and place directly with the relative magnitude of the uninvestible portion of the potential social surplus of a community; *uninvestible, that is, in socially productive outlets at home and abroad.* This law becomes manifest, especially, in an advanced capitalism where the rate of surplus-value creation is accelerated by a highly efficient, capital-saving technology in the hands of industrial monopolies and big business firms.[1] It is a law of what Marx called the capitalist tendency toward crises of overproduction.[2] It is that law expressed in the form of the overproduction of capital in its initial form—in the form of overproduction of investment funds—in the form of the creation of surplus wealth together with surplus people. Keynesians tells us that the failure to utilize to the full all of the potential social surplus (all the potential "savings" at full employment) is evidenced by the amount of unemployment. But because of their faulty definition of "savings" (following Keynes) this gives us only a partial picture of the unemployment situation.

Keynes, we remember, had defined savings as the balance between the national income and personal consumption. But his "consumption" includes that of all consumers, of productive as well as unproductive consumers, for example, "Madison Avenue," the military. His equation thus fails to account for the unproductive employment which in essence substitutes for the unemployment of productive workers.[3] In other words, to the unemployment calculated on the basis of the Keynesian equation must be added at least the standing army; the workers who are both directly and indirectly dependent for employment on the production of armaments, and of food, clothing, and housing for the military personnel and the civilian personnel of the military establishments. This unproductive employment alone is 2 to 3 times the unemployment visible to the Keynesians. (We are not

233

counting the hundreds of thousands engaged in the parasitical industries of advertising and sales promotion, for example.) We have seen p. 15 above) that in 1962 as much as 10 per cent of the American labor force was directly or indirectly employed in the defense occupations.

In a rather pathetic vein, one British economist pleaded a few years ago:

> It may be that in the immediate future the problem of rendering a moderate level of private investment consistent with full employment will be more than looked after by rearmament expenditure. But we must not shirk contemplation of the time when this will not be so; otherwise we shall be giving substance to the charge that full employment under capitalism can be assured only by war and preparation for war.[4]

In 1964, the charge still holds.

B. CONCLUSIONS

In the middle of the 20th century, American capitalism finds itself involved in a series of seemingly insoluble self-contradictions, all stemming from two independent, yet closely related, events. One of the events was the militarization of the economy as a policy of the cold war. The other was that military spending became a major means of absorbing surplus-value. The nature of the cold war has been so fully explored both east and west that it requires no further elaboration here, except to point up its political aspect.* The nature of military expenditures as an absorbent of surplus-value has been the point of departure in this book.

The cold war had its beginnings and still has its *raison d'être* not in a fear of a military attack by the Russians, but the fear that the Soviet Union will succeed in establishing a viable socialist society, wherein production is carried on for use, not for private profit, and wherein the social well-being of the people is the primary objective. In a society where unemployment is endemic and a depression always a threat, and where the social services are held down to a tolerable

---

*See, for example, my article "Why Capitalism Resists Disarmament," in *Les Temps Modernes*, January, 1962.

minimum, people may turn to the idea of socialism when times become particularly distressful. The initiating motivation of the cold war, then, has been to retard the growth of socialism abroad, or even break it up and to make it hateful to the people at home.*

To wage the cold war the nation's substance has been dammed up in the wasteland of munitions production, while the social services have been starved. We thus deny the people benefits which in the main could be the surest way to avert them from thinking socialism. In the face of the Soviet challenge in this respect, providing for the welfare of the people becomes an overriding necessity. By denying them we literally force the people to look across the seas for envious comparisons. This is one of the contradictions pressing for resolution in America.

Another lies in the fact that the very pressures of the cold war have led the Soviet people to multiply their efforts at building socialism in the shortest possible time. In their scientific, military and cultural achievements they are abreast with the United States and in some respects have surged ahead. One need but mention their achievements in Space Science to make the point. If they still lag behind us in material comforts it is because they but recently started from scratch after the expulsion of the fascist invaders. It would seem high time that we recognize these facts of life and cease wasting our good money on building a "position of strength" which no longer scares anyone, if ever it did.

A third contradiction is the growing stagnation of the economy due, in large part, to the wasting of resources in military expenditures. This contradiction lies in the fact that the military expenditures have gone to enrich a very small segment of American business, in a few favored areas of the country, while the major portion of American business, spreading across all the fifty States, pays the costs without receiving any direct benefits from munitions contracts. This has led to the neglect of civilian production of a social nature, and has contributed to the formation of innumerable "disaster areas," where, because of technological disemployment, unemployment ranges above 10 per cent of the labor force. If Administration economists really wanted to know why the rate of growth of the American economy has been so low in recent years, they will find the explanation here. Munitions production does not require plant expansion commensurate with output. These industries operate on the basis of the most advanced

---

*Simultaneously the cold war involves as well America's drive to dominance over the rest of the capitalist and the subcapitalist world.

electronic and automation techniques. The industries that still need to build the new techniques and so contribute to the growth of the economy are those that produce the goods and services for civilian consumption, both individual and social. But their resources for expansion are siphoned off in taxes for the enrichment of the munition makers and for overseas cold war expenditures. Stagnation of the American economy would be halted and economic growth stimulated if the billions now wasted in the pursuit of the cold war were diverted to the building of a healthy civilian economy. That, also, would be a sounder stance *vis à vis* the Soviet Union than our arsenal of missiles, military bases in Pakistan, Scotland and Spain, and a Pentagon bursting with Brass.

What all this means is that the American people and, first of all, American labor—white collar and blue—must make a choice and make it soon. They must demand an end to the Cold War and insist on an economy of full employment or face Armageddon. The continued build-up of evermore destructive armaments can lead but to doom.

Labor, indeed, must advance on two fronts, on the economic and the political. On the economic front it must advance beyond its struggles for day-to-day improvements in wages and working conditions, and take up the challenge of the new technologies. These are not a temporary phenomenon; indeed, they are still in their relative infancy. It is here that labor productivity is multiplied beyond the need for new capital investment. Labor cannot stop this revolutionary process, nor can it want to do so. But labor can and should insist on sharing in the heightened returns of this increased productivity. It must do so, both for the benefit of the disemployed and as a means of reducing the mounting excess social surplus, which is really the other side of the unemployment coin.

On the political front, labor must cut its ties to the policy of arms production as a major source of employment and seek to transfer present-day military expenditures to the improvement of the social services in a world of peace. As we said at the beginning of the book, the problem facing labor today is not only that of jobs; it is equally, if not more urgently, a matter also of survival. After all, talk of full employment and the Welfare State is but wind if tomorrow we may all be incinerated in a nuclear blast.

236

NOTES AND INDEX

NOTES

Abbreviations

A.E.: The American Economy
A.E.R.: American Economic Review
E.J.: Economic Journal
E.P.F.E.: Economic Policy and Full Employment
F.B.P.C.: Fiscal Policy and Business Cycles
F.E.F.S.: Full Employment in a Free Society
F.R.B.: Federal Reserve Bulletin
F.R.P.: The Falling Rate of Profit
F.R.S.: Full Recovery or Stagnation?
F.T.C.: Federal Trade Commission
G.T.: The General Theory of Employment, Interest and Money
H.E.W.: U.S. Department of Health, Education and Welfare
J.A.S.A.: Journal of the American Statistical Association
M.L.: Monthly Letter of the First National City Bank of New York
M.L.R.: Monthly Labor Review, U.S. Department of Labor
N.B.E.R.: National Bureau of Economic Research
N.E.: The New Economics
N.H.C.: National Housing Conference
N.P.A.: National Planning Association
N.Y.T.: The New York Times
Q.J.E.: Quarterly Journal of Economics
Readings: Readings in Business Cycle Theory
R.E.S.: Review of Economics and Statistics
S. & S.: Science and Society
S.E.C.: Securities and Exchange Commission
S.I.: Statistics of Income, Internal Revenue Service
S.S.B.: Social Security Bulletin, U.S. Dept. *H.E.W.*
S.C.B.: The Survey of Current Business, U.S. Dept. of Commerce
S.Y.U.N.: Statistical Yearbook of the United Nations
W.S.J.: The Wall Street Journal

Chapter 1

1. *A.E.R.*, September 1956, p. 705.
2. I present and analyze these facts in my book, *F.R.P.*, pp. 77-78 and pp. 139-144, and I shall bring them up to date later in this book.
3. For the manufacturing industries, it is known, the rate of profit per dollar of sales as well as on stockholders' equity tends to rise with the size of the industry group, measured in terms of assets. See *Quarterly Financial Report for Manufacturing Industries. F.T.C. — S.E.C.*, Tables 3 and 5.
4. See, for example, *The Operators*, the revealing book by Frank Gibney.
5. S. Melman (Ed.): *Inspection for Disarmament*, p.51, n. 20.
6. For exposé of the "pork barrel" goings on in Congress in this connection see Julius Duscha, *Harper's Magazine*, March 1964, P. 39 ff.

7. This has been the aim of the policy of containment as initiated by Professor George F. Kennan in 1946-47, that, in the words of Professor William Appleman Williams, "continued outside pressure could and would accelerate an inevitable process of dissolution" of the Soviet Union. *The Tragedy of American Diplomacy*, P. 186.

Chapter 2

1. *Marx, Marshall and Keynes.*
2. Vol. 3, p. 195b. A rather ludicrous example of this lack of definition for this concept has been the recent tendency in high political circles in capitalist countries to refer to themselves as "democracies" or "the free world," as if there were something unclean or subversive about the world "capitalist."
3. Marx included here "storing, expressing, transporting, distributing" and "packaging." *Capital*, Vol. II, p. 169 and Vol. III, p. 331. See also n. 4, below.
4. *Theories of Surplus Value*, selections by G. A. Bonner and Emile Burns, p. 194. Productive workers, wrote Marx, are "capital-producing workers . . . their labor is realized in commodities, in material wealth." Nearly a hundred years before Marx, Adam Smith wrote of unproductive services as producing "nothing for which an equal quantity of service can afterwards be procured." See p. 28 below.
5. Many a law clerk will be out of a job when the Datatrol Corporation of Silver Spring, Md., markets its legal research computer. That machine spells out in seconds laws, litigations and court decisions that would take clerks hours and days to dig up. "A major Government Agency, using computers, has cut its clerical work force from 13,000 to 3,000 workers." (John Snyder, Jr., *N.Y.T. Magazine*, March 22, 1964.)

Chapter 3

1. Thomas R. Malthus: *Principles of Political Economy*, William Pickering, London, 1836, p. 404. This is the second edition.
2. *Ibid.*, p. 398; also p. 400.
3. *Loc. cit.*, and *passim* pp. 399-413.
4. See my "Ricardo's Development as an Economist," S. and S., Summer 1956, pp. 221-225.
5. Basic to the errors of both Malthus and Ricardo was the failure of Adam Smith, whom they followed, to see that to be fully realized, surplus value must be transformed into material capital and wages in the reproduction and in the expansion of capital.
6. *The Wealth of Nations*, Book II, Chapter III, p. 265.
7. *Ibid*, Book V, Chapter III, p. 879 (1826 Ed).
8. *Treatise on Political Economy*, Tr. Prinsep, 1821, Vol. 1, p. 109.
9. For Marx's Theory of the Effective Demand, see *Capital*, Vol. II, pp. 453-611.
10. *Principles of Political Economy*, Ashley Edition, p. 731.
11. James Mill, John's father, raised a family of nine children on the small and uncertain earnings as a writer of book reviews and political and economic tracts. It was not until a year after the publication of his *History of British India* in 1818, when he was 46 years old and John 12, that he began earning a fair and steady wage as a clerk in the East India Company, a

job which his great friend Ricardo helped procure for him. Ricardo thought it very magnanimous of the Company to give Mill the job in view of the very severe strictures in the *History* of the Company's conduct in India. See Sraffa's *Ricardo*, Introductory Notes to Vol. VI, p. xvi, Vol. VIII, p. 40 and n. 1, there, and the *Encyclopedia Britannica* article, "James Mill," Vol. 15, p. 490.

12. *Loc. cit.*, pp. 51-52.
13. *Ibid.*, p. 53.
14. *Op. cit.*, p. 404. The citations from Marx will be found in his *Capital*, Vol. III, p. 568. Italics supplied.
15. Marx's identification of the "non-producing classes" is classical in design. But he extended this concept to include all the self-employed, the whole merchant class and its auxiliaries — ad men, sales promotion executives, in short, "Madison Avenue," and all of what we now call employees of the service industries. These are the recipients of revenue from the surplus-value produced by the productive classes. They draw this revenue "by grace of their social functions, for instance that of the king, priest, professor, prostitute, soldier etc. . . ." See *Capital, Vol. II, p. 429.* See also our definitions in the preceding chapter.
16. *Ibid.*, Vol. I, pp. 486 and 487, italics supplied.
17. *The Theory of Business Enterprise.*
18. *The Theoretical System of Karl Marx.*
19. See, for example, his *Economics of Unemployment.*
20. "The significant question," wrote Professor Ellis in his review of *N.E.* is, "What in the central theoretical body of the *General Theory* now survives in a fairly intact form? The present volume gives additional evidence that a number of its most central ideas have been abandoned or reformed to a state almost beyond recognition from the original." Howard S. Ellis, "The State of the New Economics," *A.E.R.*, March 1949.

Chapter 4

1. V. I. Lenin: *State and Revolution*, pp. 75-6. See also Engels in the same vein in his Preface to Marx's *Poverty of Philosophy.*
2. Quoted from their *Physiology of Industry*, in Keynes' *G.T.*, p. 367. Italics supplied by present writer.
3. Retold by Keynes in *G.T.*, pp. 365-6.
4. Quoted *ibid.*, p. 19. But as we will see later, Hobson, by another route, fell into the same error.
5. John A. Hobson: *The Economics of Unemployment.*
6. *G.T.*, pp. 367-8. Keynes' italics.

Chapter 5

1. Paul A. Samuelson in *N.E.* pp. 148-9.
2. Dudley Dillard: *The Economics of John Maynard Keynes*, p. 8.
3. *G.T.*, pp. 118-119. For a technical exposition of the "multiplier" effect, see Richard M. Goodwin, "The Multiplier," pp. 482-499 in *N.E.* Clearly, also, a decline in investment will exert a multiplier effect on the rate of a

business contraction, and it applies to consumption expenditures as well as to investment expenditures.

4. Keynes is here, clearly, describing the special phenomenon of the collapse of stock market values in America in late 1929, which he generalizes into a universal rule.

5. Keynes would not reduce wages on the downgrade, as that would cut consumer income and accelerate the decline. But he would cut *real* wages on the upgrade to improve profit expectations and so stimulate recovery. (*G.T.*, p. 17.)

6. P. 5, italics supplied.

Chapter 6

1. *Capital*, Vol. III, p. 460.
2. Ibid., p. 461. Marx returns to this theme again and again, cf, for example *Capital*, Vol. I, pp. 130-136; Vol. II, pp. 64-67, and 95, and vol. III, p. 715.
3. *The Wealth of Nations*, p. 87. Less than fifty years later, Ricardo wrote: "it [the interest rate] . . . is not regulated by the rate at which the Bank will lend . . . but by the rate of profits which can be made by the employment of capital, and which is totally independent of the quantity, or of the value of money." *Principles*, Sraffa Edition, p. 363. In this, Ricardo paraphrased Turgot who had said: "The profit that can be derived from money is doubtless one of the most frequent motives that induce the borrower to pay interest."
4. *Capital*, Vol. I, p. 155. See the same idea in his *Critique of Political Economy*, p. 198, where he writes (in 1859!): "This sudden reversion from a system of credit to a system of hard cash heaps theoretical fright on top of the practical panic . . ."
5. *Capital*, Vol. III, p. 433.
6. *Op. cit.*, p. 86, n. 17.
7. *U.S. Income and Output*, (November 1958 Ed.) p. 15.
   As M. M. Bober interprets Marx on this point: "Were interest to vanish, surplus-value would not diminish and profits (in the strict sense) would rise correspondingly." In "Marx and Economic Calculation," *A.E.R.*, June 1946, p. 356.
8. See, for example, Mordecai Ezekiel: "Statistical Investigation of Savings, Consumption and Investment," *A.E.R.*, March and June, 1942. H. D. Anderson and J. E. Meade, in *Oxford University Papers*, No. 1, October 1938, on "The Significance of the Rate of Interest."
9. "Business Investment Programs and Their Realization," by Irwin Friend and Jean Bronfenbrenner, the *S.C.B.*, December 1950, pp. 11-22.
10. For the declining interest rate through 1940 see: *Banking and Monetary Statistics*, Board of Governors of the Federal Reserve System, 1943, pp. 448 (the interest rate) and 469 (bond yields). For data since 1940 see: *S.C.B.*, current issues. See also Lawrence H. Seltzer, "Interest as a Source of Personal Income and Tax Revenue," *J.A.S.A.*, December 1955, for an observation of these tendencies treated from a somewhat different angle.
11. U.S. Department of Commerce: *Markets After the Defense Expansion*, pp. 42-43.

For similar findings consult, for example, Friederich A. Lutz: "The Interest Rate and Investment in a Dynamic Economy," the *A.E.R.*, December 1945, pp. 811-830.

The inflationary tendencies in the decade following World War II and the continued high tax rates on corporate income led to an increase in corporate funded debt and to an increase in debt payments.

12. Laughlin F. McHugh, "Financial Experience of Manufacturing Corporations," *S.C.B.*, December 1954, pp. 13-14. In the years 1956-59 internal funds accounted for nearly 70 percent of corporate investment (*S.C.B.*, October 1960, p. 17).

A McGraw-Hill survey of anticipated capital outlays in 1960 found that 80 per cent was planned to be financed from retained earnings and depreciation reserves; almost all of the financing of the manufacturing industries was to come from internal sources.

13. *J.A.S.A.*, December 1936, p. 793, n. 3.

Lawrence Klein, under the influence of Keynes' "propensities," talks (*The Keynesian Revolution*, p. 65) of business men as appearing to have "psychological preferences" for financing their investment operations from internal surplus funds!

14. A sub-caption in "The Week of Finance" by John G. Forrest in the *N.Y.T.*, January 16, 1961, tells the story most eloquently. It reads: "Stocks Soar, Jobless Rise." The connection between the two events naturally escaped him.

15. "Historical Approach to the Analysis of Business Cycles," a paper read by Professor Schumpeter at the Universities-National Bureau Conference on Business Cycle Research, November 25-29, 1949.

The quotation will be found in *Conference on Business Cycles*, N.B.E.R., New York 1951, Gottfried Haberler, Editor, p. 153.

Chapter 7

1. See, for example, "Savings in the National Economy," by Edward F. Denison in *S.C.B.*, January 1955, specifically p. 24.

2. Elizabeth W. Gilboy, "The Propensity to Consume," in the *Q.J.E.*, November 1938, pp. 138 and 140.

Also: Professor Franco Modigliani and Richard Brumberg in *Post-Keynesian Economics*, p. 430, where they assert that *"the proportion of income saved is essentially independent of income."* The authors' italics.

3. See *S.C.B.*, November 1950, p. 7, and July 1956, p. 13, Table 3.

4. See *S.C.B.*, January 1950, pp. 17-20, for a most informative study by Clement Winston and Mabel A. Smith on "Income Sensitivity of Consumption Expenditures," where the demand for different goods and services is shown to respond with different degrees of sensitivity to changes in disposable income. See also *S.C.B.*, March 1964, p. 2, "Personal Income Unchanged, Payrolls Higher."

See also *S.C.B.*, February 1962, p. 15 and *S.C.B.*, March 1963, pp. 12-13, where these parallel data are carried through 1961 and 1962, respectively. Saving as a portion of income, after personal consumption expenditures, has remained practically invariable in the years 1957-1962 as in former years, as consumers save a fairly constant proportion of their income after taxes.

242

5. For Keynes' social background, see, for example, R. F. Harrod: *The Life of John Maynard Keynes*. At one point (p. 628) Professor Harrod refers to Keynes as "the fastidious intellectual, the don, the intimate of the most refined and cultivated circle of our age."

6. *F.E.F.S.*, P. 96.
   See also Raymond Goldsmith on personal savings, minus expenditures for consumer durables, *A Study of Savings in the United States 1879-1949*. N.B.E.R.

7. See, for example, Dillard, *op. cit.*, pp. 156-159, and, Hansen: *F.R.S.?*, p. 289.

8. L. R. Klein: *The Keynesian Revolution*, p. 185.

9. *Life*, p. 418.

Chapter 8

1. Keynes' criticism of the classical assumptions permeate all sections of *G.T.* But see specifically his Chapter 2, pp. 4-22; his Chapter 14, pp. 175-185, and the Appendix to Chapter 14, pp. 186-193.

2. In *N.E.*, p. 147.

3. *Ibid*, p. 604.

4. *Ibid*, pp. 105-6.

5. *Ibid*, pp. 99-100.

6. "It is, I believe, not unfair to say," Professor Ellis concluded his review of *N.E.* cited in n. 20, Chapter 3, above, "that however great the impulse given to economic theory by Keynes . . . the formal theorems have been rejected or extremely modified."

7. *The Times*, London, May 29, 1929, p. 9. Quoted in Dillard, p. 311.

8. Henry C. Wallich, *N.Y.T. Magazine*, April 20, 1958, p. 92. Also, Seymour E. Harris: *John Maynard Keynes*, Prefatory Note, pp. IX-X.

9. Keynes was not a well man and frequently had to take long rests. He died of a heart attack on April 21, 1946, at the age of 63.

10. Recorded in Harrod's *Life*, pp. 223-224 and 440. See also Keynes' *Economic Consequences of the Peace* and his *Essays in Biography*.

Chapter 9

1. Alvin H. Hansen: *F.P.B.C.*, p. 116.

2. Seymour E. Harris, *John Maynard Keynes: Economist and Policy Maker*, pp. 192 and 193.

3. The Cleveland Trust Company *Business Bulletin*, November 15, 1940.

4. In particular by J. Steindl in his *Maturity and Stagnation in American Capitalism*.

5. Particularly, in his *F.B.P.C.*

6. *F.P.B.C.*, p. 283.

7. *F.R.S.?*, p. 296.

8. "Economic Progress and Declining Population Growth," in *Readings*, p. 370.

9. *F.P.B.C.*, p. 362, Hansen's italics.

10. *Ibid.*, pp. 39 and 41.

11. *Ibid.*, p. 360; and *Readings*, p. 377.

12. *F.P.B.C.*, pp. 360 and 361.

13. See, for example, the reports of the Committee of five economists appointed

by the American Economic Association and of the 16 economists convened
by the N.P.A.: *A.E.R.*, September 1950, pp. 503-538 and December 1949,
pp. 1263-1268, dealing with this question.

14. *F.P.B.C.*, p. 307.
15. *Saving American Capitalism*, Preface, p. 4, and elsewhere.
16. *Ibid*, p. 211.
17. *E.P.F.E.*, p. 248.

Chapter 10

1. Sumner H. Slichter, "Wall Street as a Business Barometer" (p. 40), *N.Y.T. Magazine*, October 3, 1954. Repeated by him in, "Thinking Ahead: Breakup of the Business Cycle," *The Harvard Business Review*, January 1955.
2. For this thesis see, for example, the Economists' Committee *Report*, cited earlier, p. 520. Also Alvin Hansen: *E.P.F.E.*, pp. 248-249.
3. See Richard A. Lester: "Economic Significance of Unemployment Compensation, 1948-59," in *R.E.S., November* 1960.
4. The statistics will be found in the National Income Supplements to *S.C.B.* and in *S.S.B.*
5. From *S.C.B., December* 1961, p. 13.
6. All these figures will be found in the National Income Numbers of the *S.C.B.* The "Service" industries are such diverse areas of employment as hotels and motels, households, amusement and recreation, except motion pictures, medical and health, engineering, accountants and similar professional services.
7. For example, Lester V. Chandler's article, "Monetary Policy," in *Saving American Capitalism*, p. 253 and Hansen, *F.P.B.C.*, p. 180 and pp. 289-300; also the Economists' Committee *Report*, p. 523. After all, this tax has been with us since 1914 and as far as is known has done little automatically to help stabilize the economy.
8. *E.P.F.E.*, p. 141.
9. *Ibid.*, pp. 142-44 and p. 181. The "investment tax incentive credit," of 15 per cent above current depreciation allowance, on investment in new plant and equipment was proposed by the late President Kennedy in early 1961 as a recovery stimulus. As if the country was suffering from a lack of productive capacity at the time!
10. *F.P.B.C.*, p. 293.
11. The failure to foresee the upturn after the War served a useful purpose. It created the fear of a depression which led to enactment of the "Employment Act of 1946."
12. Everett E. Hagen: "The Problem of Timing Fiscal Policy," *A.E.R., Papers and Proceedings*, May 1948, pp. 417-422. A later discussion of this question, by Professor Robert A. Gordon, will be found in *ibid.*, May 1957, pp. 117 ff.
13. Exclusive of Social Security payroll taxes, which are not a tax "revenue" available for general government expenditures. They are earmarked for the specific purpose for which they are raised and so spent. For the detailed statistics, see "National Income Supplement" to *S.C.B.*, Table 8.
14. Exclusive of Federal grants-in-aid.
15. See, for example, the annual "Survey of Consumer Finances" conducted

jointly by the Board of Governors of the Federal Reserve System and the Survey Research Center, University of Michigan. Published currently in the *F.R.B.*

The dollar amounts required to maintain basic family living standards were for 1941, $1,367 a year; for 1951, $4,165, and for 1961, over $5,000.

16. All the above figures from *S.I.*, Part I, U.S. Internal Revenue Service.

17. *Reducing Tax Rates for Production and Growth,* December 1962, p. 44. Dr. Nathan was a member of that panel.

Chapter 11

1. Gottfried Haberler, *Prosperity and Depressions,* p. 15.
2. "The Trade Cycle," in *Readings,* pp. 330-349. His forecast of the oblivion of the business cycle ends that article.
3. Quoted in Roy Harrod, *Life,* p. 346.

> "This concept of money as something contrasting categorically in its perfect liquidity with everything else," wrote Professor Howard S. Ellis in the *Annals* of November 1959 (p. 111), "was included as one piece of complete orthodoxy in the otherwise heterodox system of economics of J. M. Keynes."

4. In the fall of 1939, Professor Harrod tells us (Life, p. 489), "Keynes drafted a memorandum which included the idea of a Reconstruction Fund to be supported by the United States, on terms of unprecedented generosity, as soon as Hitler was overthrown, to prevent the spread of communism to Germany."

   Less than ten years later the American government in the form of the Marshall Plan and similar foreign aid programs undertook to do exactly that for all Western Europe. See, for example, Barbara Ward: *The West at Bay,* pp. 143-144 and *passim.*

5. See his article. "Our Unstable Dollar and the So-Called Business Cycle," *J.A.S.A.,* June 1925.
6. Charles O. Hardy: *A.E.R.,* May 1948, p. 400.
7. *F.P.B.C.,* p. 70.
8. Also *op. cit.,* pp. 518 and 519.
9. *F.P.B.C.,* p. 332.
10. *Idle Money Idle Men,* pp. 207-208.
11. The American Assembly, *Conference on United States Monetary Policy,* October 1958, pp. 62-70.

    A *New York Times* editorial, August 1, 1960, reads: "The more complex the financial structure . . . the more the quantity theory has receded into the realm of academic generalizations and the less valuable it has tended to become as a practical tool."

Chapter 12

1. *E.P.F.E.,* p. 210.
2. *A.E.,* p. 49.
3. Capital equipment depreciates even if it stands idle, as it does also through accidental damage.
4. The Account is given in the National Income Supplements to *S.C.B.*

5. All these data are based on U.S. Department of Commerce sources.
6. See the July 1959 *S.C.B.*, Table III-1 and Table III-2.
7. Geoffrey H. Moore: "Maintaining Full Employment and Economic Stability," *A.E.R.*, Papers and Proceeding, May 1959, p. 299 Italics supplied. The pattern was repeated in the 6th "contraction," that of 1960-61. See, for example, p. 115 and p. 143.
8. Cited in *M.L.*, First National City Bank of New York, May 1959.

Chapter 13

1. *Business Statistics*, 1961 Ed., and later supplements to the *S.C.B.*
2. That Hansen was not alone in these beliefs may be seen from such supporting articles as those of Professor Benjamin Higgins in the *A.E.R.*, March 1946 and *E.J.*, June 1950. Also M. Kalecki: *Theory of Economic Dynamics*, p. 159. We also recall Steindl's position on this point.
3. The statistics cited in the text are from Joseph S. Davis, "Our New Population Outlook and Its Significance," *A.E.R.*, June 1952, pp. 304-325.
4. The number of "billion dollar" corporations rose from 22 in 1950 to 54 in 1960 and the number of more than "2 billion" corporations rose from 5 to 20. *M.L.*, July 1961. Government expenditures for basic research and cold war military spending accelerated the process.
5. Wendell Berge, "Anti-Trust Policy," in *Saving American Capitalism*, *op. cit.*, p. 203 and p. 204. Is monopoly enterprise not "private enterprise?"
6. *Readings*, *op. cit.*, p. 381. Repeated in *F.P.B.C.*, pp. 363-364.
7. In *F.R.P.*, p. 71. In that connection I noted (p. 72) that industrial monopolies cannot be treated apart from business concentrations in general. "Monopoly as a one-firm domination of an industry," I wrote, "is a rarity. When one speaks of monopoly one refers to the domination of an industry by two or more if its 'giants', that is, one refers to an oligopoly," It is in this sense of "monopoly" that the present discussion is developed.
8. For an illuminating study of the nature and extent of pre-capitalist monopolies, see Earl J. Hamilton: "The Role of Monopoly in the Colonial Trade and Expansion of Europe." *A.E.R.*, May 1948, pp. 33-53.
9. Engels made a note of it at that time. See Marx's *Capital*, Vol. III, p. 142, n. 16. Lenin's *Imperialism* treats of this aspect of monopoly as it manifests itself in the international arena.
10. It is worth noting here that monopoly is not "the cancerous growth of large business units which consume small unit cells," as Professor Harris would have us believe. The non-farm business population of the United States has not been decreasing but slowly increasing — from slightly above 3 million firms in 1929 to over 4.7 million in 1961. (*Statistical Abstract of the United States.*) On the farm the number of one-family size units has been cut in half in the past 30 years because they could not provide the mechanization and chemicalization which made it possible for 12 men to produce now as much wheat, for instance, as did 34 men 15 years earlier.
11. Lenin came to this conclusion in his *Imperialism*, pp. 109-114, as far back as 1917. The method — the procedure — for that transformation does not concern us here.
12. It was the emergence of this "excess" capacity which so befuddled our econ-

omists when in the 1930's Brookings Institution studies showed that just before the outbreak of the Great Depression, American industry was operating at only about 80 per cent of rated capacity.

Chapter 14

1. Arthur F. Vinson, V.P., General Electric Company, in the *World-Telegram and Sun,* January 4, 1955.
2. Page 90 in *New Views on Automation,* a report of the Joint Economic Committee of Congress, published in late 1960.
3. K. Klimenko and M. Rakovsky, "The Technological and Economic Problems of Automation in the U.S.S.R.," in *The International Social Science Bulletin* (now *Journal*), Vol. X, No. 1: "The Social Consequences of Automation." Published by UNESCO, 1958. The citations are from pp. 45 and 50-51.
4. W. J. McLachlan, quoted by Gene Smith in "Automation Due in Power Plants," *N.Y.T.,* February 5, 1961.
5. " 'Little' Automation," article by George Melloan, *W.S.J.,* October 14, 1959. Rate of utilization of capital equipment in manufacture has increased between one-third and one-half between 1929 and the mid-1950's. *S.C.B.* June 1963, p. 8.
6. Others may be found in James R. Bright, *Automation and Management,* Harvard University Press, 1958. Also, *F.R.P.* pp. 74-79 and 139-142. A very illuminating article on automation in the steel industry here and abroad will be found in *A.E.R.,* Sept. 1964, pp. 626 ff, Professors Walter Adams and Joel B. Dirlan, authors.
   "3 Men Operate New Copper Mill" is the headline for an item in the *N.Y.T.,* June 8, 1961; and on July 5 a U.P.I. dispatch is headed, "Steel Hiring Lags as Output Climbs . . . Automation Big Factor."
7. As may be calculated from the data in Appendix 3 of *F.R.P.*
8. A detailed account of these innovations is given in *F.R.P.,* pp. 74-81.
9. Compared with a par value of between 90 and 100 in 1919, the market value of foreign bonds held by United States nationals had fallen to 57 by the end of 1940.
10. By the end of 1963, consumer credit reached the fantastic figure of $70.0 billion and the mortgage debt on 1 to 4 non-farm family homes, nearly $172.0 billion.
    According to statistics cited by Vance Packard, in *The Waste Makers,* the average American family, because of this involvement in "buy now and pay later," is "three months from bankruptcy."
11. Over 7 million new jobs would have had to be created in 1961, if the President's minimum goal of 4 per cent unemployment was to be achieved. (N.P.A.: Joint Statement on the Rise of Chronic Unemployment, April 1961.)

Chapter 15

1. J. M. Letiche, "The Relevance of Classical and Contemporary Theories of growth to Economic Development," *A.E.R.,* May 1959, pp. 480 and 483.
2. *An International Economy: Problems and Prospects* p. 1.
3. September 27, 1957, p. 3. Italics supplied.
4. September 30, 1959, pp. 4 and 5. See also a speech in the same vein deliv-

ered by Dr. Gunter Henle, a German banker and industrialist, at the second annual meeting of the Board of Governors of IFC, in New Delhi, October 8, 1958.

5. In return for a loan, President-elect Jose Maria Velasco Ibarra of Ecuador complained, "The United States demand the highest solidarity for its policy, that is inspired and directed only by them." *N.Y. Herald Tribune*, August 10, 1960.
6. From *Statistical Yearbook, U.N.*
7. The *A.E.R.*, May 1959, Papers and Proceedings, p. 169.
8. *Oxford University Papers* (New Series), February 1957, p. 5.
9. The data for this and the next table and the discussion that follows is based on material in various issues of S.C.B., articles by Samuel Piser and Frederick Cutler. See also Milton Abelson, S.C.B., November 1949.
10. This argument is repeated in the March 1963 *M.L.* (p. 33).

American International Balance Sheet for 1962

CREDITS		$7.6 bill.
Trade	$4.3	
Investment Income	3.3	
DEBITS		9.9
Military spending	2.4	} 5.9
Economic aid	3.5	
Private investment	2.5	
Short-term funds	.6	
Tourist spending	.9	
DEFICIT		2.3

Note that military spending and economic aid in 1962 exceeded our trade balance by $1.6 billion.

Chapter 16

1. *In Problems of United States Economic Development*, Vol. 1, the Committee for Economic Development, New York, January 1958, pp. 345-46. Italics supplied.
2. *The Exploding Metropolis*, a symposium by the Editors of *Fortune*, William H. Whyte, Editor-in-Chief, p. 111.
3. President Eisenhower, in his Budget Message, January 18, 1960.
4. *N.H.C. Yearbook* for 1954, p. 14.
5. *Statistical Abstract of the United States.*
6. *N.H.C. Yearbook* for 1959, tables on pp. 24 and 25.
7. Quoted by Helen Fuller in her article, "Stalled in the Lobby," the *New Republic*, March 1, 1948, p. 11. Public Housing in America began in 1935 as a P.W.A. project. In the 6 years "prior to Pearl Harbor," a total of 66,161 dwelling units were built, or an annual average of a little over 11,000. Even "twice as much" could hardly make a scratch in the private real estate market. See *N.H.C. Yearbook* for 1958, table on p. 68.
8. Cited in *N.H.C. Yearbook* for 1955, p. 17.
9. Here is the cost distribution of the construction of a hospital as estimated in a "Quarterly Survey and Unit Cost Estimating" in *Architectural Practice*, Reinhold Publishing Corporation, Third Ed., 1959, pp. 112-117:

Labor	$ 414,680.00	Overheads	$ 103,044.00
Materials	574,723.00	Profits	116,871.00
Ins., etc.	48,646.00		
Total Prime Costs	$1,038,049.00	Total	$ 219,915.00

Overheads and Profit as per cent of prime costs, 21+. These totals were computed by the writer from details in the Survey.

10. For the disgraceful goings on in slum clearance projects in New York see "The Shame of New York," by Fred J. Cook and Gene Gleason, in a special issue of the *Nation*, October 31, 1959. For their pains, both authors lost their jobs as reporters on a local daily newspaper.

11. Deputy Premier Mikhail A. Suslow, in a speech at the 11th Congress of the Italian Communist Party, held in Rome. Published in the February 1, 1960 issue of *L'Unita*.

12. From United States Office of Education Circular, No. 604.

13. U.S. Department of H.E.W., *College and University Facilities Survey* for the years 1951-55. Published in 1959.

14. Arthur S. Fleming, Secretary of the above Department, in the *Annals* for January 1960, p. 135.

15. *College and University Facilities Survey*, op. cit., p. 8. Between 1960 and 1961 the number of students pursuing doctorate degrees in education dropped 23 per cent in United States and Canadian institutions. (*N.Y.T.*, September 6, 1961.)

16. National Tax Foundation: *Facts and Figures on Government Finance*, 1960-61, p. 176.

17. *College and University Endowment Investment*, Circular No. 579, published June 1958.

18. In a Paper read before the American Economic Association meeting in Washington, D. C., December 28-31, 1959.

19. The estimates are based on data given in Table II of *Statistics of Higher Education 1955-56*, published by the Department of Health, Education and Welfare in 1959, and the enrollment projections made by Dr. Conger in the paper just cited. The $10 billion total will barely equal the amount the country spends on commercial advertising *now*. In other words, in 1959 America spent more than twice as much on commercial advertising as on all its institutions of higher learning.

20. *College and University Facilities Survey*, op. cit., Foreword.

21. As cited by *N.Y.T.* in its critical editorial, "Deficiency in Education," January 29, 1960.
    This position by the President compelled Secretary Fleming to "renege" on his department's findings, as cited earlier. On February 14, in a T.V. appearance, he denied the existence of a classroom shortage and came out in opposition to a Senate proposal for a federally-financed school construction program.

22. In the view of the executive committee of the State University Association and the American Association of Land Grant Colleges and State Universities, meeting in New York the last week of April 1960, "A debt of several thousand dollars, even on the most generous terms, is intimidating to most families and unthinkable to most 18-year-olds." Report in *N.Y.T.*, May 1, 1960.

23. Fred M. Hechinger, education editor of *N.Y.T.*, in the *N.Y.T. Magazine*, September 13, 1959. ("To Bridge the Scholarship Gap.")

24. Benjamin Fine and others, commenting on the findings of a survey on Soviet education conducted by the United States Office of Education. (*N.Y.T.*, October 27, 1957.)

25. Professor Jacques Barzun: *The House of Intellect*, p. 202. See also Policy Statement, issued in late January 1960, by the Committee for Economic Development. *Paying for Better Public Schools*, and a summary by Ralph Lazarus, Chairman, Committee for Economic Development (C.E.D.) Subcommittee on Education.

26. From a UNESCO report on libraries and museums in the two countries, published May 1961, and from a study on reading standards in the two countries by Arthur S. Trace, Jr., reported in *N.Y.T.*, May 21 and October 27, 1961, respectively.

27. Hearings before the (Kefauver) Subcommittee on Antitrust and Monopoly of the Senate Judiciary Committee late in 1959.

28. Most of the data in this section came from studies of H.E.W., chiefly from *Health Manpower Source Book* and *S.S.B.* Very useful was *Study Paper No. 5* "Trends in the Supply and Demand of Medical Care" presented by Professor Markley Roberts before the Joint Economic Committee of Congress, November 10, 1959. See also the able article "The Doctor Shortage", by Dr. Jack H. Geiger, the *Nation*, January 23, 1960.

29. *N.Y.T.*, January 14, 1960.

30. Howard A. Rusk, *N.Y.T.*, April 23, 1961: "A Career in Medicine."

31. Quoted by Dr. Roberts in *Study Paper*, p. 84. In his State of the Union Message, delivered before Congress on January 14, 1963, President Kennedy, estimated the need as a 50 per cent increase in capacity for medical schools and 100 per cent increase for dental schools.

Chapter 17

1. Collusion in "price-fixing" is so common that extensive documentation is hardly called for.

2. *M.L.R.* of the U.S. Bureau of Labor Statistics, March and July 1958. The data for 1958 and 1959 were supplied to the writer in manuscript by Arthur Jaffee of the Bureau, before their official publication. This kindness is hereby gratefully acknowledged.

3. Joint Economic Committee of Congress, Committee Print: *Productivity, Prices and Income*, 1957, p. 89. Also, U.S. Bureau of Labor Statistics, *Bulletin* #1249, "Trend of Output per Man-Hour."

4. "The inflationary process is essentially an administrative one. It arises from a largely autonomous upward pressure on wage rates relative to the cost of living." Professor Gardner Ackley, The University of Michigan, in *A.E.R.*, Papers and Proceedings, May 1959, p. 428. The whole section "Administered Prices Reconsidered," pp. 419-461, in these Proceedings, is pertinent to this connection.

5. For example, an editorial in *N.Y.T.*, November 16, 1959, called attention to the fact that the dairy industry upon granting a raise to its employees that would run up to a total of $105,000 a week, raised the price of milk to yield $210,000 a week, twice the amount of the raise in wages.

And this practice, it seems, is common to industry as a whole, not just milk. "As far as production workers are concerned," writes Dr. Gardiner C. Means, "only a small part of the 10 per cent increase in industrial prices between 1955 and 1957 can properly be attributed to the increase in wage rates. See his *Administrative Inflation and Public Policy*, p. 30.

6. I demonstrated this phenomenon as applying to pig iron some 37 years ago in *Business Barometer #2, The Price of Pig Iron*, the University of Pittsburgh Press, 1927.

7. Examples of this bafflement were detailed by Edwin L. Dale, Jr. in his article, "Basic Inquiry into a Baffling Inflation," *N.Y.T. Magazine*, August 25, 1957, and in *M.L.* of the First National City Bank of New York for August 1957. In a letter to *N.Y.T.*, dated July 9, 1957, United States Senator Estes Kefauver raised the question: "How can prices go up in the face of declining demand and excess capacity?"

8. This is how the First National City Bank of New York, *M.L.* November 1958, explained the developing recovery from the 1957-58 recession:
   Greater industrial efficiency arising from new equipment, improved operating methods, and elimination of wasteful and inefficient practices has made possible reductions in the work force. *Numerous firms have found that not all workers laid off need to be rehired.* [italics supplied]

9. At a forum conducted by the Whig-Cliosophic Society at Princeton University, December 17, 1946.

10. For an advanced treatment of this thesis, see the very able article by Jacob Morris: "Unemployment and Unproductive Employment." *S. & S.*, Summer 1958.

11. This, as we know, was the official position of the Eisenhower Administration. See for example, Walter Lippmann in the *Herald Tribune*, January 22, 1959; also Edwin L. Dale, Jr. who wrote in *N.Y.T.*, January 21, 1959: "Administration economists said they expected the upward movement to continue through 1959, with 1960 being even better. They conceded there might be 'some lag' in the return to full employment, but said *a rise in the economy of less than the boom proportions of 1955 would be desirable.*" (italics supplied)
   See again, n. 8, above.
   The source of this thinking was Professor Galbraith's *Affluent Society* in which he asserted that the choice now lay between inflation and "consigning some part of the working forces to joblessness and inferior income." (p. 291.)

12. August 9, 16 and 23, 1952. Italics supplied.

13. *A.E.R.*, May 1951, pp. 182-83.

14. *Op. cit.*, p. 535.

15. *Ibid.*, p. 536. It was still an "unsolved problem" ten years later when, in the Spring 1957 issue of the *British Universities and Left Review* (p. 66), Mrs. Joan Robinson wrote: "Indeed, it must be freely admitted that the problem of finding the policies that produce full employment without inflation has not yet been solved either on the plane of theory or on the plane of practice."

251

Chapter 18

1. *Allocating the Tax Burden by Income Class*, Tax Foundation, Inc., New York, May 1960.
2. After the war, laws were enacted to restrict the free immigration of labor, chiefly from Eastern and Southeastern Europe. It was feared that these nationals would bring along the Bolshevik bacillus, with which many of them had become infected as a result of the October Revolution in Russia. One need but recall the "Palmer raids" to appreciate capitalist fears at this time. For a longer treatment of this question, see the present writer's article, "Statistics and the Race Hypothesis," *Journal of Social Forces*, June 1926.
3. Thus, for example, they oppose an increase in the social security tax rate to cover medical care for the aged. They scare the people by calling it a "wedge to socialism."

Chapter 19

1. The rising tendency of the rate of surplus-value between the two World Wars is documented in *F.R.P.* See also p. 15, n.3. The economy would drown in surplus-value, as it nearly did in the 1930's if, for instance, the 50-hour week were to prevail today as it did then.
2. See, for example, *Capital*, Vol. III, Chapter 15: "Unraveling the Internal Contradictions of the Law," of the falling rate of profit.
3. Keynes' definition of savings as national income minus consumption puts into question the whole construction of the national income account in capitalist countries where government expenditures, as well as all unproductive expenditures, are treated as contributing components of the GNP (Gross National Product.) But government expenditures do not contribute to the building up of the national product. They are, on the contrary, a deduction from it by way of taxation. Similarly, all expenditures of an unproductive nature are deductions from, not a contribution to the surplus-value of a community.
4. R. C. O. Matthews: "Capital Stock Adjustment Theories of the Trade Cycle and the Problems of Policy," in *Post Keynesian Economics*," p. 191.

INDEX

253

26169